THE SHIFT SERIES BOX SET TWO

—·—

IMAGINATION MASTERY, SEVEN STEPS TO RIGHT THINKING, PERCEPTION MASTERY, BLOOMING YOUR LIFE

BECA LEWIS

PERCEPTION PUBLISHING

CONTENTS

IMAGINATION MASTERY

WHAT OTHERS SAY ABOUT THIS BOOK

*W*hat I found to be especially true and beneficial in this book was working through the exercises, stretch my thinking beyond what the physical senses or limited mind was reporting. I learned that looking forward with good expectations enabled me to find answers even when I had been feeling blocked. Wow. It really isn't my responsibility to figure things out.

I learned how to listen, trust, then act on the angel messages. Since beginning this practice, there are paradigm shifts happening in my day to day experiences that have brought (and continue to bring) measurable healing results, small and large.

I now know and trust that the answers have always been present. Thinking imaginatively has helped me realize my freedom from worry. I am learning to trust that good is all powerful. I am very grateful that I am becoming an Imagination Master! —Barbara Budan

— · —

Author Note

When you start to develop your powers of empathy and imagination, the whole world opens up to you.—Susan Sarandon

This book grew out of the *Imagination Mastery* class that I first taught in the spring of 2019.

I wanted to share how imagination, used in the right way, can—and does—completely transform our life experiences.

Once the class was over, because I already had most of the worksheets, I thought it would be easy to turn them into an actual book.

I imagined it would be easy. The joke was on me.

It wasn't easy at all, because when I am teaching a class, I am speaking what I want the members of the class to know and do.

To convey the same information in a book means I have to write it. Of course. That's a duh.

But I hadn't realized how many concepts needed explanation until I started writing them out.

That meant I had to write this book in a different style than most of my other books. I wrote it as if I was teaching the Imagination Mastery class, and you, my reader, was in that class.

In my mind's eye, I am with you as you read this book and work through the lessons.

As you read this book, you'll see there are a lot of worksheets.

If you would prefer to not write in the book, I have a free download of a PDF version of just the worksheets for you. No other writing. Just the worksheets.

You can follow along in the book. You can either print them out or write on them on your computer.

Even if you are reading a hard copy of the book, and the worksheets are in it, you might still want those worksheets, so you don't have to write in the book.

That way, you can do the exercises over and over again. You can get the *free workbook pages* for this book in two places, at or where you can also find videos that will teach you how to do Quality Word lists and I Choose sheets.

I would love to hear what happens, and what works for you.

Imagining with you, ~ Beca

SECTION ONE

Why Imagine

ONE

— • —

AN IDEA

B efore you begin...

This course is a fantastic one to do with a group of friends or a mastermind group.

Even one other person would be great.

You'll keep each other on track and accountable, something that we all need. Besides, later on, there will be an exercise to do that is best with a partner.

If you can, find someone, or a group of people, **that have your best interests in mind**. People who have the same desires as you to shift their life, and who you trust to keep your "secrets."

Don't think you know anyone like this? Don't worry!

Do the course on your own, knowing that it will help you find those people. ecause like-minded, like-souled, people find each other when the time is right.

If you need help, let me know. There might be a group going on that you can join, or I could be teaching a live class just as you begin this. Find the class and community at https://perceptionu.comfor now, though, don't wait. Get started.

Things will shift to bring you what you need and want if you are faithful to the practice and to yourself.

Two

⸺ ◦ ⸺

Wings Of Imagination

The man who has no imagination has no wings.—Muhammad Ali

Here is the question you might, and probably should be, asking yourself.

Why bother with learning how to be an Imagination Master? What practical use could being a master of imagination be in the "real" world, or daily life?

Perhaps you are wondering why you would waste the next few months of your life practicing how to imagine.

I mean, after all, what will your friends and family say? Perhaps they would ask you if there aren't more productive ways to spend your time.

And then there is always the chance that, like me, imagining is something you were supposed to stop doing. Or at least hide that you are doing it.

I can't tell you how many times a teacher, or parent, would catch me staring into space and ask me, "Are you daydreaming again?"

Yes. Yes, I was, and it was fun!

After all, I was a reader of fairy tales and science fiction, and it all seemed so marvelous. It seemed so much better than sitting behind a desk in a square room.

I asked myself what it would be like if I were a fairy in the forest? Or if there was a unicorn waiting for me to ride home.

They were the imaginations of a little girl. What good were those imaginations to me, other than to make life more fun?

And what good will being a master of imagination be for you, or me, as an adult?

Sure, now that I am long past grown-up, I can turn my imaginations into stories, and then books, and that seems like a practical thing to do after all.

But that is only one small use for it. It doesn't answer the question of why you, or I, would want to be an Imagination Master at any age over ten.

There is such a good reason that it is almost shocking.

Especially since we have been taught that the world is only what we see or experience through our five senses. That we need to grow up and make a living. That success can be measured.

What if that was all wrong?

9

Imagine this. It is!

Imagination is actually where our future lives. Imagination is what creates inventions that make our lives better.

Imagination brought us Einstein's equations, airplanes, the internet, electric lights, the smartphone, and countless other inventions that have changed our life.

Imagination had us take a chance on love, on finding friends that don't look like us and visit the moon. All because of imagination.

But there is still more than that.

And it's all because of this:

The Subconscious mind can not tell the difference between what's real and what's imagined. — Bob Proctor

Think about this, and you'll know it's true.

Have you ever watched something on TV and started to laugh, cry, or feel afraid?

Have you ever cried because you heard a sad story? It had nothing to do with you, but you felt it?

Have you ever worried over something that never happened? Been afraid, and then discovered that what you were afraid of was a story someone made up?

Yes, you have. We all have. That is imagination at work.

Our minds, our subconscious minds, our rational minds, do not know the difference between reality and imagination.

Even our memories are not accurate. We have re-imagined the past in a way that works for us.

The horror of that moment," the King went on, "I shall never never forget!"
"You will, though," the Queen said, "if you don't make a memorandum of it. —The White King and Queen, Through the Looking Class by Lewis Carroll

Imagine that. Imagine what that means! It means we could imagine what we want to be real. We can rewrite the story of our lives any time that we want to.

Wait? What?

Yes. It's true. So why don't we use imagination more often to design how we want to live?

John Kennedy, in his famous speech on May 25, 1961, dared us to dream of going to the moon. He used a trick in that speech to get us to imagine it. Over and over again, he repeated the phrase, "We choose to go to the moon."

What was he doing? **He was reprogramming the nation's belief system.** We all imagined what going to the moon would look like. But most of all, we imagined what it would feel like.

And what happened? We went to the moon.

Many people say that John Kennedy's death was a turning point in our world. What would our world be like if he kept on forcing us to imagine a better future for all humankind?

It's probably why mourning for him has lasted so long. We mourn for what could have been.

He can't imagine a better future for all the earth anymore, but we can.

The subconscious mind is far more powerful than the conscious mind. But it will stay in pre-programmed ruts and direct our lives without our knowledge unless we learn to change it. Expand it. Use it to reveal a reality that works.

How do we do that?

We become Imagination Masters, again. Because we already are, or were, as children. It's time to get back to it—on purpose.

What you perceive to be reality magnifies.
That's just the way it is. So let's imagine.

However, in this book, we are not going to imagine, or visualize, what we already know.

We will not turn our daily imaginations into either an "I want this" or a "to-do" list.

No. We are going to do so much more.

We are going to imagine what we don't know—what we haven't seen before. Ride moonbeams. Summon a magic carpet and visit the fairies who used to live in our backyard.

What good will this do? It will turn on the spigot to new ideas and a new reality. In more practical terms, it creates new neural pathways in our brains. Everything gets easier, brighter, more fun, more successful.

Less discord. More imagination.

As humans, we are spectacularly good at imagining the "what if" scenarios of disaster, or ill health, or worry-filled days.

Stop it! Not just because it is a waste of time, but because that is creating a reality for you to experience, and is that the one you want?

Instead, think "what if" and imagine glorious things. Good things. For you and everyone.

Don't make it happen. Imagine it. Step back. Feel what it would be like if it were true.

Then imagine again.

That's what we are going to do together for seven weeks.

Perhaps when you've finished, you will do it again, until imagination becomes what drives your day.

Imagine a different way to solve a problem, to speak a hard truth to a friend, or heal an illness.

Have I convinced you of the value of taking just a few minutes out of your day, every day, to become better at the one thing that can change everything?

If not, convince yourself. Give it a try.

Imagination. Not Visualization.

One more thing, before you begin.

Imagination is not visualization. This is not a book called Visualization Mastery for a good reason. They are two different things.

Visualization is an excellent tool when we are working on something we want to make better. There are many studies about how visualization improves everything from golf games, to performing better on stage.

Imagination is outside of what we already know.

When we imagine, we take ourselves out of the world as we know it.

We are not trying to make things better by visualizing them. We are not trying to get something by visualizing.

We are imagining because within our small limited viewpoint of the world we are missing most of what is really going on.

By imagining, we'll begin to see more, experience more, and it will be greater than we could ever have visualized.

Have fun with it. Don't be serious. Be childlike. Imagine, the best, most amazing—whatever—that you can. It will only get better as the days go by.

Let's get started.

I'll see you on the other side.

THREE

— · —

QUALITY WORDS

I magination should be used, not to escape reality, but to create it. —Colin Wilson

Shall we begin? Let's create a new reality together. But first, let's talk about a few of the essential tools that you will be using in this course.

There are two of them that you might not have ever done before, or at least the way that we will be using them. So, let's take a moment and talk about what they are and how to use them.

Quality Lists and I Choose sheets.

These two tools are invaluable, so don't skip them!

Let's start with quality words.

I know you know that thoughts are things, but using the concept of quality words, we are going to work backwards to that idea.

We are going to find the qualities of things first, and then translate them back into things.

That means that the "things" in your life will more accurately reflect what you want after using this tool.

This includes everything from the shoes you are wearing to the people that you love.

17

Yes, I know people are not a "thing," but they are a set of qualities, like everything that we see and experience.

However, to get us started, we won't start with people. We'll begin with easier things, like birds, trees, stones, flowers, and animals.

After that, people will be much easier to translate into qualities. Well, everything will be. You'll see.

After a while, I hope you will get into the habit of using quality words all the time, especially when you are looking for ways to make a decision or a shift in your life.

I promise that their use will make changes much easier, and the outcome more in alignment with what you desire.

However, for now, you are going to use them in your Imagination Mastery work and become an expert at using them.

What Are Qualities?

Here's what they are not.

Quality words are not sentences.

If you find yourself having to write a sentence, or even a few words, to describe what you see or feel, you haven't hit the quality yet.

Keep listening within, and trust what you hear. You can always change your mind.

Remember, we are translating things back to thoughts, which is where they originate. If we shift our thoughts and beliefs, the "thing" has to respond to that shift.

Here's what quality words are.

Quality words describe in one word the essence of something.

You'll discover as we go along how important these words become. It takes a bit of practice, but after using this idea for a few weeks, it will make so much sense you'll wonder how you got along without them before.

By the way, there are no right or wrongs with what words you choose.

You don't have to explain what the words mean to anyone, including yourself.

In fact, please don't. Qualities are a feeling, an emotion, an intuition, an inner knowing. These things can't be described, and there is no need to do so.

The quality word is a place marker for all that it represents.

If you are working with a friend or mastermind group to do this course, go ahead and share your quality words.

However, don't try to describe them. Let them exist on their own. And don't suggest words to each other.

Discover them by working together, not by one person knowing more than someone else.

Your quality words are personal, as are theirs. No corrections are necessary unless they come from within yourself.

How To Do A Quality Words List

Why do we complete a list of quality words after every week of imagining?

Because all that we want, or imagine, has to be **translated back** into what it really means to us.

Doing this means we will stop wasting time searching for material things to make us happy.

Using quality words, we will discover what we truly want.

Often we'll find we already have it. We simply didn't recognize it because we were looking for the wrong thing.

All things are, in essence, composed of qualities.

When we translate things back into their qualities, a fantastic thing happens. We become conscious of what is already present for us. It may not look like we thought it was going to look, but it will be what we wanted.

But first, we have to find out what our heart wants.

Quality words will become a way of life once you experience the power of them. So, let's get started and make you an expert at using quality words to shift your life.

Here are the steps:

Step 1: Take a moment and list 8 to 10 qualities of something you want to see, or experience.

Remember, use one word to express each quality. If you are using sentences, you have not come to the heart of it.

Step 2: There are two kinds of quality lists: You can either list the qualities of what the thing looks like, or you can list the qualities of how you will feel when you have it.

For example, buying a car.

Your quality list for the thing—or car—might contain ideas such as red, fast, inexpensive, safe, etc.

If you choose to make a quality list of how you will feel when you drive this car, it might read "wealthy, secure, free, joyful, etc."

For this Imagination Mastery course, you will be using the lists you will make at the end of each week.

Step 3: Now that you have the quality list, the next step is to put these qualities in order. Why is this important?

Have you ever been at a place in your life where nothing happens towards what you want no matter what you do?
This is most likely because you have a quality or value block.

If you have two values that feel equal to you, your core-self will be confused as to which one to provide.

Continuing with the car example, let's say you list the qualities of luxury and frugal. Until you know which quality is first, you'll be stuck, and nothing will happen.

This is because, at first glance, they appear to be conflicting.
However, once your list is in order, you can receive, or see, all of what you have listed, because in an unlimited big R Reality, everything has already been provided for you under the law of God's Grace.

Critical Next Step

You need help to put the list in order!
Doing this is critical, and that is why having a partner while doing this course would be very helpful.
Someone else needs to help you put them in the order that your intuition, heart, internal voice, guidance wants them to be.

This order will not be the same order that your intellectual mind put them in while making the list.
Don't look at your list while this person is working with you, as this will engage brain and logic.
What you want to engage is your heart and inspiration.

21

BECA LEWIS

The person with your list will ask you the following question:

"Which is more important to you?" and will give you two words on the list to compare.

The person must not give you any other verbal or physical cues. Don't listen to anything except your inner voice. Respond with the answer it tells you. Don't argue with it.

If you are unable to choose one as more important than the other, the person should ask you, "Which one can you not live without?"

Notice that your mind tells you that if you choose one, you might not get the other.

That fear is coming from the point of view that there is never enough and that you don't deserve everything you want.

Since neither statement is true, notice these thoughts and move on. The truth is, once you are clear about what you desire to see, you will be able to see and receive all these qualities, in a form that is appropriate for you.

Each word **must be compared with every word** until you have an ordered list. You will probably be surprised at the order if you have stayed with your heart and trusted your answers.

Here is how I do this.
(Don't worry, this is a step-by-step process. Not hard. Don't let worry get in the way. And if you would like to watch videos of how to do this you can find them at .)

22

Take a sheet of paper. Draw a line down the middle. Write the quality words on the left.

Put your finger on the first word on your partner's list. (This is so you don't lose your place.)

Ask the "which is more important" question, comparing the first word on the list to the second one.

If they say the first word, move on to comparing the first word to the third word.

What if they say the second word is more important? Great. Cross it off and move it to the right side of the page.

Now compare the first word to the third word. If they say the first word is more important, move on.

What if they say the third word is more important than the first? Great. Cross it off.

But before you move it to the right side of the page, you have to find out if it is more important, or less important, than the word that is already over there.

To do that, ask the "which is more important" question between those two words on the right.

Let's say the third word is more important than the second, so write it above the second word.

Go back to the left side of the list.

Your finger is still on that first word. Compare it to the fourth word, and so on down the list until you have done the entire left side of the list.

If you have found more words that are more important than the first one, they will go to the right side after you compare them to that list, from the bottom up.

For example:
You have two words on the right. The third word is first, and then the second.

Now you have a new word. Compare it to the second. If it is more important, compare it to the third. If it is more important, put it at the top, if it isn't, it goes in the middle.

(Here's where you realize you need lots of spaces between the words on the right because you never know where the list is going.)

After you have completed comparing the first word all the way down the list on the left, you will have some crossed-out words on the left, because they are now on the right in their right order.

Cross out the first word, and add it at the bottom of the list on the right.

Draw a line under that list. You are done with those words.

Go to the list on the left. Put your finger on the first uncrossed out word. Compare it with the next uncrossed out word below it.

Do the same thing with the words that you did before.

When you are done doing that with the new words, put a line under the list and start again on the left.

Usually, this is done in two or three passes. But keep going until all the words are crossed out on the left and in order on the list on the right.

Now you can move to how to use this list.

Remember, you can't ask yourself these questions. Otherwise, you will answer the question with the same mind that made it, the intellectual mind.

We need the heart, gut, intuitive mind answering to get the list in the correct order.

Even if you don't have a friend doing this course with you, you can still hand someone this "how to do this" information and let them walk you through your list.

I have a video for you to watch on how to do this here: perceptionu.com/the-library/**how-to-shift**/ You'll also find the workbooks here too!

How To Use A Quality Words List

Now that you have a quality word list, how do you use it? Of course, you could ignore it and hope things change. But now that you have put so much work into the list why not make the most of it?

Here are the four simple ways to use your list. Use it and get ready to experience more than you might imagine.

1. Use the qualities as a filter.

25

If something appears that you think might be what you are looking for and does not have at least the first four qualities—with the first one first and the rest following in order, it is not "it!"

Think of the time you will save if you can eliminate quickly and easily what is not right for you.

For example, you discover that safety is first on your quality list for a means of transportation and the car you are looking at has a very low safety record, don't buy this car no matter how much you love it.

If you buy it, you will eventually be unhappy with it, and somehow you will unconsciously figure out how to get rid of it.

2. See the qualities everywhere.

See the qualities in everything, not just in what you're seeking. Notice that they're always with you in many forms.

You have always had, and always will have, each quality on your list if you practice looking and expect to see it.

A quality does not have to belong to you. It can appear anywhere. All of what you see is your world. The goal is to notice that the quality you're looking for already exists everywhere, and since you can see it—it exists for you—now.

3. Be grateful for each quality as you see it.

Be grateful for these qualities each time you see them, no matter where they occur. If the person you dislike most has one of these qualities, be grateful that you have seen this quality in your life.

Know that if it is "out there" it was first "within here" and therefore always available, and always part of your life.

4. Be and live these qualities yourself.

Now that you have begun to live with these qualities I know that you are discovering that having the "thing" you wanted is no longer as important.

You have found that It already exists as thoughts—qualities.

As we express gratitude for this fact, we are living within Grace. The result?

Sometimes we realize we don't actually need the thing we were asking to see, or it turns up in another package, or it appears in a way more excellent than we could have dreamed.

Whichever way this happens, you have begun by seeking the essence of the "thing" that you want. That beginning cannot help but produce in your world whatever you need at the moment. You have always had it.

None of us have ever been abandoned, nor could we ever be. Looking for qualities opens our eyes to what has always been and always will be ours.

That changes everything.

FOUR

— · —

I CHOOSE

I choose, therefore I am.—Amit Goswami, The Self-Aware Universe

I wanted to change the world. But I found that the only thing one can be sure of changing is oneself.—Aldous Huxley

We choose to go to the moon. We choose to go to the moon in this decade and do the other things, not because they are easy, but because they are hard, because that goal will serve to organize and measure the best of our energies and skills, because that challenge is one that we are willing to accept, one we are unwilling to postpone, and one which we intend to win, and the others, too.—John F. Kennedy

At the end of each week, I have included a chance to do an I Choose sheet. If you feel no resistance at all to what you have discovered you want, then you could skip this step.

However, that is not likely, is it?

It is our resistance that keeps us stuck.

Sometimes that resistance is so apparent we are well aware of it. Other times, it hides in the shadows, and we only know it's there

28

because of the symptoms of lethargy, anger, and discouragement, to name a few.

I could spend a long time talking about resistance, but instead let me send you to Steven Pressfield's book, *The War Of Art*.

Although he is talking about resistance in terms of an artist, it applies to every one of us all the time.

So, let's assume that you have some resistance to living a better life, whether it is buried or noticeable.

Doing this extremely simple-to-do *I Choose* exercise works what others might call miracles.

One of those miracles happened to me many years ago. My husband had left, and I was clueless that was going to happen. I came home from a trip and he was gone.

I didn't know what to do. All my get up and go, had got up and left, too.

I was struggling to pay bills, feed my family, and support a home that I had just purchased.

I loved that house. I can still walk through it in my mind and tell you everything that was there because I designed the whole thing to be exactly how I wanted it to be.

I knew I needed to sell it because I couldn't afford the payments, but I resisted that idea until one day my oldest daughter, who was in her last year of high school, said, "Mom. Sell the house. You have no other choice."

I knew she was right. I had to do it. So I put into practice all the things that we are talking about in this book.

I gathered a small group of people I knew, loved, and trusted who also had some difficult decisions to make.

We formed what we called a flash mastermind group with the express intention of doing what we had been resisting, and doing it quickly.

We made *Quality Word lists,* and *I Choose* sheets. I did *I Choose* sheets every moment I had a chance to write. I sat in meetings and wrote them instead of taking notes. I covered sheets and sheets of paper.

Our flash mastermind group disbanded a month later after meeting only four times. We had all completed the task we had been resisting.

For me, my house sold at a higher price than my realtor thought was possible. It was the first offer, and it was for cash.

I never looked at those sheets after I wrote them out. There was no reason to rehash old thoughts.

It would have been like looking through the garbage.

Have I convinced you to try this out?

Consciously choosing will allow your life to unfold effortlessly.

We set ourselves up to fail in most of our choices or resolutions because we don't stop and listen to the monkey voice's response to the choice.

It always resists. **Always.** So unless we deal with our resistance, we struggle more than is necessary.

Let's Choose

At the end of each week in this book, you will have already set up what you want to choose. Using an *I Choose* sheet will move it forward.

Here's an example of what that might look like using an example that I think most people will relate to.

Begin by stating what you want as a choice.

Say this: *I choose to have a good-looking and healthy body.*

Now stop and listen!

Perhaps the voice says:

"Ha, well sure you may want to have this body, but you will have to exercise to get it."

Respond something like this:

I choose to exercise.

Listen again. Perhaps the voice says:

"You hate to exercise."

Respond:

I choose to love to exercise.

Listen again. The voice may say:

"You don't have the time to exercise."

Respond:

I choose to have the time to exercise.

The voice:

"You don't have anything to wear to exercise."

Respond:

I choose to have something to wear to exercise.

See how this works?

The list can, and probably will, run on for a page or two for just one simple choice.

Some of mine have gone on for days and days filling multiple sheets of paper.

Note: ONLY write your response. Do not write what that voice says.

What we are doing by choosing consciously is uncovering, without attachment and emotion, all the hidden choices and beliefs that have kept us from actually doing the thing we thought we had resolved to do. We are shifting our perception.

If you are doing this *Imagination Mastery* book with someone, share what you have chosen.

31

Then watch each other to make sure that you don't do or say things that contradict what you have chosen. You will become protectors of each other's dreams.

Remember, you can never consciously choose too often.

I have a choice in every moment to keep my heart open or closed, to live in love or fear. More than any other specific practice, I have found that maintaining the awareness of choice is the most important factor in keeping an open heart, for every action, every thought, every moment contains the potential for bringing us closer to either intimacy and healing or isolation and suffering. —Dean Ornish, M.D., Love and Survival: The Scientific Basis for the Healing Power of Intimacy

There is a vitality, a life force, a quickening that is translated through you into action, and there is only one of you in all time, this expression is unique, and if you block it, it will never exist through any other medium; and be lost.

The world will not have it. It is not your business to determine how good it is, nor how it compares with other expression. It is your business to keep it yours clearly and directly, to keep the channel open.

You do not even have to believe in yourself or your work. You have to keep open and aware directly to the urges that motivate you. Keep the channel open. No artist is pleased.

There is no satisfaction whatever at any time. There is a queer, divine dissatisfaction, a blessed unrest that keeps us marching and makes us more alive than the others. —Martha Graham

Unless this thing is consistent with the highest right, I do not want it; and if it is, I can trust God's law to establish it. —The Lord Thy Confidence (pamphlet from 1912)

SECTION THREE

Practice

FIVE

— • —

IMAGINATION IS EVERYTHING

*Y*our *imagination is everything. It is the preview of life's coming attractions.* —Albert Einstein

Now that you have the basic tools, are you ready to get started?

Each week has a different focus, but the imagination exercises each day will remain mostly the same.

Try not to get behind, but if you do, it's okay.
This is not a race. The turtle always wins because it stays focused.

If you get your rational mind out of the way when you start these exercises, you can complete each day's assignment within five to ten minutes.
Don't worry. Let go. Imagine.

Be like the White Queen!

"I can't believe that!" said Alice.
"Can't you?" the Queen said in a pitying tone. "Try again: draw a long breath, and shut your eyes."

Alice laughed. "There's no use trying," she said: "one can't believe impossible things."

"I daresay you haven't had much practice," said the Queen. "When I was your age, I always did it for half-an-hour a day. Why, sometimes I've believed as many as six impossible things before breakfast."

Every day we are going to be like the White Queen. She was quite the Imagination Master, wasn't she?

She was continuously trying to get Alice to become an Imagination Master, too. In this passage from Alice In Wonderland, the White Queen gives Alice a task.

Imagine six impossible things before breakfast.

So we are going to follow her advice but do it differently.

We are going to imagine seven impossible things every day for the next seven weeks.

Except, it doesn't have to be before breakfast, or even all at one time.

You can fill out your daily imagination forms as you go through your day, or all at once. Whichever way works best for you.

Personally, I like to sit down first thing in the morning and write out everything that comes to mind. When I allow my thoughts to flow, not judge them, I can complete this assignment within five minutes.

Perhaps it will take you longer at first, but pay attention. Is that part of yourself being like Alice and saying, "I can't believe that."

Remember we are not trying to be rational or use our intelligence, we are imagining!

By the way, here's how you can tell if you are in your rational mind as you do this.

When what you are writing doesn't feel impossible. Or it feels as if everything you imagine is stupid. Or silly. Or a waste of time.

Come on, let go.

Just for a few minutes a day, in the safety of your own life, imagine that life is full of glories, possibilities, that are entirely invisible to the rational mind.

Be irrational. Imagine what that will feel like. Be free!

Why seven impossible things, instead of six?

Because, years ago, when I first started teaching this exercise, everyone liked the number seven better.

It's a number that represents completion, so we are going with that!

Why imagine yourself as all the different kinds of beings that we are going to imagine ourselves to be each week?

Because we aren't birds, trees, animals, stone or flowers, therefore, we don't have preconceived notions about what it would be like to be one.

It's an all-new experience. It's out of our rational, controlling mind.

This workbook is all about expanding our imagination. We are going beyond what is evident to the senses so that we can break out of ruts and stuck places.

Don't fight it. Go with it.
By the end of this book, if you have done the work, all your questions about "why" will be answered.

Not by me, but by you and what you have discovered.

Go boldly where you have never gone before. Imagination. It's the final frontier!
It's where everything changes.

Six

— · —

Week One

I magination is more important than knowledge. Knowledge is limited. Imagination encircles the world. —Albert Einstein

Let's start our first week of imagining with these beautiful citizens of the sky—our bird friends.

Yes, this week you are going to imagine that you are a bird.

Maybe you know birds. Perhaps you don't pay any attention to them.

None of that matters in imagination.

Be the bird that arrived in your mind. **The one you just thought of as you read this.** Take that one. It has a message for you.

Don't bother telling me that no bird popped into your mind. One did. Accept it. Go with it.

Still, don't know what bird? Don't try to figure it out. If you are stuck, imagine that a bird did choose you. See. That worked.

This process will be correct for each week as we imagine ourselves to be something we are not, from birds, trees, stones, or flowers.

They will choose you. Let that happen.

Remember you are doing this to break out of what you have been doing all your lives.

Only then can you move into a new version of life, a better one. One that exists beyond our imagination right now. You are going to change that.

Ready to leap? Let's go!

Week One Set Up

Live out of your imagination, not your history.—Stephen R. Covey
Today's Date:_____
Remember: **Do not try to figure this out!**
Allow the divine, the creative force, imagination, to move your pencil.
Play with the idea of being your bird. What does it feel like? You can fly this week. Where are you flying to? What is your home like? What song do you sing?
This week I imagine myself to be this bird:_____
How would you feel if you were this bird? Listen within to hear the answers. Try for ten qualities! (This is your unordered quality words list.)
1._____
2._____
3._____
4._____
5._____
6._____

7. _____
8. _____
9. _____
10. _____

My bird looks like this to me: (Go ahead. Draw, paste, scribble, your bird. No, it doesn't have to look like it. Don't judge, Play!)

Check back to *Chapter Two* on Quality Word lists to remind yourself how to put these words in order and then how to use them.

My quality words in order for how I would feel if I were this bird.
1. _____
2. _____
3. _____
4. _____
5. _____
6. _____
7. _____
8. _____
9. _____
10. _____

Fantastic! Now that you have these qualities—use them. Imagine yourself as this bird this week instead of your ordinary self. Let this bird help you do your daily imaginations.

Week One: Day One

Today's Date:_____
My Seven Impossible Things Before Breakfast.

1._____
2._____
3._____
4._____
5._____
6._____
7._____

Week One: Day Two

Today's Date:_____
My Seven Impossible Things Before Breakfast.

1._____
2._____
3._____
4._____
5._____
6._____
7._____

Week One: Day Three

Today's Date:_____
My Seven Impossible Things Before Breakfast

1._____
2._____
3._____
4._____
5._____
6._____

7._____

Week One: Day Four

Today's Date:_____
My Seven Impossible Things Before Breakfast

1._____
2._____
3._____
4._____
5._____
6._____
7._____

Week One: Day Five

Today's Date:_____
My Seven Impossible Things Before Breakfast

1._____
2._____
3._____
4._____
5._____
6._____
7._____

Week One: Day Six

Today's Date:_____
My Seven Impossible Things Before Breakfast

1._____
2._____
3._____
4._____
5._____
6._____
7._____

Week One: Day Seven

Today's Date:_____
My Seven Impossible Things Before Breakfast

1._____
2._____
3._____
4._____
5._____
6._____
7._____

First Week Review

The world is but a canvas to the imagination. —Henry David Thoreau

Now that this first week is over, it's time to review what happened.

First, look over all the impossible things that you wrote. You have forty-nine of them to pick from, a treasure trove of abundance!

Did you do some more than once? Don't worry. Don't judge. That's just what happened.

Go ahead, pick the one you like the most and write it below. Can't decide? Just pick one. You can't go wrong.

Then spend a few minutes to write about it.
Again, I'll say it repeatedly. Don't judge. This isn't a writing contest.
No one will see it but you. Write it the way you want to. The important part is putting pen to paper and letting go.

What's happening here? We are training ourselves to be aware of what we are thinking and doing.
No matter how aware we might think we are, there is always room for improvement.
What if you discover you aren't aware? That's good news, too. It means you will experience the joys of awareness to an even greater extent as we travel through imagination together.

My Favorite Impossible Thing For The Week:

_____

_____

_____

_____

_____

Things I noticed:

_____

_____

_____

_____

_____

_____

What has changed?

_____

_____

_____

_____

_____

_____

First Week I Choose

Imagination will often carry us to worlds that never were. But without it we go nowhere.—Carl Sagan

Take one of your impossible things, perhaps your favorite one, choose it, and use it to do this exercise.

No matter how far "out there" it may be, use it anyway.

In this exercise, we are stretching out our minds just as we do our bodies. We can't get past our habits by staying in the same mindset.

I Choose sheets are another vital tool for being mentally flexible.

Remind yourself how to do this by reviewing Chapter Three, the I Choose chapter in this workbook. Have fun with this!

(This might be where you grab a piece of scrap paper and start writing. It's possible this could go on for pages!)

I Choose This Impossible Thing:

_____

_____

_____

_____

_____

_____

First Week Recap

If you did the work this week, you might be surprised by what happened. And imagine this, you have only just begun.
(If you haven't done it yet, don't fret. You can do it now!)

Here is what you have done this week.

You spent seven days imagining seven impossible things. You made a quality list of what you would feel like if you were the bird that picked you.

You chose your favorite imagination, thought about it, commented on it, and did an I Choose sheet, using it as a jumping-off point.

Did you notice that sometimes your daily assignment took only a few minutes a day?

Sometimes it took much longer. Neither is right or wrong.

This imagination work is not about how much time it takes to get it done, but overcoming the resistance to doing it.

When you run across resistance, tell it to go outside and play and leave you alone.

This is the most important kind of work you can do every today because it will make everything else easy, or unnecessary, and definitely more expansive.

Here are some quick "tricks" you can use to defeat that resistance.

- Don't judge how or what you write.

- Don't question it.

- Do follow the internal voice that is guiding you.

- Don't try to make it important.

- Don't try to write something to make it happen.

- Do let go.

- Do allow yourself to be delighted.

Yes! You can have more than seven imaginations a day. Seven primes the pump.

If your imagination starts to flow, go with it!

This entire workbook is designed to get the imagination juices going. If the flow of creativity starts acting like a raging river, grab a raft, and hang on for the ride of your life.

On the other hand, a quick reflection pool could be the perfect place to hang out.

Wherever you find yourself, be grateful. You have the ability to imagine. That in itself is a gift.

Reality is for people that lack imagination.—Hayao Miyazak

Seven

— • —

Week Two

I magination is the true magic carpet. —Norman Vincent Peale

Welcome to your second week of Imagination Mastery!

Just as the benefits of consistently doing any exercise changes you, so will doing these imagination exercises.

As with all exercise, sometimes the results are immediately noticeable.

Other times, we have to wait patiently and trust that what we are doing is working. But always, always, there will be results when we do the work.

With that in mind, shall we get started?

Pick Your Symbol

This week you are going to pick a tree, or you are going to allow a tree to choose you.

Stop a second. Even if you don't know the name of the tree that popped into your heart, choose it.

Take the time to learn more about your tree this week. What's its official name? How does it grow?
Allow the tree to give you messages that you can apply to your own life.

Perhaps your bird from last week visits your tree. What do they teach and share with each other, and with you?

Adding Something New

We are adding something else to your morning routine. Meditation.

To be more specific, *imagination meditation.*

Try to spend at least fifteen minutes every day and let yourself feel an imagination. It doesn't matter which one of your imaginations that you choose, anyone will do. None are more important than others.

Or imagine yourself to be a tree or your bird. What would that be like to live as a tree or a bird?

As you do your imagination exercises this week, don't try to make something happen, don't wish you were better than you are at imagination, don't want what you imagine to be important.

Nothing is more important than another. Everything counts equally.

Just let go.

For your meditation, find some place quiet that feels safe to you.
Let the thoughts go by without trying to do anything about them.
Allow yourself to drop into your feelings.

Enjoy this time. It will feel delightful once you get the hang of it.
Don't cheat yourself by leaving this out of your day. Even if you end
up having only two minutes, take those.

Remember, as always, no judgment—starting with yourself.

Week Two Set Up

Everything you can imagine is real. —Pablo Picasso

Today's Date:_____
Play with the idea of being your tree.
What does it feel like? This week you will stay in one place. Or do
you? Maybe you have a magical tree that walks. It at least sways. Trees
feed and care for the entire world. Look up the symbol of your tree.
How does that relate to you?

This week I imagine myself to be this tree:_____
How would you feel if you were this tree? Listen within to hear the
answers. Try for ten qualities! (This is your unordered quality words
list.)

  1._____
  2._____
  3. _____
  4. _____

5. _____
6. _____
7. _____
8. _____
9. _____
10. _____

My tree looks like this to me: (Go ahead. Draw, paste, scribble, your tree. No, it doesn't have to look like it. Don't judge, Play!)

Check back to *Chapter Two* on Quality Word lists to remind yourself how to put these words in order and then how to use them.

My quality words in order for how I would feel if I were this tree.

1._____
2._____
3. _____
4. _____
5. _____
6. _____
7. _____
8. _____
9. _____
10. _____

Fantastic! Now that you have these qualities—use them. Imagine yourself as this tree this week instead of your ordinary self. Let this tree help you do your daily imaginations.

Week Two: Day One
Today's Date:_____
Today's Meditation Focus:_____
My Seven Impossible Things Before Breakfast.
1._____
2._____
3._____
4._____
5._____
6._____
7._____

Week Two: Day Two

Today's Date:_____
Today's Meditation Focus:_____
My Seven Impossible Things Before Breakfast.

1._____
2._____
3._____
4._____
5._____
6._____
7._____

Week Two: Day Three

Today's Date:_____
Today's Meditation Focus:_____
My Seven Impossible Things Before Breakfast.

1._____
2._____
3._____
4._____
5._____
6._____
7._____

Week Two: Day Four

Today's Date:_____
Today's Meditation Focus:_____
My Seven Impossible Things Before Breakfast.

1._____
2._____
3._____
4._____
5._____
6._____
7._____

Week Two: Day Five

Today's Date:_____
Today's Meditation Focus:_____
My Seven Impossible Things Before Breakfast.

1._____
2._____
3._____

4._____
5._____
6._____
7._____

Week Two: Day Six

Today's Date:_____
Today's Meditation Focus:_____
My Seven Impossible Things Before Breakfast.

1._____
2._____
3._____
4._____
5._____
6._____
7._____

Week Two: Day Seven

Today's Date:_____
Today's Meditation Focus:_____
My Seven Impossible Things Before Breakfast.

1._____
2._____
3._____
4._____
5._____
6._____
7._____

Second Week Review
You need imagination in order to imagine a future that doesn't exist. —Azar Nafisi

Two weeks of imagining!
Can you feel your imagination's muscle getting stronger? Are some of your old viewpoints beginning to dissolve?

Did anything happen that surprised you this week?

What happened during your meditations?

Just make a note of it, but don't worry about what happened. Or even celebrate it. Because it will always be different, and it will always be perfect for the day.

Now is the time to pick one of your favorite imaginations and write about it. Why it's your favorite doesn't matter. What and how you write doesn't matter.

Remember, what we are doing is training ourselves to be aware of what we are thinking and doing. And then we are allowing our imaginations to bring us into unlimited possibilities.

Doing this is not work. It is a celebration!

My Favorite Impossible Thing For The Week:

_____

_____

_____

BECA LEWIS

_____

_____
_____
_____

Things I noticed:

_____
_____
_____
_____
_____

What has changed?

_____
_____
_____
_____
_____

Second Week I Choose

Worry is a misuse of imagination.—Dan Zadra

Take one of your impossible things, perhaps your favorite one, choose it, and use it to do this exercise.

No matter how far "out there" it may be, use it anyway.

In this exercise, we are stretching out our minds just as we do our bodies. We can't get past our habits by staying in the same mindset.

I Choose sheets are another vital tool for being mentally flexible.

Remind yourself how to do this by reviewing Chapter Three, the I Choose chapter in this workbook. Have fun with this!

(This might be where you grab a piece of scrap paper and start writing. It's possible this could go on for pages!)

I Choose This Impossible Thing:

_____

_____

_____

_____

_____

_____

Second Week Recap

Pat yourself on the back for making it this far in your workbook!

Starting a new habit and then sticking with it is hard. Acknowledge that to yourself.

Our human, old self, does not want to let go. It's going to do everything it can to distract us from changing.

When you notice this in yourself, try not to give this resistance more power by berating yourself for not being perfect.

Let it go. It's not you. Move on.

Instead, go back to your workbook. Fill in what you might have missed. Take a breath and begin again.

Be like a child that falls, laughs, and rises again.

That's you!

Let's review what we did this week.

You spent seven days imagining seven impossible things.

You meditated every day.

You made a quality list of what you would feel like if you were the tree that picked you.

You chose your favorite imagination, thought about it, commented on it, and did an I Choose sheet using it as a jumping-off point.

Did you miss any of this?

Don't worry. Don't give up. Keep going.

If you are in a mastermind group, perhaps you all could set a way to check in daily to make sure you've done your imagining for the day.

If you don't have someone to do this with, set your own type of reminder!

I know you won't let yourself down, and if you do, you'll pick yourself up and keep on going. You know why?

Because you are an Imagination Master, that's why!

EIGHT

— · —

WEEK THREE

I *magination and creativity can change the world.*—Anonymous

Perception Rules

Before we begin our week, let's take a moment and briefly examine one of my favorite topics: perception. There are two modes of perception—*state of mind and point of view.* Our point of view is what we believe to be true and want to be true.

It's what we intentionally, or unintentionally, use as the building blocks of our lives. However, points of view become ruts and habits, if not consistently examined, and too often we become prisoners of our point of view.

In this course, we are stepping out of ruts by stretching our point of view into something that better aligns with the concept of an infinite Intelligence, a loving God, an abundant life.

This shift will open our self-imposed cell doors and begin to change our lives for the better. If that were all it took, it would be fantastic.

But as I said, there are two modes of perception, and they have to agree with each other. Which means if we desire a permanent change, we also have to shift our state of mind perception.

State of mind refers to our emotions and feelings. It's what we feel to be true, either out of a form of joy or out of fear. Guess which mode is stronger. You're right. It's the state of mind perception.

We can believe that God is good all we want, but if our internal emotions and feelings reside in either fear or doubt that it is true for us, our outside world will more closely match that state of mind rather than our point of view.

This need to align our perceptions is why I have added so many exercises like meditation, writing, and choosing in this course. To do this, we have to feel what we believe and want. Once we get our state of mind perception in harmony with our point of view perception, we are in-sync, or in-flow with the universe.

Here's what we want to do. We want to bring our state of mind and point of view into harmony. Until our emotions and feelings are the same as our point of view, it will be hard to make changes. And if we do succeed, it will be hard to do.

Why? Because we had to make it happen by fighting our hidden perceptions. When our perceptions aren't in harmony with each other, what we accomplish won't be as satisfying or as long-lasting. Doing this work, we are not making anything happen. We are getting out of the way.

If you would like more about perception, my book *Living in Grace: The Shift To Spiritual Perception* lays the whole idea out in an easy-to-understand form. My book *The Four Essential Questions: Choosing Spiritually Healthy Habits* looks at these two modes of perception in another way, with the focus of breaking out of limiting ruts and paradigms. Find these two books anywhere you get your books.

Welcome to your third week of Imagination Mastery!

We are more often frightened than hurt, and we suffer more from imagination than from reality.—Seneca

Are you settled into a routine for getting your daily imagination work done? Are you using your quality words to see your life differently? Have you taken the time to put them in order? It's so important to do this.

Often in our lives, we make choices based on a preference that we think we have. Habits and expectations are easy to follow. Like taking the same road to work every day. But what if that isn't the best road for you to take?

Using your ordered quality words as a tool to make decisions will help break those habits and dissolve those expectations that don't fit who you are, or what you want.

If you are new to Quality Word lists, I Choose sheets, and meditation, then these new tools might feel strange at first. But eventually, you will discover they are incredibly useful tools to use in your daily life.

I mean, who doesn't need a hammer, a wrench, and a screwdriver in their house? These tools are the same. Simple, easy to use, perfect for almost every situation.

However, like all tools, they only do you good if you use them.

Pick Your Symbol

This week you are going to pick an animal, although by now you might be aware that it is often the symbol that chooses you.

There is one other problem with picking an animal. It is so tempting to choose one that you already love, or you have a relationship with. No. Not that one, even if it was the one that popped into your head. Instead, pause, listen again, and let it be something new.

Maybe it will be an animal that you don't even like or know anything about. It doesn't matter, go with that one.

Remember, this course is all about shifting, locked in perceptions, and points of view. Every animal has something to teach us, and qualities to share.

Something New!

We are adding one extra element to your imagination workbook. After the week is over, you are going to write a short imagination. Notice that I didn't say a short story because I don't want you to worry about the quality of what you are writing.

This is a short imagination. Perhaps include your bird, tree, or animal. Maybe use one of your imaginations as a jumping-off spot.

Whatever you use, don't worry about proper writing style, spelling, grammar, etc. This writing isn't for anyone but you. Perhaps one day it will grow into something more, but for now, it is a mind-stretching exercise.

Oh, and don't forget your meditation time. Maybe your animal will hang out with you, maybe under the tree, or in the tree with you, along with your bird.

Goodness, you are attracting quite a family, aren't you?

Enjoy your week!

Week Three Set Up

The best use of imagination is creativity. —Deepak Chopra

Today's Date:_____
Play with the idea of being your animal. What does your animal do? How does it move? How does it take care of its young? Where does it live? Look up the symbol of your animal. How does that relate to you?

This week I imagine myself to be this animal:_____

How would you feel if you were this animal? Listen within to hear the answers. Try for ten qualities! (This is your unordered quality words list.)

1._____
2._____
3._____
4._____
5._____
6._____
7._____
8._____
9._____
10._____

My animal looks like this to me: (Go ahead. Draw, paste, scribble, your animal. No, it doesn't have to look like it. Don't judge, Play!)

Check back to *Chapter Two* on Quality Word lists to remind yourself how to put these words in order and then how to use them.

My quality words in order for how I would feel if I were this animal.

1._____
2._____
3. _____
4. _____
5. _____
6. _____
7. _____
8. _____
9. _____
10. _____

Fantastic! Now that you have these qualities—use them. Imagine yourself as this animal this week instead of your ordinary self. Let this animal help you do your daily imaginations.

Week Three: Day One

Today's Date:_____
Today's Meditation Focus:_____
My Seven Impossible Things Before Breakfast.

1._____
2._____
3._____
4._____
5._____
6._____
7._____

Week Three: Day Two

Today's Date:_____
Today's Meditation Focus:_____
My Seven Impossible Things Before Breakfast.

1._____
2._____
3._____
4._____
5._____
6._____
7._____

Week Three: Day Three

Today's Date:_____
Today's Meditation Focus:_____

My Seven Impossible Things Before Breakfast.

1._____
2._____
3._____
4._____
5._____
6._____
7._____

Week Three: Day Four
Today's Date:_____
Today's Meditation Focus:_____

My Seven Impossible Things Before Breakfast.

1._____
2._____
3._____
4._____
5._____
6._____
7._____

Week Three: Day Five

Today's Date:_____
Today's Meditation Focus:_____
My Seven Impossible Things Before Breakfast.

1._____
2._____
3._____
4._____
5._____
6._____
7._____

Week Three: Day Six

Today's Date:_____
Today's Meditation Focus:_____
My Seven Impossible Things Before Breakfast.

1._____
2._____

3._____

4._____

5._____

6._____

7._____

Week Three: Day Seven

Today's Date:_____

Today's Meditation Focus:_____

My Seven Impossible Things Before Breakfast.

1._____

2._____

3._____

4._____

5._____

6._____

7._____

Third Week Review

Happiness is not an ideal of reason, but of imagination. —Immanuel Kant

Three weeks in, and things are changing. Have you noticed?

Did anything happen that surprised you this week?

What happened during your meditations? Are you forgetting to do them? Why? Just observe what happened.

Read the imagination story that you wrote. What does it tell you about yourself and the world around you?

This is all about awareness of what perceptions drive our reality, so that we can allow our lives to stretch into the infinite.

Third Week I Choose

The true sign of intelligence is not knowledge but imagination. —Albert Einstein

Take one of your impossible things, perhaps your favorite one, choose it, and use it to do this exercise.

No matter how far "out there" it may be, use it anyway.

In this exercise, we are stretching out our minds just as we do our bodies. We can't get past our habits by staying in the same mindset.

I Choose sheets are another vital tool for being mentally flexible.

Remind yourself how to do this by reviewing Chapter Three, the I Choose chapter in this workbook. Have fun with this!

(This might be where you grab a piece of scrap paper and start writing. It's possible this could go on for pages!)

I Choose This Impossible Thing:

_____

_____

_____

_____

_____

_____

Remember, what we are doing is training ourselves to be aware of what we are thinking and doing. And then we are allowing our imaginations to bring us into unlimited possibilities.

My Favorite Impossible Thing For The Week:

_____
_____
_____
_____
_____
_____

What has changed?

_____
_____
_____
_____
_____

Here's your new assignment for the week:

Write a short imagination. Be your bird, tree, or animal. Or take one of your daily imaginations and write what would happen if it were true.

_____
_____
_____
_____
_____

Third Week Recap

Congratulations on keeping up with the Seven Impossible Imaginations every day. If you sometimes struggle with this, perhaps do them a different way.

Instead of writing them down in your workbook, write somewhere else. Or record them. Or draw them. The point is to imagine.

Why not imagine all the different ways you can do an assignment? Not just this one. What about "life" assignments? How can you do them differently, so they bring meaning and joy to you?

Did you also play with your animal? Maybe you rode on its back through the forest. Imagine. Anything.

Don't get serious.

Don't judge.

Let it flow. Let imagination use you for the Divine's purpose of being creative.

If you still struggle, pay attention to what is stopping you. Noticing it is the first step to resistance losing its power.

Let the play and joy of imagination transform your daily life and expect to experience and see things you have never seen or experienced before!

And let the imagination story you write at the end of each week tell itself to you. You will be surprised at what happens!

Here's what you did this week:

- You spent seven days imagining seven impossible things.

- You meditated every day.

- You made a quality list of what you would feel like if you were the animal that picked you.

- You chose your favorite imagination, thought about it, commented on it, and did an I Choose sheet using it as a jumping-off point.

- You wrote an imagination story.

It was a good week, wasn't it?

NINE

— · —

WEEK FOUR

I magination is the true magic carpet. —Norman Vincent Peale

Welcome to your fourth week of Imagination Mastery!

How did your short imagination writing go for you this week? Was it easy? Hard? Did you judge everything that you wrote or just let it flow?

As a fiction writer, I love the moments when I get into the story, and my imagination takes me away to some place I have never been before. Even as you write these little "stories" for yourself, let that happen.

Leave the world as you think it is, and let that part of you that knows there is more open up.

As I have mentioned before, it's not about how good your imagination writing is, it's that you do it, and then let the doing of it transform you.

So even though writing your imagination adds a few extra minutes onto the last day of each week, take the time to do it.

Actually, it doesn't have to be at the end of the week. Any time you get an idea, flip to your page and start writing. Or write on your computer, or on your phone, or record it.

Whatever you way you choose to imagine, is the right way for you.

Pick Your Symbol

This week you are going to pick a stone.

What? A stone? Yes, a stone.

Stones are amazing. They were here on this Earth long before we arrived. They hold the history of our world. Maybe our universe.

It doesn't have to be a special stone, like a gemstone. It could be a rock in your garden or one that you picked up at the beach or a walk in the woods.

See if you can discover what kind of stone it is by searching the internet for information. What are its qualities? What does it symbolize? Every stone has a story. Let it tell it to you.

You could even use the story of the stone for your imagination writing this week.

Week Four Set Up

But, I nearly forgot you must close your eyes, otherwise...you won't see anything.—Alice, Alice in Wonderland

Today's Date:_____

Play with the idea of being your stone. What would that feel like?

This week I imagine myself to be this stone:_____

How would you feel if you were this stone? Listen within to hear the answers. Try for ten qualities! (This is your unordered quality words list.)

1._____
2._____
3. _____

4. _____
5. _____
6. _____
7. _____
8. _____
9. _____
10. _____

My stone looks like this to me: (Go ahead. Draw, paste, scribble, your stone. No, it doesn't have to look like it. Don't judge, Play!)

Check back to *Chapter Two* on Quality Lists to remind yourself how to put these words in order and then how to use them.

My quality words in order for how I would feel if I were this stone.

1._____
2._____
3._____
4._____
5._____
6._____
7._____
8._____
9._____
10. _____

Fantastic! Now that you have these qualities—use them. Imagine yourself as this stone this week instead of your ordinary self. Let this stone help you do your daily imaginations.

Week Four: Day One

Today's Date:_____
Today's Meditation Focus:_____

My Seven Impossible Things Before Breakfast.

1._____
2._____
3._____
4._____
5._____
6._____
7._____

Week Four: Day Two

Today's Date:_____
Today's Meditation Focus:_____
My Seven Impossible Things Before Breakfast.

1._____
2._____
3._____
4._____
5._____
6._____
7._____

Week Four: Day Three

Today's Date:_____
Today's Meditation Focus:_____
My Seven Impossible Things Before Breakfast.

1._____
2._____

3._____

4._____

5._____

6._____

7._____

Week Four: Day Four

Today's Date:_____

Today's Meditation Focus:_____

My Seven Impossible Things Before Breakfast.

1._____

2._____

3._____

4._____

5._____

6._____

7._____

Week Four: Day Five

Today's Date:_____

Today's Meditation Focus:_____

My Seven Impossible Things Before Breakfast.

1._____

2._____

3._____

4._____

5._____

6._____

7._____

Week Four: Day Six

Today's Date:_____
Today's Meditation Focus:_____
My Seven Impossible Things Before Breakfast.

1._____
2._____
3._____
4._____
5._____
6._____
7._____

Week Four: Day Seven

Today's Date:_____
Today's Meditation Focus:_____
My Seven Impossible Things Before Breakfast.

1._____
2._____
3._____
4._____
5._____
6._____
7._____

Fourth Week Review

Imagination takes you everywhere.—Anonymous

You did it! You completed your fourth week. Stand in front of the mirror and thank yourself for showing up.

I'm not kidding. Really. Go do it. How about doing it right now. I'll wait.

It was weird, wasn't it? But empowering. You can trust yourself to do what you said you would do.

I know there will be times you won't, but every time you do, it strengthens that muscle.

Imagine that you can show up for yourself all the time. What would that feel like?

Pretty good, right? It will only get better, so keep going!

Fourth Week I Choose

Imagination creates reality.—Richard Wagner

Take one of your impossible things, perhaps your favorite one, choose it, and use it to do this exercise.

No matter how far "out there" it may be, use it anyway.

In this exercise, we are stretching out our minds just as we do our bodies. We can't get past our habits by staying in the same mindset.

I Choose sheets are another vital tool for being mentally flexible.

Remind yourself how to do this by reviewing *Chapter Three*, the I Choose chapter in this workbook. Have fun with this!

(This might be where you grab a piece of scrap paper and start writing. It's possible this could go on for pages!)

I Choose This Impossible Thing:

_____

_____

_____

_____

_____

_____

Remember, what we are doing is training ourselves to be aware of what we are thinking and doing. And then we are allowing our imaginations to bring us into unlimited possibilities.

My Favorite Impossible Thing For The Week:

_____

_____

_____

_____

_____

Things I noticed:

_____

_____

_____

_____

_____

What has changed?

_____

_____

_____

_____

_____

_____

Write a short imagination. Be your bird, tree, animal, or stone. Or take one of your daily imaginations and write what would happen if it were true.

_____

_____

_____

_____

_____

_____

Fourth Week Recap

The only limit to your impact is your imagination and commitment.—Tony Robbins

What did you and your stone do this week?
What information did you learn from it?
Perhaps patience?
Or the use of pressure and "hard times" to transform you and your life into something that shines.

It's been a busy week. Here's what you did:

- You spent seven days imagining seven impossible things.

- You meditated every day.

- You made a quality list of what you would feel like if you were the stone that picked you.

- You chose your favorite imagination, thought about it,

commented on it, and did an I Choose sheet using it as a jumping-off point.

- You wrote an imagination story.

You are over halfway through. Things are changing, aren't they?

TEN

— • —

WEEK FIVE

I magination is an instrument of survival.—Rogier Van Der Heide

Welcome to your fifth week of Imagination Mastery!

Perhaps by now doing imagination work every day has become part of your routine.

But if not, don't worry about it. Don't allow that mean voice in your head to berate you for what you haven't done. Instead, start now, even if you have to begin in the fifth week. Just start. Or go back and begin again. It's okay to start over.

The hardest part of doing anything is showing up. No one is judging your imaginations, or writing, or habits. So don't do it to yourself.

Just show up for yourself over and over again until the showing up part becomes part of your nature. Everything will evolve from there.

Use the tools that you are learning to be present for yourself. Perhaps do an I Choose sheet that begins with something like—I choose to show up for myself. Or this one—I trust to do what is right for me. Or the simple version, I trust myself.

The results might surprise you.

Pick Your Symbol

This week you are going to pick a flower. This one should feel pretty good. Who doesn't want to be a flower?

Are you going to be a flower you know or a new one? What does it mean to you? Why?

Remember, it doesn't have to be a showy flower. What about the tiny flowers we walk on without noticing? Or the ones that spread fragrance in the air but their blooms are barely noticeable.
Of course, there are the ones that spark our gardens into something spectacular. How do they do that?

Where does your flower like to grow? How many of its qualities can you find within yourself?
What does this flower symbolize to you? To the world?

Enjoy the idea of flowers this week. Let it be a beautiful one.

Week Five Set Up

What is now proved was once only imagined.—William Blake

Today's Date:_____
Play with the idea of being your flower. What would that feel like?

This week I imagine myself to be this flower:_____

How would you feel if you were this flower? Listen within to hear the answers. Try for ten qualities! (This is your unordered quality words list.)

1._____
2._____
3. _____
4. _____
5. _____
6. _____
7. _____
8. _____
9. _____
10. _____

My flower looks like this to me: (Go ahead. Draw, paste, scribble, your flower. No, it doesn't have to look like it. Don't judge, Play!)

Check back to *Chapter Two* on Quality Lists to remind yourself how to put these words in order and then how to use them.

My quality words in order for how I would feel if I were this flower.

1._____
2._____
3. _____
4. _____
5. _____
6. _____
7. _____

8._____
9._____
10._____

Fantastic! Now that you have these qualities—use them. Imagine yourself as this flower this week instead of your ordinary self. Let your flower help you do your daily imaginations.

Week Five: Day One

Today's Date:_____
Today's Meditation Focus:_____

My Seven Impossible Things Before Breakfast.
1._____
2._____
3._____
4._____
5._____
6._____
7._____

Week Five Day Two

Today's Date:_____
Today's Meditation Focus:_____

My Seven Impossible Things Before Breakfast.

1._____
2._____

3._____
4._____
5._____
6._____
7._____

Week Five: Day Three

Today's Date:_____
Today's Meditation Focus:_____

My Seven Impossible Things Before Breakfast.

1._____
2._____
3._____
4._____
5._____
6._____
7._____

Week Five: Day Four

Today's Date:_____
Today's Meditation Focus:_____

My Seven Impossible Things Before Breakfast.

1._____
2._____
3._____
4._____

5._____

6._____

7._____

Week Five: Day Five

Today's Date:_____

Today's Meditation Focus:_____

My Seven Impossible Things Before Breakfast.

1._____

2._____

3._____

4._____

5._____

6._____

7._____

Week Five: Day Six

Today's Date:_____

Today's Meditation Focus:_____

My Seven Impossible Things Before Breakfast.

1._____

2._____

3._____

4._____

5._____

6._____

7._____

Week Five: Day Seven

Today's Date:_____
Today's Meditation Focus:_____

My Seven Impossible Things Before Breakfast.

1._____
2._____
3._____
4._____
5._____
6._____
7._____

Fifth Week Review

When one paints an ideal, one does not need to limit one's imagination. —Ellen Key

Congratulations! You've completed your fifth week of being an Imagination Master.

I hope you are as proud of yourself as I am of you. By now, things should be moving around in your life enough to see that this simple idea changes lives.

If you are working with a friend or a group, this may be an excellent week to pause and appreciate the power of community.

If you are doing this by yourself, you are still in a community.

There are hundreds, maybe thousands, of other people doing this course, too. Imagine that they are present for you, as you are for them.

You are always being watched over.

How do I know?

Because we are all connected, we are all an integral essence of the One Divine Intelligence.

Imagine that!

Fifth Week I Choose

To raise new questions, new possibilities, to regard old problems from a new angle, requires creative imagination and marks real advance in science.—Albert Einstein

Take one of your impossible things, perhaps your favorite one, and choose it to do this exercise.

No matter how far "out there" it may be, use it anyway.

In this exercise, we are stretching out our minds just as we do our bodies. We can't get past our habits by staying in the same mindset. I Choose sheets are another vital tool for being mentally flexible.

Remind yourself how to do this by reviewing *Chapter Three*, the I Choose chapter in this workbook. Have fun with this!

(It's possible this could go on for pages!)

I Choose This Impossible Thing:

_____

_____

_____

_____

_____

Remember, what we are doing is training ourselves to be aware of what we are thinking and doing. And then we are allowing our imaginations to bring us into unlimited possibilities.

My Favorite Impossible Thing For The Week:

_____

_____

_____

_____

_____

_____

Things I noticed:

_____

_____

_____

_____

What has changed?

_____

_____

_____

_____

Write a short imagination. Be your bird, tree, animal, stone, or flower. Or take one of your daily imaginations and write what would happen if it were true.

_____

_____

_____

_____

_____

_____

Fifth Week Recap

Now that we are at the end of the fifth week, don't forget to spend some time with your imagination story.

You can write, draw, or speak into a recorder an imagination about the five elements you have imagined yourself to be so far. You've been a bird, tree, animal, stone, and flower.

See, you've been many parts of nature. Has it inspired you to take a walk, or sit in nature more? Perhaps do your meditation in nature. Feel what it is sharing with you. Rest in the fact that you are always part of this Oneness.

Here's what you did this week:

- You spent seven days imagining seven impossible things.

- You meditated every day.

- You made a quality list of what you would feel like if you were the flower that picked you.

- You chose your favorite imagination, thought about it, commented on it, and did an I Choose sheet using it as a jumping-off point.

- You wrote an imagination story.

Here we go... Week six coming up.

ELEVEN

— · —

WEEK SIX

R *eality leaves a lot to the imagination.*—John Lennon

Welcome to week six of Imagination Mastery

If you are here, congratulations, you rock!

Now that you are truly becoming an Imagination Master, don't forget you can do these assignments in whatever way works for you.

This workbook is a guide, not a rule.

Let your imagination run wild. Imagining won't hurt anyone or anything, as long as you always begin with the intent to be—and do—good.

If for some reason temptation snuck in to imagine bad things, don't go there.

That's the what-if of worry, or revenge, or competition, or winning at someone else's expense.

No matter what, don't let that imagination take over. Although it may look as though some people get away with that kind of behavior, it won't last, and no matter what they say, they are not happy.

Stay in the lane of choosing the best for everyone. Don't let the claim of being better than someone else remove you from the joy of experiencing infinite Love.

We all are tempted sometimes. And sometimes, we make the mistake of succumbing to that temptation.

But we can all come back, and be stronger for it. Imagine yourself, and everyone that your thoughts rest upon, as a child of the Divine. Imagine that and all will be well.

Pick Your Symbol

This week you are going to imagine yourself having at least one superpower. You can keep that superpower all week, or change it daily, or even twice a day.

Do you think that you have no idea what superpower you would choose?

You know I don't believe that. I believe that all of us harbor a desire to be more, have magic, do things we can't normally do.

Movies and TV shows filled with people with superpowers are everywhere. That's because it taps into all our desires.

So go ahead. Have a superpower. Imagine using it in your daily life. What would you do with it?

That's what you are going to imagine each day!

Let yourself feel child-like, open to imagination, and the joy it brings.

At the end of the week, write, draw, speak into a recorder, an imagination about you with your super, or magical, powers.

Week Six Set Up

Imagination will often carry us to worlds that never were. But without it we go nowhere.—Carl Sagan

Today's Date:_____

Play with the idea of having a super power and or being magical. Perhaps you are a wizard? Or a shapeshifter?

What would that feel like? What could you do? How would you live life differently?

This week I imagine myself to have this superpower:_____

How would you feel if you were this superpower? Listen within to hear the answers. Try for ten qualities! (This is your unordered quality words list.)

1._____
2._____
3._____
4._____
5._____
6._____
7._____
8._____
9._____
10. _____

My superpower feels—or looks—like this to me: (Go ahead. Draw, paste, scribble, your superpower. No, it doesn't have to look like it. Don't judge, Play!)

Check back to *Chapter Two* on Quality Lists to remind yourself how to put these words in order and then how to use them.

My quality words in order for how I would feel if I were this superpower.

1._____
2._____
3. _____
4. _____
5. _____
6. _____
7. _____
8. _____
9. _____
10. _____

Fantastic! Now that you have these qualities—use them. Imagine yourself as this superpower this week instead of your ordinary self. Let your superpower help you do your daily imaginations.

Week Six: Day One

Today's Date:_____
I have this superpower:_____

Seven Things I Could Do With It.

1._____
2._____
3._____
4._____
5._____
6._____
7._____

Week Six Day Two

Today's Date:_____

I have this superpower:_____

Seven Things I Could Do With It.

1._____

2._____

3._____

4._____

5._____

6._____

7._____

Week Six: Day Three

Today's Date:_____
I have this superpower:_____

Seven Things I Could Do With It.

1._____

2._____

3._____

4._____

5._____

6._____

7._____

Week Six: Day Four

Today's Date:_____
I have this superpower:_____

Seven Things I Could Do With It.

1._____
2._____
3._____
4._____
5._____
6._____
7._____

Week Six: Day Five

Today's Date:_____
I have this superpower:_____

Seven Things I Could Do With It.

1._____
2._____
3._____
4._____
5._____
6._____
7._____

Week Six: Day Six

Today's Date:_____
I have this superpower:_____

Seven Things I Could Do With It.

1._____
2._____
3._____
4._____
5._____
6._____
7._____

Week Six: Day Seven

Today's Date:_____
I have this superpower:_____

Seven Things I Could Do With It.

1._____
2._____
3._____
4._____
5._____
6._____
7._____

Sixth Week Review

If you can imagine it, you can achieve it. If you can dream it, you can become it.—William Arthur Ward

Phew. Six weeks wrapped up and finished! Do you realize that you have written two-hundred and ninety-four imaginations?

Plus, you have added into your life at least one superpower. Maybe more.

Imagine that!

You did this by doing one day at a time. Steady. No rushing. This is how things that last are accomplished.

And you have cracked the code.

Congratulations!

Sixth Week I Choose

The world is but a canvas to the imagination. —Thoreau

Take one of your impossible things, perhaps your favorite one, choose it, and use it to do this exercise.

No matter how far "out there" it may be, use it anyway.

In this exercise, we are stretching out our minds just as we do our bodies. We can't get past our habits by staying in the same mindset.

I Choose sheets are another vital tool for being mentally flexible.

Remind yourself how to do this by reviewing *Chapter Three*, the I Choose chapter in this workbook. Have fun with this!

(It's possible this could go on for pages!)

I Choose This Impossible Thing:

_____

_____

_____

_____

_____

_____

_____

Remember, what we are doing is training ourselves to be aware of what we are thinking and doing. And then we are allowing our imaginations to bring us into unlimited possibilities.

My Favorite Impossible Thing For The Week:

_____

_____

_____

_____

_____

Things I noticed:

_____

_____

_____

_____

_____

What has changed?

_____

_____

_____

_____

_____

_____

Write a short imagination about being your superpower. Perhaps add in your bird, tree, animal, stone, or flower. Or take one of your daily imaginations and write about what would happen if it were true.

_____

_____

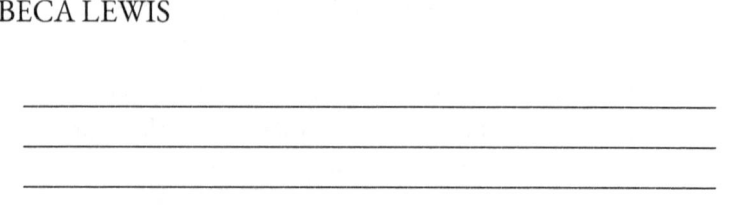

Sixth Week Recap

Superpowers are fantastic. Being magical is lovely. But doing what we say we are going to do has more power than all of that.

So if you are here, you already have a superpower —the ability to keep going in spite of temptations, distractions, distress, or even success.

You have kept a promise to yourself. There is magic in that!

Here's what you did this week:

You spent seven days imagining having superpowers.
- You meditated every day.

- You made a quality list of what you would feel like if you were that superpower that picked you.

- You chose your favorite imagination, thought about it, commented on it, and did an I Choose sheet using it as a jumping-off point.

- You wrote an imagination story.

Just one week to go. And because I know how much fun having superpowers can be, we'll continue with that for one more week, and then we'll wrap it up and see what we have done.

If you have a habit of stopping before you finish something, notice that, and keep going. Finish this. Trust yourself to do what you promise yourself that you will do.

Ready? Let's go!

Twelve

— • —

Week Seven

A *nyone who lives within their means suffers from a lack of imagination.* —Oscar Wilde

Although unplanned by me, our seventh week landed on the eleventh chapter. There are always signs and symbols waiting for us and I love this one.

What do these two mean?

Number seven is considered the number for completion, and eleven is often associated with moving from personal power to spiritual power.

Perfect, right?

Because after this week, you will have completed seven weeks of imagination, and that has moved you from thinking you are in charge and into more of an acceptance that the Divine is in charge.

As we erase our biases and locked in perceptions, we experience more of that Reality as the doors of our perception open into the Infinite.

Take this last week and luxuriate in the opportunity to do this kind of work.

It's an opportunity to shift your life by doing nothing more than shifting your perceptions and then following the residual guidance into what you do with your daily life.

Pick Your Symbol

This week we are staying with superpowers. Try out a few different ones. Perhaps, ones you might never have thought of before.

What if you could make yourself as small as an ant, or as large as a building? What if when you blinked, the world changed colors, or you waved your hand, and everything stood still except you.

For your seven impossible things every day you'll be imagining what you could do with your superpowers.

How would you change your world?

Have fun—no judgment or listening to the mean voice in your head. Ever. But this week I have your attention, so I can remind you.

Play!

Let the Divine creative force move through you this week.

Imagine how that feels and flow with it.

Week Seven Set Up

Imagination is the beginning of creation. You imagine what you desire, you will what you imagine, and at last, you create what you will.—George Bernard Shaw

Today's Date:_____

Play with the idea of having a super power and or being magical. Perhaps you are a wizard? Or a shapeshifter?

What would that feel like? What could you do? How would you live life differently?

This week I imagine myself to have this superpower:_____

105

How would you feel if you were this superpower? Listen within to hear the answers. Try for ten qualities! (This is your unordered quality words list.)

1._____
2._____
3._____
4._____
5._____
6._____
7._____
8._____
9._____
10._____

My superpower feels—or looks—like this to me: (Go ahead. Draw, paste, scribble, your superpower. No, it doesn't have to look like it. Don't judge, Play!)

Check back to *Chapter Two* on Quality Word lists to remind yourself how to put these words in order and then how to use them.
My quality words in order for how I would feel if I were this superpower.

1._____
2._____
3._____
4._____
5._____
6._____
7._____
8._____

9. _____
10. _____

Fantastic! Now that you have these qualities—use them. Imagine yourself as this superpower this week instead of your ordinary self. Let your superpower help you do your daily imaginations.

Week Seven: Day One

Today's Date:_____
I have this superpower:_____

Seven Things I Could Do With It.

1._____
2._____
3._____
4._____
5._____
6._____
7._____

Week Seven Day Two

Today's Date:_____
I have this superpower:_____

Seven Things I Could Do With It.

1._____
2._____
3._____
4._____

5._____
6._____
7._____

Week Seven: Day Three

Today's Date:_____
I have this superpower:_____

Seven Things I Could Do With It.

1._____
2._____
3._____
4._____
5._____
6._____
7._____

Week Seven: Day Four

Today's Date:_____
I have this superpower:_____

Seven Things I Could Do With It.

1._____
2._____
3._____
4._____
5._____
6._____

7._____

Week Seven: Day Five

Today's Date:_____
I have this superpower:_____

Seven Things I Could Do With It.

1._____
2._____
3._____
4._____
5._____
6._____
7._____

Week Seven: Day Six

Today's Date:_____
I have this superpower:_____

Seven Things I Could Do With It.

1._____
2._____
3._____
4._____
5._____
6._____
7._____

Week Seven: Day Seven

Today's Date:_____
I have this superpower:_____

Seven Things I Could Do With It.

1._____
2._____
3._____
4._____
5._____
6._____
7._____

Seventh Week Review

Reality can be beaten with enough imagination. —Mark Twain

Since we are in our seventh and final week, we have a slightly different review.

It involves all those quality word lists that you have done these last seven weeks.

You are going to take the top word from each of your ordered lists and *bring them into one quality word list.*

If you have duplicates, don't put them in twice. Instead, use the word below that in this master list.

At the same time, make a separate list of the duplicate words. In a minute, we are going to do something with both those lists. But, like all quality word lists, they are first unordered and then they must be ordered.

There are only a few more things to do. Remember how good completion feels.

Enjoy doing this. It's like designing the blueprint of the "house" you want to live in from now on.

Do the lists, then we'll talk about how to use them at the end of the chapter.

This is your unordered list of the top quality words from the last seven weeks.

1._____
2._____
3. _____
4. _____
5. _____
6. _____
7. _____

This is your ordered list of the top quality words from the last seven weeks.

1._____
2._____
3. _____
4. _____
5. _____
6. _____
7. _____

This is your unordered list of the duplicate words from the past seven weeks.

1._____
2._____
3. _____
4. _____
5. _____
6. _____
7._____

This is your ordered list of the duplicate words from the past seven weeks.

1._____
2._____
3. _____
4. _____
5. _____
6. _____
7. _____

Seventh Week I Choose

Imagination is the power of the mind over the possibilities of things.—William Stevens

Yes, one last *I Choose* sheet.

You have seven weeks of things from which to choose.

You could always go back and re-choose something you chose before.

After all, you are different now.

Or choose something new. By now, I Choose sheets are second nature for you.

You can write them on scraps of paper, on the paper placemat at the restaurant while you wait for your food, or say them into a recorder.

Do them in a way that works for you, but do them!

Consciously choosing is one of the most powerful things that we can do.

Sometimes it feels like life, and the world is choosing for us. Here's your chance to change that.

I Choose This Impossible Thing:

_____

_____

_____

_____

_____

_____

My Current Favorite Impossible Thing:

_____

_____

_____

_____

_____

Things I noticed:

_____

_____

_____

_____
_____
_____

What has changed?

_____
_____
_____
_____
_____
_____

Here's your last imagination. It is your chance to imagine something you have never imagined before. Be something other than yourself. Let your imagination run wild.

We live in an infinitely expanding universe. There is no reason to keep ourselves inside of a story that is limiting in any way. No one will know what you write here unless you want to share. Let joy and goodness lead the way. Imagine that!

_____
_____
_____
_____

THIRTEEN

— • —

RECAP

*B*ring ideas in and entertain them royally, for one of them may be the king.—Mark Van Doren

You did it!

You completed seven weeks of imagining! As a result, your outside life is changing.

Have you noticed? It had to have happened because when you change, so does your life.

All you have to do is notice, and celebrate it, and then keep practicing.

But before we end our seven weeks together, we have those last two quality lists to discuss.

We can't leave them out because they are like the treasure at the end of the rainbow.

These last two quality lists can travel with you for the rest of your life.

Or you can replace or add to them if you do this class again. As you change, evolve, see things differently, your lists may change.

Just like we can turn around when we realize we are on a journey to a destination we don't want, we can do that in life, too.

But we need a place to start.

So, yes, you can do this course over and over again. You can take time off or immediately begin again.

But for now, let's talk about what to do with your ordered quality words that ended up on your master list.

Obviously, they mean a great deal to you. Because with all the quality words vital to you, the ones on this list made the top seven.

What does that mean to you?

It means that by using these quality words as guides, you can now consciously choose what you want to experience in life.

Here are two examples of what that might mean:

It might mean you change the chairs in your living room because comfortable is the top word on your master list, and although the chairs are beautiful, they are not comfortable.

Or perhaps the top word on your list is valued.

If so, that might mean you need to examine your relationships to discover if they value you. (I mean it. You have to. Now that you are conscious of what you desire, you can't ignore it.)

If they don't, or you don't, why not? Pay attention. Is it them, or you?

Did you think you don't deserve more, or are they unwilling or incapable of valuing you? Maybe it's a mix of both.

No matter. Now you can choose consciously.

Do you want to stay unvalued? Of course not.
So you can do an I Choose sheet that begins with something like, I choose to be valued. Then release all the reasons why you block yourself from feeling valued.

If you still aren't being valued, then you can choose to let go of those relationships or jobs. Sometimes, by doing this work, this kind of thing takes care of itself. Other times you will need to take action.

What's important is that you take this Master Quality List seriously. It is the key to transforming your life to match who you are and what you desire.

Go through the how-to-use the list in Chapter Two again, and follow the four steps outlined there.

I can make you a promise that if you do this work, things will change in the direction of your conscious intent.

If I had told you that this *Imagination Mastery* book is a class in learning how to be a wizard or a magician, then no matter how much work it entailed, you probably would have agreed it was worth it.

Well, these simple things do work like "magic."
Not because we are breaking any laws of the universe, but because we are tapping into the one that can't be altered.

What you perceive to be reality magnifies.

In the Enneagram, The Stages of the Work, it's stated slightly differently,—"If you were transformed, the world would be transformed."—but it's the same.

Now for the second list that you made.

This is the list of the duplicate words. I think you already know why I had you separate them from your Master List.

These qualities are more than important to you, they are essential. So much so, that they ended up at the top of more than one list.

Ask yourself if you are honoring your basic life needs represented by these quality words.

Have you, and are you, designing your life around them? Or are you ignoring them? If so, you are doing it at the risk of your own unhappiness.

But I know you aren't going to do that anymore. You are an Imagination Master, and you have the tools at your fingertips to help you with whatever you need to do.

Let's say that the top quality on your duplicate list is love.

The word love is so all-encompassing that it needs more of your attention. What kind of love? From whom? In what way?

It would be a fantastic idea to do a quality word list for the way that you would feel if you were experiencing the kind of love you meant when you chose that word.
Then, you will have a clearer idea of what you want love to be like in your life.

Clarity and conscious choosing are imperative.

What if by the quality of love you mean you would like to spend more time with your family but to feel more valued at work, you work harder?

Or you believe that your family needs the money more than time with you? Are these beliefs undermining the quality of love in your family?

By becoming clear about what you want and putting your quality words at the forefront of your choices, everything begins to work together in harmony.

I could go on and on about the importance of this work, and how to use it.
That's why I have written more books on the subject. So perhaps pick up one of those books, if you would like to learn more.

But for now, not to worry.

What you are doing within this Imagination Mastery book will transform your experience of life, if you let it.

Let me know if I can help. ~ Beca

PS
Don't forget that you can get the free workbook pages for this book in two places either at becalewis.com or perceptionu.com/the-library/workbooks where you can also find videos that will teach you how to do Quality Word lists and I Choose sheets.

Go confidently in the direction of your dreams, and live the life you have imagined.—Henry David Thoreau

Fourteen

— ◆ —

Acknowledgements

M y heartfelt thanks to the *Imagination Mastery* class for being the beta testers for this book.

And for those wonderful members of the *Beca Book Community* who checked this book (and so many more) for accuracy.

Thank you especially to Jet Tucker and Jamie Lewis for cleaning up all my errors, and always being there when I need them to check up on me.

SEVEN STEPS TO RIGHT THINKING

—•—

WHAT OTHERS SAY ABOUT THIS BOOK

I *have read several of Beca's books and taken many of her classes.*
Each one gets better and better as I grow and begin to understand
my spiritual journey. The Right Thinking book was one of my
favorites. While perfect at any stage of your life, it helped me start the
transition from working to retirement. For a person who has worked
all her life and loves her career, the idea of retirement was scary. I felt
like I would be losing my identity. In the end, I was able to realize that
my life's purpose did not stop at retirement. I am now enjoying my next
stage of life. Thank you, Beca!!!! — Patricia Kearney

Whether you take it with a group or read the book on your own, this
course is so helpful if you are like me. I tend to overthink things, so I
need simple, practical guidelines for any learning process, especially
in the spiritual arena. Beca took me through all the steps, in sequence,
helping me to build a solid foundation on which to ground myself and
live a much more graceful life—a life of truly Right Thinking! — Jet
Tucker

SECTION ONE

Preparation

FIFTEEN

— · —

PREFACE

This system of Right Thinking is deceptively simple. Only seven steps. There is no need to go into lengthy explanations of each step. They are easy to understand.

The only thing difficult about the process is doing it.

Without telling you exactly what to do, which never works for anything, especially for something like this, my intent is to give you enough guidance to easily find your way through this process.

You are in charge during this process—you and your God. Trust that. Listen to your heart, try out the logic, and do the work. The results will speak for themselves.

NOTE: Although this book has a "workbook" section in it, if you would like an actual workbook where you can write in the answers, I have a free one for you here: https://perceptionu.com/the-library/workbooks/

Sixteen

—•—

Preparing

Trust is the first step to love. — Premchand

Before you begin, there are a few things I would like you to know.

Please treat this book as a workbook for life. You can apply this Right Thinking system to any situation.

I would say to heal it, but really it produces a shift in thinking and that shift reveals what is actually going on, which results in what appears as healing.

This could be an emotional, physical, or mental healing because all healing begins the same way. By thinking rightly, which leads to the right action to take.

There is always action required. We have to participate. What that participation looks like depends on you and the situation.

But by applying Right Thinking, it will much more likely result in the right action.

Yes, Right Action is one of the seven steps, and we'll talk about it more when we get there, but in the meantime, it's essential to know that action will be required of us.

And since this book is about Right Thinking, it's clear that if we stick with what is Right, it will be the Right Action.

Because I have structured this book as a system, this book works well within a mastermind group or with a friend or two.

A like-minded community will help keep you on track, and as in all communities that support and listen to each other, it will magnify and hasten the results.

So see if you can find someone, or a group of people, to do this Right Thinking system with. Choose people that have your best interest in mind. I mean that last part. Be sure they have your best interest in mind.

Even the best family member or friend does not always have that intent. Choose carefully.

Find people who have the same desires as you to shift their lives and who you can trust to keep your "secrets."

Don't think you know anyone like this? Don't worry!

Read and follow this system on your own. I know that someday you will find people like that because like-minded, like-souled people find each other when the time is right.

If you need help, let me know. There might be a group going on that you can join, or I could be teaching a live class just as you begin this. You can find me at becalewis.com.

Take this time for deep thinking and the chance to rejuvenate your life. Don't wait. Get started.

Things will shift to bring you what you need and want if you are faithful to the practice and yourself. It always starts there.

With yourself. And faith.

Not sure you have it? You do. Or you wouldn't have opened this book.

That's enough faith right there.

He who believes himself to be far advanced in the spiritual life has not even made a good beginning. — Jean Pierre Camus

I remember the day I first taught this Right Thinking system. I had been playing with the concepts and steps on my own for a few years, and I was excited to see what others thought about it.

In my mind's eye, I can see the room that I rented in a tiny motel near Carlsbad beach in Southern California in 2003.

A small group of men and women joined me. We were off in the corner of a dark room, but none of us noticed. We were in the middle of applying something that could shift our thinking from what wasn't working to what would work.

Everyone in the room already knew me, and most of them were very familiar with The Shift System that I had been teaching for many years.

So I didn't have to explain the background of what we were doing. I just had to explain the Right Thinking steps to them.

We spent the day experiencing the shift of perception that the awareness of Truth brings. We rejoiced, knowing that we had taken the right steps towards healing.

And that's what we are doing together here—in a book instead of a class.

We are walking our thinking through *Seven Steps of Right Thinking* that will shift us out of our limited human belief systems and into the infinite possibilities of big T Truth and big R Reality.

Now, as then, as we keep our thought process within big T Truth, it results in an improved situation, whether it is a mental, physical, or an emotional problem.

Yes, these steps can be applied in any order, depending on the circumstances. But I have my favorite order, which is what we'll be doing in this book.

Often the work we do will affect areas we didn't expect to get better.

Why? Because everything is connected. And as we willingly shift our perceptions to a higher understanding of Truth, it affects everything in our world.

Shifting to big T Truth, we replace a false belief and perception that has hidden the Divine's perfection from us. And that produces what looks like healing.

However, beliefs and perceptions are stubborn, often persistent. Accepted as normal. But when we stop thinking of problems as something we have to fix, and instead as only a perception we have to shift, it becomes easier.

Before we begin, it's essential to understand that just because it is a belief or a perception doesn't mean it's not being experienced.

We are not discounting the experience of a belief while we shift it. That would be cruel and unkind. Beliefs and perceptions are real to the person experiencing them, including ourselves.

Compassion, kindness, and practical help are essential components of Right Thinking.

And just because we call it a belief is not a reason to say to ourselves, or someone else, that we caused it because of our flawed thinking, or mistaken beliefs, or misperceptions. No.

Problems are never, ever, ever something we made happen. We, and they, are not to blame. No, sir. Never. Our choices may have kept us in a problem or put us there, but we didn't create them. We just took a road to where we didn't mean to go.

As soon as we fall into blame-thinking, we are back into the problem for ourselves or others.

Actually, we have made it worse because we have accepted it as reality. Then guilt and judgment are in charge because it would have us believe that we are God and can cause or create something.

Do you know what is really happening? We are misperceiving the Creation that the Divine Intelligence that is Love has put into place.

No. I don't know why. And I try not to care because as soon as I go there, whoops. There I am again, back into the belief of a problem.

Where I want to be is in the Mind of Love. I want to see the world the way Infinite Intelligence sees it. Experience it the way omnipresent Love experiences it.

When we achieve that state of being—bam—what appears as a problem dissolves.

Is it this immediate? Sometimes.

If we get that glimpse of the Truth that these seven steps reveal and hold on to it, that problem has nowhere to exist.

But often, it is working through the so-called problem that gets us somewhere.

We have to recalibrate our perceptions and our beliefs. Realign ourselves with Truth repeatedly. Argue for Truth like a lawyer.

And since this is the way healing often happens, we might as well get every teeny bit of goodness out of the time it takes.

Like Jacob wrestling with the Angel, we can say, "Let me learn this lesson. I want wisdom. I want my eyes fully open to Truth."

Since that first class, I have taught the Seven Steps To Right Thinking course many times. Each time I learn more about how it works and better ways to present it.

The result? It's finally ready to be a book. This book. Only seven steps. Use them any way that works for you.

When it's a class, it's seven weeks. If it is you at home, it's seven seconds, seven minutes, seven hours, seven days. Whatever it takes.

Systems are only guidelines. Not rules.

Let your intuition, the quiet voice within, guide you. You can't go wrong. I mean it. You can't go wrong.

You and I are the action, the expression of Divine Love.

And Love is never wrong!

Remember, problems are only a misperception. And we can shift that.

One more thing.

Because I think of this book as a course, I am writing it as if I am speaking to you in a class. I am thinking of you—yes, you—as I write.

You and I are One. That's the Truth. Now let's practice that Truth together using these seven steps and watch the world shift for the better. Not just for us, but for everyone.

I'll see you on the other side.

SEVENTEEN

— • —

PERCEPTION

There are things known and there are things unknown, and in between are the doors of perception. —Aldous Huxley

There is no getting around it. Perception is reality. Perception creates reality. That means to get anything done or live a life of meaning and purpose, we have to continually shift our perceptions.

If you have read any of my other books, you have run across this idea before, but it bears repeating because it is easy to forget.

We are never trying to make something happen or stop something from happening.

What we are always doing is practicing, working on, shifting our perceptions towards the Infinite.

From there, everything falls into place.

But first, we have to be willing.

And then, if we are smart, and of course we are, we choose a point of view perception of the highest, best, most perfect life possible, and then we shift our state of mind perception to match.

Why not? No one wants to live in fear, or poverty, or ill health, or unhappiness.

However, we have all experienced someone who refuses to see a solution because their point of view perception or paradigm does not include that solution.

We've heard the excuses. "People are not meant to fly. No one can run a four-minute mile. Go to the moon? Impossible."

Usually, our shifts aren't this huge. But every shift of perception, every moment of willingness to admit that something better is possible, changes our lives.

Yes, every change in perception, from trying a new brand of a product to letting go of how we used to do something and trying a different way, shifts our experience.

However, it doesn't do any good to choose a new perception that only includes a new point of view. We have to align our entire belief system with it. I call this the state of mind perception.

Our point of view and state of mind perceptions must be in harmony with each other. Otherwise, it's a push-pull process that keeps us stuck in the problem.

Shifting our point of view perception is what the *Bible* might call the letter of the law. Good to have, but it's not what brings healing. It's the spirit of the law that does, and our state of mind perception is just that.

Not putting the two together is like calling ourselves a good person and then harming another on purpose—something we see all too often in the world.

Religious wars are a misalignment between point of view and state of mind perceptions.

Thinking others must conform to our perspective because it is what God wants of us, by hating and destroying those that don't believe as we do, is often the result.

That is not Right Thinking and is what we want to rewrite for ourselves.

For example, we could have the point of view that the Divine supplies all our needs, but wake up each morning in fear of not having enough.

That is a misalignment between our point of view and state of mind, and that misalignment will not allow us to experience the healing that we desire.

Emotion, or state of mind, overrides our point of view.

Advertisers know this. That's why they use techniques to bring our feelings, wants, and desires into alignment with what they want us to believe—that their product is the best one available, and we need it.

Using this Right Thinking system, it becomes easier and easier to not agree with anything that isn't for the highest good, not only for ourselves but also for others.

First, we need to choose the highest point of view that we can imagine.

Here is the point of view I am using throughout this book.

Perfection is already present. Everywhere. There is only one creation, and it is Spiritual. It is the universe in which we live.

Yes. I know. It doesn't feel like this most of the time. That's okay. It's still Truth.

The Divine is the intelligent omnipresence of Love and is the one and only creator. Not the creator of our material perception. It is the creator, designer, infinite intelligence of Spiritual Reality.

Sounds good, right? It is. I love it. I believe it. It is, with no equivocation, my point of view.

I choose this point of view because I know that what I perceive to be reality magnifies, and I want, need, and desire to live a life filled with purpose, love, creativity, plenty, etc.

Yes, I have to remind myself of this point of view all the time. It takes practice since it is not the worldview.

Now comes the next part.

We want to move our state of mind into alignment with this point of view, and we need tools to do this. We need ways we can get better at the practice.

Right Thinking is one of those ways.

If we can bring our point of view and state of mind into complete alignment with the Truth of everyone's perfection as the idea, expression, reflection, of the Divine Principle of all Life, then the illusion of a problem falls away, and we experience what is called healing.

Sometimes that happens in a moment, and sometimes the problem takes time to fade away.

Sometimes we will be so engrossed in Truth we'll forget that we had a problem. Because even though healing is the expected result, our desire lies in understanding more about our true Spiritual nature as the reflection of the Divine.

Practicing this point of view means we have to give up how we—within the belief that we are human—think it should be.

This is because we could never, in our wildest dreams, come up with a better outcome than what letting go of our ego will reveal.

Before we start, let me take a moment and say how grateful I am for you.

Everyone who chooses a path of Right Thinking, the spiritual path, is a light for everyone else. As you shift your perception, it helps the entire world move into the harmony of Divine Love.

You have chosen the path of a spiritual warrior, a singer of harmony, a dancer of Spirit. Thank you.

EIGHTEEN

— · —

YOUR WAY

To live content with small means; to seek elegance rather than luxury, and refinement rather than fashion; to be worthy, not respectable, and wealthy, not rich; to listen to stars and birds, babes and sages, with open heart; to study hard; to think quietly, act frankly, talk gently, await occasions, hurry never; in a word, to let the spiritual, unbidden and unconscious, grow up through the common–this is my symphony. — William Henry Channing

Are you ready to begin? You can decide now how long you want to take to go through this book. Take one step a day, or one step a week, or one step an hour.

Do what works for you. However you decide, it will be perfect for you. If it's not, make adjustments until it is.

A few years ago, I thought I would emulate some of my author friends and write a book every six weeks. Yes, some of them were doing it even faster than that, but with everything else I was doing, I knew six weeks was my limit.

I lasted through three books.

And then I discovered that writing that quickly wasn't satisfying for me. At all. I felt rushed continuously and always worried and anxious.

For what? I asked myself. To be like someone else? To make more money?

I knew that if those were the reasons, it would never work. I would eventually sabotage myself to make it stop. This is not a good way to live.

Through the next few books, I kept fiddling with the process until I discovered my timing.

And yes, I still have to remind myself to keep writing when it gets too hard. But that's true for anything, even if it is something we love to do.

It was the rhythm of it I was after. What could I do that kept me motivated but not overwhelmed?

Do this system of Right Thinking the same way. Stay motivated. But don't make yourself crazy, trying to keep a schedule that isn't yours.

One way to figure out what works for you is to ask yourself if what you are doing is sustainable. Can you keep it up?

That's what I did with writing. I changed to a schedule sustainable for me. I keep adjusting the schedule so I can keep doing this without making myself so overwhelmed that I have to fight the desire to quit.

Not to get overwhelmed is a good intent for me. Ask my husband. He can tell when I have made myself crazy by making myself a list that no one can keep up with for long.

Of course, he doesn't like it when I am reacting to being overwhelmed because he has to work around it. I know you know what I mean.

When we are not paying attention to what works for us, not only do we make life hard for ourselves but also for those around us.

No one should become stuck in the status quo. But don't give yourself so much to do that it becomes debilitating. Life is not static. We can, and continuously must, keep adjusting what we do to fit the changing dynamics of daily life.

Do this system. Practice it. But do it your way.

In the process, don't harm yourself or anyone else. Always aim for the next right step. You can tell if it's the next step because it will bring more joy for anyone your life touches—starting with your own.

Alright. Now that you have chosen a schedule that you think will work for you, knowing that you can change it, we will spend some time together doing the most important thing we can do—shift our everyday habitual thinking to Right Thinking.

Right Thinking is the thinking which begins and ends with the desire to raise our understanding of the Infinite, and experience the results in our lives and the lives of those around us, both near and far.

We begin with the first step of Right Intent.

Where else would we start? We have to begin with Right Intent in order for everything else to begin with the correct Principle.

We start with our desire to choose a clear intent for every thought and action. To ground it in the first commandment of "Thou shalt have no other Gods before me."

Years ago, I discovered a prayer that helps me establish my intent in every action, but especially in the ones I am afraid to do or don't want to do, which—not surprisingly—are often the same thing.

It is part of a poem written by Mary Baker Eddy, and it goes like this, "... my prayer, some daily good to do for Thine, for Thee; and offering pure of Love whereto God leadeth me."

What a great place to start!

To make things easy, I'll assume you are doing this system one step at a time for a week. Doing it this way, the first time through this, will give us time to absorb each step's meaning and practice it.

For this first week, let's be sure we are thinking and acting from Right Intent.

To do this, we must pull in all our perception skills. Don't worry. We will have lots of practice.

As you do this course, pause often, observe without judgment, and listen deeply.

Here we go!

SECTION TWO

Seven Steps

Nineteen

Step One - Right Intent

The most difficult thing is the decision to act, the rest is merely tenacity. The fears are paper tigers. You can do anything you decide to do. You can act to change and control your life; and the procedure, the process is its own reward. — Amelia Earhart

No matter what we do, it is always best to start with our Right Intent.

Many people start with a goal or a to-do list, but not us. We always begin with intent. We will get to goals and to-dos later.

But why do we start with intent?

Because our goals can change, and if our goals change, then so do the to-dos for reaching those goals. That is a good thing because it means we are adjusting to changing circumstances.

But intents stay the same. We may change our intent to a different one, but once we have an intent, then the goals and to-dos will naturally fall into place.

Another way to see the difference is that intent is not measurable, although you will see and feel the difference. Goals and to-do lists are.

For example, as a writer, I intend to communicate clearly, entertain, and shift thinking to infinite possibilities.

How many books, what kind of books, when to publish them, how to write them, and how to sell more books, fall into goals, and to-do lists, and are things that I can measure. They grew out of my intent.

Remember, actions are measurable, intents are not. Remembering that will help us decide if what we want is a goal or an intent.

We must always, always begin with intent.

Not only will we be more focused, but with clear intent, we will be more content with whatever we choose to do.

Think of your intent as the why behind the action,

For example, to write this book or teach the class, I had to set an intent. You might say that I had a goal to teach a class. Sure. But why? Because without that why, I could easily lose interest or get pulled off track.

So first, what was my intent for putting together this *Seven Steps for Right Thinking*?

I wanted to have a path to walk for when I, or anyone else, needed to experience healing.

It's the "anyone else" that I always want to be present in my intents. I want my intents to align with what I have accepted as a mission: share ways to shift thinking and lives towards the Infinite.

Yes, I could have said this was my goal, but since it is the reason, or the why behind the action and is not measurable, I recognize this as my intent.

However, although intent—or the why—is always powerful, we are interested in Right Intent.

Someone who has lost their moral compass could set an intent to do harm.

That is never our intent.

So let's review what we mean by Right.

Look for strengths in people, not weaknesses; for good, not evil. Most of us find what we search for. — J. Wilbur Chapman

All the words that we will use in this system are familiar: intent, premise, reasoning, practice, action, etc. We use these words and do these actions all the time. What makes this system work is that we put the word Right in front of them.

When the word Right is an adjective, it includes the words justified and acceptable.

Do we want to use the words justified and acceptable in our definition? Usually not. At least we have to see them as warning signs to look deeper.

If we have to justify our decisions, intent, and actions, we may be heading down the wrong path.

Justification is a warning sign to ourselves that we are probably not making the right choice. We are making a more comfortable choice, a more familiar choice. When we do that, we have to look again to make sure it is the right choice.

And is doing only partially the right thing acceptable? Usually not. And yes, sometimes we have to make concessions and compromises. But even then, we need to base them on the Right Intent.

Which brings me back to religious wars, well, actually any war. Wars have to be justified by the ones declaring them. They need to make their actions acceptable to themselves first so they can convince others.

On a smaller scale, we may justify why we cheat, look away when someone needs our help, or gossip instead of help.

This doesn't mean that sometimes we have to justify our actions when we need to do something that others might consider wrong.

Is it wrong to steal bread when you are hungry?

Or was it more wrong to allow situations where someone is hungry and then punishing them for doing their best to survive?

We know the answer.

We always have to see actions from a higher Intent, and it is the highest right we currently know and considering the circumstances.

But if that still small voice says that it isn't the right thing to do based on the law of Love, it's best to stop and reexamine the motive behind the intent.

As a noun, the word Right means that which is morally correct, just, or honorable.

And that's what we mean by it, too. But that brings us back to questioning what is morally correct, just, and honorable.

I think we know it when we see it. Or understand it when we feel it. It's right when it doesn't break Spiritual laws or the spirit of another being.

We will discover more about what is morally correct, just, or honorable to us during this practice.

And why does it matter?

There are three principal reasons.

First, because when we don't choose the morally good, correct path, everything eventually falls apart.

And second, because we intend to be good people. How do I know that is one of your intents? Because you wouldn't be reading this book if you didn't want that for yourself.

And the third reason is that we know that *what we perceive to be reality magnifies.*

That means that if we believe and act as if it's true—that good is the only power—then good we get. When we give morally ambiguous choices the power, that's what we get.

Which brings me back to the first reason for choosing the highest Intent we know in each moment.

If we don't, eventually, everything falls apart.

While I was writing this book, the world was in the middle of the 2020 pandemic. For the first time in recorded history, everyone in the world stopped doing what they were doing.

COVID 19 literally stopped the world. It gave us all both a microscope and a wide-angle view of human nature and people's choices. It gave us a chance to reset everything.

We discovered that some people, perhaps unconsciously, wanted to express their personal freedom more than they cared about possibly hurting others. That's not a Right Intent.

It was "I have a right to do this" point of view and involved justification and rationalization.

When we make these kinds of choices, we may overlook the broader interpretations of what our actions mean and their consequences.

Everyone made hard decisions. But only the solutions made with the safety of everyone as a community in mind could be called Right Intent.

We discovered that most people are kind, caring, and thoughtful. Most people go out of their way to help. We also found that it was easy to be caught up in fear. To lash out and call it a right of freedom.

Everyone had to rethink their lives and make choices about what to do next. The decisions and choices made from our highest understanding at the time of the right thing to do were Right Intent.

In this book, that is what we will practice doing.

The more we practice, the better we will be at it. We'll change our intents as we gain wisdom, which will indeed happen.

Remember, the intent is an overall decision. It's why we do things. It is not a goal. It is not a list of to-dos.

As we set our intents, we'll do our best to select morally good, just, kind, and expansive ones.

However, as we gain insight and wisdom, we will also expand our awareness of what we are doing and have a clearer understanding of if it is right.

That is a good thing. An intent to move into a higher understanding of our true spiritual nature underlies everything about *The Shift System* and *Right Thinking*.

Narrowing it down, so we don't have so many words to say, we use the word Right.

So now that we know what we mean by Right, let's get started with setting Right Intents, and that begins with ourselves.

TWENTY

— • —

PERCEPTION

We are social creatures to the inmost centre of our being. The notion that one can begin anything at all from scratch, free from the past, or unindebted to others, could not conceivably be more wrong. — Karl Popper

We need to add a few steps to this Right Thinking process before going any further.

It would be lovely if by merely choosing our intent, everything would fall into place with no more effort on our part.

But you and I know it doesn't work that way. Too many old beliefs and habits get in the way. So we need to address this problem. We need to root out those old perceptions and replace them with ones that will let us experience the Right Intents that we are setting.

Remember the point of view and state of mind modes of perception that we talked about in Chapter Two? They are the key to making these shifts, so I have some thinking exercises for you to do for both these modes.

Don't pass these exercises by thinking they aren't necessary. They are.

First, an explanation or two, and then I'll use Sally as an example of how they work.

Because what we don't know does hurt us, we need to discover what hidden perceptions have been driving our lives around without our conscious consent.

Although sometimes we are aware of these perceptions, beliefs, and habits, we usually ignore them, either because we don't think they are doing us any harm or changing them seems too difficult.

Sometimes we don't change them because we don't think it is allowed, or shifting them will take us into uncharted territory.

Yes, we have the Divine's permission to change our beliefs, because otherwise, how will we move to a higher understanding of Love?

And yes, we will move into uncharted—for us—territory. But help is always waiting for us.

And it shall come to pass, that before they call, I will answer; and while they are yet speaking, I will hear. — Isaiah 65:24

Yes, life will change. That's the point, after all. But it will change for the better.

Shifting Our Point of View

Much of what goes on in our lives begins with the point of view we have accepted about ourselves.

Happily, we have a choice about how much of it we want to keep. We can change it. We don't have to accept anything about ourselves if it doesn't align with our true spiritual natures.

None of us has escaped this problem. So as we work on Right Thinking, let's discover what is not right thinking.

Although we will address what is Right Identity as one of the seven steps, we first have to uncover those perceptions, beliefs, and habits that we have accepted as accurate about who we are.

Start a written list of what you say to yourself about who you are. Include what others tell you about who you are, and what the worldview says you are.

This list is essential to uncovering the beliefs that underlay everything we believe about ourselves. If you had a mouse in your house, would you search it out before it did damage? What about a raccoon? Or a moose?

Hidden thoughts and beliefs are the same. They do damage to our lives. Root them out. To get started, all you have to do is write them down. It's an observation practice.

Some are good things to identify with, others not so much. It doesn't matter, add them all to the list. Keep writing.

The most important thing of all—besides noticing—is not judging. Just notice. Give this exercise your physical attention, but not your emotional attention. This exercise will continue all our lives. It's part of re-writing our story. Don't worry. I'll remind you to do it.

Shifting Our State of Mind

But what about our state of mind?

In our world, there are so many things going on that affect how we feel that it's imperative to pay attention to our state of mind.

There are many techniques to calming the mind and bringing us back to the harmony that underlies all of Life.

We could meditate. Go for a walk. Sit in nature. Listen to bird songs. Breathe. Our intent is to quiet the mind and the thoughts that tell us we are not doing it right.

Some people call this the inner critic, the judge, the monkey mind. It always lies.

TWENTY-ONE

— • —

YOU FIRST

When you move, the Universe moves. When you reach, it reaches. When you stretch, it stretches. But always, you must go first. — Mike Dooley

I mentioned that my intent behind putting together this *Seven Step System for Right Thinking* was because I wanted to have a path to walk when I—or anyone else—needed to experience healing.

Notice how my intent starts with me and then reaches out to others.

I point this out because I want you to start with yourself too. Not stay with yourself, start with yourself.

Too many of us were trained to accept that we must think of others first. But doing it that way does not work in the long run, because it's not sustainable.

The commandment to do unto others as we would have them do unto us means that we better be taking good care of ourselves first because that is the only way we can continue to do good unto others.

Sure, some people don't need to be reminded to think about themselves first. These are the people who don't care how their actions affect others. I doubt if they are reading this book.

But we all know them. And if you are part of one of these people's lives, the likelihood that you suffer because of them is high.

Because without the desire to assist others, those people are dangerous to themselves and the world.

Right Intent must be an intent that does no harm and blesses everyone it touches.

Too many people get lost in the desire for power and lose their awareness of their connection to Divine essence and their obligation to care for others as themselves.

Can this system be applied to healing a person or situation harmful to you personally or the world? Absolutely.

However, it will be your perception of them that heals. We are not in charge of what that will look like. However, we know it will be better for you and them—if they are willing.

The underlying and motivating intent behind Right Thinking is spiritual renovation.

To give you an example of what Right Intent could look like, this is the one I made for the class and for this book:

- To practice clean, clear thinking, which will, in turn, dissolve the darkness of fear and ignorance.

- To renew hopes and aspirations within ourselves and share it with others.

- To pour out a cleansing flood of spiritual Right Thinking for ourselves, our families, the world.

- To rejoice together, knowing that the reign of harmony is already within us, and present for everyone, everywhere.

- Within the class, we added this intent: To fully participate in this community of like-minded souls so that every member feels the support and encouragement of walking with a group of people on the same path with everyone's best interests in mind.

To make this book as practical as possible, because spirituality is useless if it's not practical, I made up a person, I've named her Sally, and I will walk you through how she might apply this system to her problem(s).

But first, let's look at some examples of what people who took the class stated as their intent.

Then we'll move on to Sally's and yours.

Sample Right Intents:
- To live, hear, and share Truth.

- To live in this world as Joy and Grace

- To exude Enthusiasm.

- To be grateful for God's blessings.

- To listen carefully.

- To be productive.

- To express joy each day.

- To use technology to further my life's purpose.

- To know I can share my gifts.

- To notice where my attention has been going.

- To block all negative influences from my life.

- To accept and recognize joy around me.

- To feel the divine energy of Spirit.

- To stay in the Now.

- Wherever God leads me, I shall go.

- To find focus.

- To dance for exercise & meditate for relaxation.

- To reconnect to my inner plug.

- To transform myself and my life.

- To get more organized.

- To stay present.

- To be grateful and reset everything that matters.

- To put my foot down and say no to error.

- To focus on love, not fear.

- To make a daily productive schedule.

- To embrace my "new normal."

- To celebrate going within.

- To develop a life full of happy, healthy choices.

- To grow deep roots.

- To keep in touch with family and friends.

You can see that these intents cover a wide range of desires for what they wanted to get out of the class.

So let's begin with you. Take a moment and ask yourself, "what is my intent for reading this book and learning this system?"

So as not to get overwhelmed and to be sustainable, pick just one for now.

This system is not going anywhere. Once you get familiar with it, you can run through it in a flash as many times a day as you desire.

For now, you'll pick just one overall intent for the practice.

But first, let's meet Sally.

Twenty-Two

Sally's Intent

Our fictional friend Sally may feel familiar. That won't be surprising. We all have the same kinds of issues or problems or situations to work through at different times in our lives.

If not us, someone we know and love may have experienced them.

Hopefully, Sally's walk through this system of thoughtful thinking will be helpful for your practice.

Okay. Story time.

Sally has more than one problem on her mind and has trouble deciding which one to focus on first.

She doesn't feel all that healthy. She's gained weight over the years and doesn't have consistent exercise habits. In general, she hasn't been feeling well for years, and now she is worried that she might have something seriously wrong with her.

Her children often test her patience. She wishes she could do more for them, while not interfering with their ability to find their own happiness.

Work. Well, it could be better. She feels under-appreciated and underpaid. Besides, people act in ways that upset her at work, and she often brings that upset home. Sally is tempted to quit her job and do something that brings her more joy, but what?

Besides, she and her husband need to make sure they make enough money for their future. And the world seems to be going crazy now, so who can trust anything?

And even if she knew what she wanted to do, she can't choose to change her life right now. Her mother is getting older and will need more care. Who will do it if not her?

Her husband isn't much help.

He has become increasingly fearful. It's hard for her to admit that he is spending money on things that help him escape. And he takes out his anger and fear on her. Sometimes he scares her. Mostly he annoys her.

Sally has things going on, doesn't she?

There are many things she can choose from for this first pass through this system.

She takes a few days, but finally, Sally decides on her overall Intent. Here's what Sally decided.

- Overall Intent: *Get my health back.*

Just writing her desire to get her health back as the overall intent for this practice made Sally feel better. She was going to do it. Finally.

Sally figures that she will have the energy to deal with the other problems in her life if she begins with how she feels about her health.

She had been putting off dealing with her health for far too long. Each year that has gone by has not made her body feel better. Now all she wants is to wake up in the morning and not be upset about what she sees in the mirror. She wanted to be able to walk to the mailbox without something hurting.

Maybe she could never feel or look like she did at eighteen, but she would try. How could it hurt?

Sally laughed when she said that to herself. It might hurt. Because getting her health back meant she would have to find out why she had let herself get to this point.

That was what she needed to find out first. Sally grabbed some sheets of paper and stuck them around the house, ready to write down what she believed about herself and her health habits.

Sally realized she didn't really want to do find out what she believed and had accepted as truth. It was work. And hearing all those beliefs in her head was probably going to make her feel worse.

But she did want to get her health back and feel better, so she just wrote them down anyway and tried not to judge herself.

Some thoughts were in her own voice, others were things she had heard her parents say, and some of it was what she assumed was a worldview, like genetics.

After a few days, Sally noticed that there weren't as many thoughts as she imagined there would be. Most of them were simply a variation on a theme that she was a failure and a loser.

However, Sally made careful notes about the details of why she was letting herself be called a failure and a loser.

Sally figured that they were ideas she would be re-writing as she practiced Right Thinking.

It was hard to keep from being upset with what she was hearing, but Sally knew that wouldn't solve anything, and she was ready to let go of the past and move on. To help her point of view, Sally sat outside every day for a few minutes and watched the clouds go by. She started listening to a meditation tape during her lunch break. Five minutes made a big difference.

By the end of the week, the list was long but less threatening. Now that she was noticing what was driving her thoughts, she felt better. Sally always knew something was going on without her knowledge, and now that she was looking right at it, she felt more in control.

The intent to feel better and get her health back seemed possible. Sometimes, for a few minutes a day, it even felt real. That made it easy to write out her Right Intent.

BECA LEWIS

Here's what Sally decided.

Overall Right Intent: *Get my health back.*
Right Intent: *To feel better.*

TWENTY-THREE

PRACTICAL INTENT

I arise in the morning torn between a desire to improve the world and a desire to enjoy the world. This makes it hard to plan the day. — E. B. White

Since we are intentionally setting intents, we get to be very clear about what we are choosing.

I used to call this first step, Right Desire. So if you substitute the word desire for intent, it might be easier. What is it that you want? What is it that you desire?

These intents, while remaining morally correct (which means by you choosing it, others will eventually benefit, and no commandments are broken) are all about you.

All of this work is all about you.

This is a Right Intent. Because when we get ourselves straight, the world around us straightens out with us.

Instead of starting from the outside, we begin from the inside. So, what do you desire? Feel the answer. Spend time with it. Does it bring you joy? Remember, emotion will drive the outcome.

It's okay that thinking about this brings fear or worry. Stretching out of comfort zones can do that.

But when fear or worry set the intent, we will never get to what we desire, and we, and the world, will not benefit.

However, if fear and worry follow the intent, or try to stop you from choosing it, you just might be on the right track.

Being emotionally comfortable is never the intent. We aim for spiritual growth, wisdom, understanding, possibilities, and expansion, which often feels uncomfortable.

However, it will be worth it. And don't worry. We'll deal with the fear and worry later.

Just move forward, take a deep breath, and set your Right Intent. And as always, as you gain wisdom and understanding, you can change it.

Change is good. And since change is always going on, that is the premise we are going to adopt.

Practical Intent

I am writing this book as a weekly practice, but you can choose the time frame that works for you.

However, doing it as a weekly practice at least the first time around gives you time to pay attention to your thinking and the outcomes.

Remember that these intents are meant for you. They have to be right for you. Be careful to not choose an intent that someone else said is correct, or gave to you, or you grew up with, or that's how it has always been, or it will gain you points, or what everyone else is doing.

These assignments for each step of Right Thinking will help ground the system, repair old beliefs, build habits that work for you, dissolve untruths about yourself and others, and reveal your true self to yourself.

Step One: Right Intent
My overall intent for reading this book:
My Right Intent:

Begin a list as to how you find yourself identifying yourself. Notice what you say to yourself. Notice what others say about you. Write it down! Note which ones are always being said. We will do this for a few weeks. Listen. Don't judge. Just keep notes.

Choose at least one way that you will calm your thinking, quiet the mind and bring it into harmony with your intent. Perhaps meditation of some kind. Walking by yourself. Sitting in nature. Listening to bird songs.

Intent Review

Before we head into the next week's Right Thinking step, take a moment and review what happened in the past week.

Maybe this seems like a step you could skip, but please don't. Remember, it's what we don't notice that drives our lives without our consciously choosing it.

Reviewing the week helps ground the work into something tangible, and although our intents are not measurable, progress is.

Even if the progress doesn't feel good, note that too. Everything is relevant for shifting our perceptions.

Things I noticed:

Ways I am stuck:

Things that have changed:

Twenty-Four

Step Two: Right Premise

A nd God saw every thing that he had made, and, behold, it was very good. — Genesis 1:31

Old premises and perceptions that keep us stuck are habits. We are going to shift them.

Our neighbor across the street always backs out into the road. It makes both Del and me crazy. He has a turnaround in his driveway, so it would be easy to come into the street in a way that isn't a hazard to himself and others. Why is he backing out when he doesn't have to?

Is it a habit, or is he not paying attention, or is he only thinking of himself? Or all three?

As we pay more attention to our habits and preconceived ideas, better ways of doing things will pop up in our thinking. We'll want to smack our foreheads and ask ourselves why we didn't see that before.

Because habits and unconscious choices act as blinders, we only see what we expect to see. As we shift our perceptions to a more expansive view, many things we never saw before appear before us.

Using the practice of Right Thinking we will search for, and root out of ourselves, habitual thinking. As we do so, more and more evidence of infinite possibilities will become evident.

Last week, we set a Right Intent, and now we are moving to Right Premise.

But what is a premise?

Let's start again with the dictionary definition. As a noun, the word premise contains a logic that goes like this: If the premise is true, then the conclusion must be true.

Or it's a proposition which forms the basis of a theory. As a verb, it works as a base for a theory.

Both definitions work with what we are going to do with our premise.

However, to get to the Right part of it, we need to do a quick review of how the two modes of perception—point of view and state of mind—work because they form a premise.

We know that what we perceive to be reality magnifies, which means we get more of what we believe to be true. Some people call this a self-fulfilling prophecy. Either way, it's how human life works.

Our human brains filter out anything that doesn't match what we believe or want to know. It's probably for the best because there is no way we can take in all that is going on around us.

However, since you are reading this book, I will assume that you have a sense that something, we can call it God, or infinite Mind, or the Great Mystery, or the Divine, exists, and we are Its creation.

Even though our human senses can't sense this, or no one can "prove" it, we know that it's true.

And we yearn to know more of this Truth and have our lives more closely match this Infinite One, which has to be harmonious and Good.

I argue why this is true in all the books in The Shift Series, so for now, let's agree on this: There is an Infinite Intelligent One that is omnipresent Love. Good exists and is the only power.

We are choosing this point of view because it's true. And even though we don't fully understand how it could be true, it is what we want to experience.

We want to experience Intelligent omnipresent Love. We want to rest in the knowledge that Good is the only power. We want to experience a life that results from that point of view.

So we've done it. We've chosen our point of view. It is also the basis for everything that follows from here, starting with Right Premise.

A reminder. Yes, the more we hold to this point of view, the more we should experience the ultimate harmony that this point of view promises.

And we will.

Except, if our state of mind does not accept this point of view as a valid premise, instead we let worry, guilt, self-pity, or fear take over, those emotions will control how much we experience it.

Of course, all these emotions exist for all of us and will probably coexist with us until we break the bonds of a human perspective. But they don't have to be in charge.

Whatever moves us into the state of mind where we can hear and experience the harmony of the Life, that's what we need to do.

Because—and this is a huge because—we remember that if our state of mind is not in agreement with our point of view, it is our state of mind that will project more of what we experience.

At all times, we must fight to stay within a common point of view and state of mind that Good and harmony are in charge of this moment and every moment.

We always have the opportunity to reset ourselves to a better point of view and bring our state of mind into harmony with it.

That said, now we are ready to set our Right Premise for the Right Intent that we are focusing on this week.

It doesn't have to sound "spiritual." It just has to be set into a premise that begins with the point of view and state of mind that we wish to experience.

If we worry about whether we are right, it's not—right, that is. Because worry, guilt, fear, shame, and uncertainty are trying to set the premise.

We can change our premises as we learn more, even if it is only a minute from now.

In fact, we have to keep changing it, because there is no way that what we believe and know right now is absolutely correct.

We can't expect that we know everything in this moment any more than a baby knows what it will know after fifty years of experience.

But we can keep stepping forward.

Before we set our Right Premise, let's look at how Sally is choosing hers.

Twenty-Five

Sally's Premise

It's been an interesting week for Sally. There were days she forgot to pay attention to her Overall Intent to get her health back and her Right Intent to feel better. When she remembered, she was often doing the exact opposite thing she intended to do.

Sally thought that setting the intent to get her health back and feel better would motivate her to eat better, maybe exercise a little every day, but that only happened the first day. After that, it was a struggle. Instead, it felt as if everything worked against her. Her husband didn't like the meal she cooked. She stubbed her toe, so it was hard to walk, and in general, she felt terrible.

Sally was tempted to stop doing this Right Thinking practice if it was going to make things worse, but she knew she was tired of how things were. Besides, she was always giving up on what she wanted for herself. This time she would stick it out because she really wanted to feel better.

Sally's list of things she said about herself had grown to stacks of little pieces of paper scattered around the house. When she read them over, she couldn't believe how often she told herself that she was a loser.

Sally knew she wasn't supposed to judge, but she felt like a loser, so it was hard not to agree with that voice in her head, making her feel even more like a loser.

She had to give herself a pep talk every morning. And when she started feeling sorry for herself, she had to write that down too, trying not to agree with, or judge, what seemed so true. She had made a mess of her life.

The one thing she managed to do almost every day was sit quietly on her back porch for a few minutes before she left for work. Sometimes she sat in the dark because she was getting up earlier. It was strange, but she liked it. She didn't know if that was meditation, but it felt good, and she planned to do more of that.

Sally was definitely ready to begin her second week of Right Thinking. She was ready for things to get better. Figuring out the Right Premise to add to her Right Intent seemed strange. And difficult. She would have to say something that didn't feel true to her, especially after such a hard week.

But eventually, she came up with something she hoped would help. Sally decided that since she was supposed to state a Right Premise with the point of view that everything was already perfect and good, that meant that she must be feeling good despite all appearances to the contrary.

She loved that she didn't have to make something happen, she only had to let go and see what was already true, even if it seemed fanciful. However, it would be wonderful if it turned out to be true.

After thinking it through, Sally decided that since she was the Divine's perfect reflection, she must reflect perfect health. Did she believe it? Her rational mind did not, but Sally decided to trust the process. If what she believed to be true magnified, she would stop the habit of thinking of herself as a mess and start seeing herself as already healthy.

And, she vowed to herself, she would spend time actively shifting her state of mind into harmony with that perception which meant, she decided, more meditation time and perhaps a trip to the park to sit outside and listen to the birds.

It couldn't hurt, and it just might help, she told herself.

Here's where Sally is so far:
Overall Right Intent: *Get my health back.*
Right Intent: *To feel better.*
Right Premise: *I am already healthy and I feel great.*

TWENTY-SIX

---•---

FACE AND REPLACE

The human mind is composed of chasms and sunless abysses, layer upon layer in which there are secret chambers where alien natures can hide undetected. — Thomas De Quincey

We have to do something with that list of perceptions we have been collecting about ourselves.

We are going to face them head-on. And then, replace those negative perceptions with what is true, using two perception shifting tools, I Choose sheets and Quality Words lists.

This week we will add the I Choose tool to face what we say to ourselves and replace it consciously.

Doing I Choose sheets will help bring our state of mind into harmony with our point of view, and we know how important that is!

Remember, it's our unconscious choices that are building our current life experience. We have been uncovering our unconscious hidden choices and perceptions and beginning to choose consciously.

In the early 1800s, Thomas De Quincey invented the term *unconscious*. He maintained that thoughts and emotions we don't know we have can control us.

Yes. Not that they can—they are. Therefore, uncovering and eliminating hidden thoughts and emotions, or shifting the ones that don't serve us, is imperative.

Consciously choosing, we are aware of our thoughts and emotions. And standing in the premise we have chosen, we are moving away from our perception of ourselves as human and into our true spiritual nature.

Yes, consciously choosing looks like affirmations, but they are even more potent because instead of overlying a truth on top of something, we are cleaning out the mess first.

Let's use Sally to see what that would look like.

Sally keeps hearing that she is a loser. She says it to herself all the time.

First, she faces it.

She listens and hears:

I am a loser.

Now she chooses to replace it.

I choose to see myself as a winner.

She listens and hears the monkey voice, inner critic, and judge say,

"You've been a loser since the day you were born."

Sally:

"I choose to know that I am a child of God."

Monkey Voice:

"You don't have a right to choose."

Sally:

"I choose to have a right."

Monkey Voice:

"Everything you do turns out wrong."

Sally:

"I choose that everything I do turns out for the best."

Monkey Voice:

"Your parents thought you were a loser, too."

170

Sally:
"I choose to see myself as a child of the One Father-Mother God."
Monkey Voice:
"There is no God."
Sally:
"I choose to know that there is One, and It doesn't create losers."

Okay, you get the idea. And yes, I Choose sheets could go on for pages and pages and veer off into multiple directions.

But always, always, Sally is going to consciously make her choices based on the best point of view that she can imagine.

Twenty-Seven

—·—

Practical Premise

Now it's your turn.

These assignments for each step of Right Thinking will help ground the system, repair old beliefs, build habits that work for you, dissolve untruths about yourself and others, and reveal your true self to yourself.

These pages are designed to build on each other. First, Right Intent, then Right Premise.

You'll notice that I keep saying this week's. Why? Because if you wish, you could change your intent, etc., every week.

However, for the first time through this system, I suggest you stick with one. After you get the hang of it, feel free to change it up.

And yes, we keep writing them out. Writing things down over and over again helps override the programming that says otherwise.

Step Two: Right Premise

My overall intent for reading this book:

My Right Intent:

My Right Premise:

- Continue noticing how you are self identifying, and how others see you.

- Start an I Choose sheet, and keep it going until that voice has nothing left to say.

- Choose at least one way that you will calm your thinking, quiet the mind and bring it into harmony with your intent. Do a meditation of some kind. Walking by yourself. Sitting in nature. Listening to bird songs.

-

Premise Review

Before we head into the next week's Right Thinking step, take a moment and review what happened in the past week.

Maybe this seems like a step you could skip, but please don't. Remember, it's what we don't notice that drives our lives without our consciously choosing it.

Reviewing the week helps ground the work into something tangible, and although our intents are not measurable, progress is. Even if the progress doesn't feel good, note that too. Everything is relevant for shifting our perceptions.

Things I noticed:

Ways I am stuck:

Things that have changed:

TWENTY-EIGHT

— • —

STEP THREE: RIGHT IDENTITY

K now thyself. — Inscribed on The Temple of Apollo at Delphi

To know thyself is the beginning of wisdom. — Socrates

Knowing others is intelligence, knowing yourself is true wisdom. — The Tao Te Ching

This above all, to thine own self be true. — William Shakespeare

Right Identity is not our human identity. It's our identity as the expression of the Divine.

It's hard to see, let alone feel and know in our hearts and minds, our Divine identity, and then be faithful to it.

Since we live in what appears as a human identity, let's talk about that first, because it will give us clues to who we truly are.

As humans, we stand in front of a mirror and see a face and a body. Sometimes we like it. Most often we don't.

As time moves on, we see and feel the changes that the belief of time invokes. Once again, sometimes we like those changes. Most often, we don't.

However, our mirror is not the only way to see our human selves. We can also use profile tests, astrology, the Chinese Zodiac, etc. as mirrors. Sometimes we like what they tell us. Sometimes we don't.

However, in all cases, it's essential to pay attention to what the reflection is telling us because only then can we change our perception about ourselves, whether it is what we believe or what others believe about us.

Worldview is a powerful belief system. We need to look at that mirror because we won't consciously shift what we don't know is being claimed about who we are.

Looking in an actual mirror, we can determine how we want to appear to the outside world. We make sure our shirt is not on inside out, and our hair isn't sticking out at weird angles.

Profile tests, and other mirrors like them, help us in the same way. They show us things about ourselves.

Once again, it doesn't matter if we like those things or not.

Since all reflections only reveal to us what our human self or the worldview believes, liking it or not liking it isn't the issue.

Knowing about it gives us the power to shift it and become more aware of our pure spiritual essence.

These reflection instruments can reveal our unique gifts to us. Once we see them and accept them, then we can take those gifts and expand them.

Reflections also reveal our weaknesses so we can strengthen them. They provide "ah-ha" moments that can shift the way we live in the world.

As an example, when I learned that I'm an introvert, it shifted everything for me. I understood why I did things and how I had not set up my life to fit who I am.

At the time, I was a Certified Financial Planner. I loved the work, but not how I was doing it.

Realizing that as an introvert I "gassed up" by myself to spend my energy with people meant that the way my extroverted trainer—who "gassed up" by being with people—was teaching me to run my business, made me want to quit. Adjusting my days to match what I needed, I designed my business into one I loved.

Mirrors also reveal to us how other people perceive us.

Knowing this means we can adjust how we present ourselves to communicate more clearly based on what we are trying to accomplish. And since we are always responsible for how and what we communicate, this is essential information.

Other information these reflections convey can help us combat temptations that drag us away from or hide our true spiritual nature.

The mirror called the Enneagram, does this exceptionally well. It not only reflects to us our true spiritual nature, but it also reveals unhealthy behavior, so we can stop giving in to it or accepting it as accurate about ourselves.

We can see them as temptations and not realities.

And since much of our behavior is not something we notice, it's good to have any mirror that alerts us to it.

Even the best of friends will not tell us all about the irritating and ungodlike behavior that we may exhibit, and often are not aware that we are doing it.

Since we intend to discover and live as the Divine's expression, these are things we need to know.

Not knowing is not a strength; instead, it leaves us vulnerable.

There is another crucial reason for paying attention to what reflections reveal to us.

Anything that tells us something about our human expression, whether or not we believe it, the worldview does. Most of humankind does. And that hidden perception, energy, point of view—whatever we want to call it—does impact us.

If we don't know about it, we often do it and accept it as truth without consciously being aware that we are doing so.

When I learned that people believe that Tauruses don't like change, I made a conscious choice to not agree with that perception. I love change, new directions, and expansion.

And if I am being stubborn (after noticing that I am), I can ask myself if I am giving in to a belief about myself or being stubborn because I am not moving off of Truth.

If I don't feel like participating, is it because there is an untrue belief that an introvert stays silent, or because I am afraid to speak out and be present?

Reflections are not excuses to not do something we need to do or want to do. Nor are they traps or prisons. Most of all, we can not use them to justify limiting how we are expressing ourselves or treat others.

We don't give them power. We learn from them. And face and replace them as necessary.

The question always is: are we acting as the expression of the Divine? Or are we acting out of personality, ego, and beliefs about our human self?

None of us are alike—either humanly or Divinely.

Choosing our Right Identity, we become even more unique, not as a personality, but as our true spiritual nature.

We are a unique expression of Love. Love doesn't move through us. We are Love Loving Itself.

Light doesn't pass through us. We are Light.

We are the Abundance of God in action. We are the presence of Kindness.

Looking in any mirror is a good thing. Stand in front of the profile, the mirror, the belief system, and be grateful for the information.

But also be grateful that you are more than what can ever be seen with the human senses, or reflected in a human mirror of any kind.

Never born and never dying; we are rewriting the story we live in and what appears as life in matter.

As we do this, it becomes more and more apparent that there are not two universes, material and spiritual. Just one. Spiritual. We are not material. We are Spiritual.

We use human tools to discover this. Reflections of all kinds—mirrors, profiles, books, people, nature—reflect both our beliefs and Truth.

And as we learn this, we can celebrate what we know about ourselves and be grateful for the chance to play this earth game, because not playing will not make it go away.

Seeing through it is the answer.

All of this is why we are tracking what we say to ourselves about ourselves. Why we pay attention to our habits—moving them closer to spiritually healthy habits.

We pay attention to what we accept about what others say about us. Is it a clue, or a mistaken perception?

And in the end, here's where we are going. We are letting go of everything that describes us humanly, even the good stuff.

As we do this, we must be patient with ourselves, kind to ourselves, and enjoy the process. As they say in yoga classes, "Don't wish for this moment to be over." Be present. Receive the gift that the moment is offering.

In big R Reality, we have never left what we have called heaven. All we are doing now is letting go of what's hiding our present perfection from us, which is only a mistaken perception.

In the meantime, let's follow the wisdom of the Arab saying attributed to Mohammad, "Trust in Allah (God, the Divine, the Essence, Love), but tie up your camel."

Before we head into choosing your Right Identity statement, let's do more with the tool of Face and Replace, and then we'll check in with Sally.

TWENTY-NINE

— · —

FACE AND REPLACE

Quality Word Lists

We've been noticing how we identify ourselves and how others see us. Now, it's time to claim our true Spiritual identity.

Everyone has one, so don't try sneaking out of this.

Each of us is a unique expression of the Divine. Each of us has gifts that are the essence of our being. They are not something we have to earn. They are like the fragrance of a flower, the slow, steady rhythm of a turtle, the sweet song of the robin. They are part of us.

All of nature naturally expresses its gifts. Except for humans. Crazy, right? Instead, we deny what comes naturally to us, suppress it, run from it, or misuse it.

This book isn't about why we do that. I'm not sure it matters. What matters is that we notice it and shift it.

This book is about a practice that will dissolve that habit, belief, perception, and let our unique spiritual blessings shine forth.

Our next tool for doing this is something I call Quality Word lists. The concept is simple. Replace negative beliefs and thoughts about ourselves with positive qualities.

Remember, *what we perceive to be reality magnifies,* so why not?

179

However, we aren't making these up or wishing for them. We are noticing what's already present. They are already our gifts, our essence, but we've been denying or ignoring them.

What if a beautiful red rose started acting and thinking like a human and believed that it was ugly, dull, useless, and prickly? We could easily see that it is mistaken. Its essence is beauty, the color red, and sweet fragrance.

We are the same. Our qualities are baked into who we are. We only have to stop acting and thinking like a human. Yes, I laughed here. You can, too, if you want too. But we can do it! And we will.

To help us along, we'll use the Quality Word list tool as part of our Face and Replace process.

There are two kinds of quality lists that we could make: the qualities of how something looks and the qualities of feelings.

In this Right Thinking practice, we will focus on feeling qualities.

These qualities will help us bring our state of mind perception into harmony with our point of view.

Each quality is one word that contains the essence of what we mean.

If it takes a sentence to describe it, keep feeling it, and pare it down to one word. No one but us needs to understand what we mean by that quality.

It's a feeling, and trying to explain it brings it back into the human element, which is extremely limited.

The question to answer is: *If I were the identity that I am claiming, how would I feel?*

If you haven't done this before, this may take some time to sink in. Allow yourself to feel how wonderful that would be.

We'll be making a second list, too.

We will make a Quality Word list that directly replaces the negative things we have heard about ourselves with a positive quality.

Let's see what Sally does with this perception shifting tool.

Thirty

Sally's Identity

This week Sally felt a little better, although saying she was already healthy still felt like a lie most of the time. Especially if she looked in the mirror or got upset with herself for only being able to walk around the block a few times.

But it was beginning to make sense to Sally that it was what she had been saying to herself, or others said about her, or the worldview, that had kept her in the habit of not doing healthy things for herself.

The I Choose tool for Facing and Replacing helped her see those habits as thoughts first and then choosing different ones seemed too easy to do to make a difference. But it seemed to work.

So Sally decided to make her choices more specific. She did an I Choose list that began with *I Choose to walk every day.*

She couldn't believe how many things she had unconsciously put in the way of doing what she wanted to do. Things from not having the right shoes, not having enough time, to what would people think.

It was a long list, but Sally kept consciously choosing. She chose to have the right shoes, to have enough time, and to have people support her choices.

Doing nothing other than Consciously Choosing, she started walking and loving it. Mostly.

But sometimes she wondered what good it would do. However, once she recognized that it was also a habit of thinking, she went right back to the Right Thinking steps and Consciously Choosing.

Sally found that when she said to herself that since God was Health Itself, and she was a reflection and expression of God, it meant that she was already healthy and that kept her in the right frame of mind to keep going.

As Sally got ready to claim her Right Identity, she realized she had already been doing that by saying she was God's reflection and expression.

That's when Sally realized that every step of Right Thinking was embedded within each other.

That doing these simple exercises would change her health seemed impossible to her, but Sally was determined to do it. She had started this process, and she would finish it.

She was ready to use the second Face and Replace tool, Quality Word lists, so she started with a list about how she would feel if she were healthy.

One thing she knew was if she felt healthy, she would feel free. So she wrote that word down on her list. It was a beginning, and strangely, she felt freer just by starting her Quality Word list.

And that feeling started bringing up more feelings, and as she distilled those feelings into qualities, Sally felt as if this practice might actually work.

Sally also started her second list that would replace the negative of what she had noticed about what she said and thought about herself with the opposite positive quality.

This list was easier for Sally. To replace loser, she wrote "winner." To replace the negative idea of being too picky she wrote "precise."

Sally enjoyed making these lists and decided it was the same as designing a room. Take out the old furniture and bring in the new.

Here's what Sally wrote to continue her practice.

Overall Right Intent: *Get my health back.*
Right Intent: *To feel better.*
Right Premise: *I am already healthy and I feel great.*
Right Identity: *I am the expression of health.*

THIRTY-ONE

— · —

PRACTICAL IDENTITY

To answer the question, can I change my Right Thinking choices, the quick answer is *yes, of course.*

Even though this is called Right Thinking, there is no right or wrong way to do it. I call this a thoughtful system, not a Right System, or the only way to do it system.

I expect us to keep thinking, wondering, and asking questions.

Think of this book as a path with signs that help you get where you are going.

However, once you know the territory and the habit of listening to the still small voice kicks in, you might find yourself mixing up the order, or using just one of the steps, or changing the words in each step every time.

I often find myself starting with one Intent or Premise or Identity and then changing them every time I repeat them.

Let that happen. Follow your internal guidance.

As long as we begin from our highest understanding of the Divine at each step, it is still Right Thinking.

I rarely keep the same wording twice. But that's because I have practiced walking myself through all the steps so many times it has become second nature.

Once you get the hang of this system and hear those Angel Ideas, change as needed.

When you feel grounded in the Principles of this practice, get out on that dance floor and dance!

However, taking one focus all the way through can be very powerful, and that's what we are doing here.

That said, let's review how your practice went this week.

Practical Identity:

It's time to claim your true spiritual nature. Intent, then Premise, and now Identity.

And yes, we keep writing them out. Writing things down over and over again helps override the programming that says otherwise.

Step Three: Right Identity

My overall intent for reading this book:
My Right Intent:
My Right Premise:
My Right Identity:

- Continue noticing how you are self identifying, and how others see you.

-

- Keep your I Choose sheets going for anything that you are working on.

- Start your Quality Word list to replace the negative things you hear about yourself.

- Start a Quality Word list about how you would feel if what you chose as your Right Identity were true.

- Choose at least one way that you will calm your thinking, quiet your mind and bring it into harmony with your intent. Do a meditation. Walk by yourself. Sit in nature. Listen to bird songs. Breathe.

Identity Review

Before we head into the next week's Right Thinking step, take a moment and review what happened in the past week.

As always, don't skip this step. Remember, it's what we don't notice that drives our life without our consciously choosing it.

Reviewing the week helps ground the work into something tangible, and although our intents are not measurable, progress is. Even if the progress doesn't feel good, note that, too. Everything is relevant for shifting our perceptions.

Things I noticed:

Ways I am stuck:

Things that have changed:

Thirty-Two

Step Four: Right Resistance

A sinner is not reformed merely by assuring him that he cannot be a sinner because there is no sin. To put down the claim of sin, you must detect it, remove the mask, point out the illusion, and thus get the victory over sin and so prove its unreality. — Mary Baker Eddy

We all know about resistance. Usually, we think of it as that quality that keeps us from doing something. We talk about resistance as a negative and work on overcoming it.

But what about good resistance? Yes, resistance has a positive side.

We resist the urge to put our hand on a hot stove, or run in front of a car, or say hurtful things on purpose. These are examples of good resistance.

So obviously, there are two ways to look at resistance—two kinds of resistance—the kind we say no to and the kind we say yes to.

We say no to the resistance that stops us from doing what we love to do, or want to do, or must do.

That is the kind of resistance that we want to overcome.

But here's the thing.

It's still a form of good resistance because our unconscious mind thinks it's working on our behalf. And it will continue to do so until we change what we believe to be true about ourselves and others.

We can't blame resistance for doing what we have asked it to do. Instead, we have to change ourselves so that resistance supports our genuine desires rather than thwarting them.

Intent, Premise, and Identity put us on the path to accomplishing that shift. By Consciously Choosing these first three steps, we gain insights into what we believe and accept as accurate about ourselves, others, and the world.

These first three steps in Right Thinking help us break habits that hold us back or keep us in stasis and the status quo.

Without changing our belief systems and habits, resistance works on our behalf to keep us stuck because it thinks that's what we want.

Therefore, it's obvious what we have to do. Shift our beliefs and habits to ones that work in our favor.

To make this kind of shift takes practice.

We practice setting spiritually healthy habits.

We practice overcoming paradigms, biases, and prejudices that hold us back or take us in a direction that is not safe, healthy, or happiness producing.

What we want to notice at all times is what we're resisting and why.

Are we resisting the call to move us into a clearer understanding of our true spiritual nature?

Let's say no to that resistance.

And we use yes resistance or Right Resistance to do so.

We are saying yes to learning how to resist what we need to resist. Not passively. But with conviction—the stomping our foot kind of resistance.

We use Right Resistance to not give into unhealthy temptations.

Yes, it's tempting to give in to temptations. It takes Right Resistance to say no to them, to call temptation a liar. That is the kind of resistance that we want.

We say yes to resisting lies, and liars, and doing harmful things to ourselves and others.

In the Say Yes class that I teach, we have discovered that saying no needs to happen more often than saying yes.

We can't say yes to what we want unless we make room for it.

That means we have to take the time to discover what is most important to us and say no to anything tempting us away from it.

In this book, that's what we did first; we set our Right Intent.

In doing so, we actively and consciously chose what is important to us—from how we make our beds to how we want to make our "mark" in the world.

Then we chose what Right Premise and Right Identity we need to stand in to make room for it to happen.

It is a practice of adjusting and refining our state of mind and point of view.

In this book, we are taking the time to look at ourselves to see what is coloring our perception. What paradigm, what belief systems are driving our lives without our being aware of them?

We are breaking the habit of staying in false, or no longer useful, perceptions about ourselves (which always overflows to others).

We are facing and replacing them with an improved version. This is Right Resistance.

And as our understanding grows, we continue to repeat this process over and over again. We replace what isn't true with quality words that are the essence of ourselves as expressions and reflections of the Divine.

We face and replace anything that claims evil has more power than Good. We face and replace the belief that we are anything less than the perfect representation of that Good.

Right Thinking is a skill that must be practiced and used every day and in every moment. Because as long as we exist in what we believe to be a human form, we must practice.

Spirituality is not magic.

We can't sprinkle fairy dust and have it change everything. However, we can imagine that fairy dust is God's essence, and that will shift our perception. So do it, but do it consciously, holding to a correct Intent, Premise, and Identity as you do so.

We have to practice resisting the temptations that are always around us. To do so, we can use the mirrors we have set up. They can alert us to what the temptations might be for us. They give us clues about the language that the liar speaks that will appeal to our human self.

That way, when we encounter these temptations, we will recognize them as temptations trying to pull us away from our True Identity.

Christ Jesus was tempted three times. He was tempted to put himself in danger so that God's angels would save him. He was tempted to declare himself King, in other words, claim human power. And he was tempted to worship false gods, to put his faith in what he knew was not true.

He used Right Resistance to say no. He claimed his True Intent, Premise, and Identity, showing us that we can do the same thing.

Yes, this is yes resistance in action. Right Resistance is when we say, "I resist what is not true."

And once we claim our Right Intent, Premise, and Identity, this gets much easier.

We are looking at error not to focus on it and have a conversation with it, but to replace it with what is True.

The kind of resistance that looks like war or fighting will never work in the long run because it is not replacing the error with Truth.

Our form of resistance is to remove the mask of all lies, beliefs, perceptions, temptations, and then throw the water of Truth, the light of the Divine on them, and let anything unlike Good dissolve away into nothingness.

Go forth, put on the armor of Truth, and resist temptation by shifting the story about yourself and the world to one that is only about the power of Good.

THIRTY-THREE

— • —

WHOSE VOICE

Since for Right Resistance to work, we need to recognize which voice is telling us the truth, let's look at the ways we can tell them apart.

Temptation that takes us away from our true nature always—not sometimes—always disguises itself as a voice we will trust.

Its favorite disguise is to "speak" to us in the same way we talk and think. It has to choose this method, because the only substance it has is our belief in it.

Which means even the most aware person can sometimes be confused or fooled.

However, once we know it's not God's voice speaking, we can stop listening, stop being curious, stop obeying. It will be easy when we claim for ourselves that all that really exists is Love.

To make the recognition easier, here are eleven ways to tell which voice is speaking.

There is the Angel voice reminding you of your true spiritual nature, let's call that voice God, or the Devil voice wanting to stop you from knowing big T Truth.

- 1. It's not God when you say or think: "This is the way I am."

192

God has placed no limits on who we are and what we do.

God does not know us as human creations that fit within categories.

It is our human sense of ourselves that states we can only be one way and not the other.

When the voice says, "You are too shy to do that," or "You are good at that but not this," or "You are too young, too old, a mother, a father, a woman, a man, a sister, a brother" or any other description that is limiting it is not God's voice.

We are all the full and unlimited expression of the Infinite One called God. Limitation is not God speaking.

It is God when you hear, "You are free from that limitation."

- 2. It's not God when it is based on conditional, biased Love.

God does not judge.

It is our human sense of God that has made God into a parody of our humanness. We have made a god in our likeness.

But like the sun which shines on all equally, God, as Infinite Love, loves equally. We do not have to meet any material conditions to be loved.

When we act out from a human understanding of God, we may find ourselves judging, wishing or wanting, feeling hate, sorrow or revenge. However, conditions and judgment are not God.

It is God when you hear, "Only Love and Love only."

- 3. It's not God when you hear, "Why bother? Nothing I do makes a difference."

You have a unique talent that must be expressed.

Feelings that no one will notice or appreciate it, or that the world can do without it, are a blatant lie.

God is all there is to Life. We are all necessary for the fullness of God to be expressed.

Since it would be impossible for God to not be expressing Itself, in Truth we, too, are always expressing our unique talent.

Once you stop listening to the "Devil" the world will unfold new and wonderful ways for you to be noticed and make a difference. Do them; you are the only one who can!

It is God when you hear, "Live your gift."

- 4. It's not God when you are hoping for a material outcome.

Since God is eternal unlimited Spirit, what does It know of matter or our material needs? Nothing!

Using God to improve our lives is a sham. We are only fooling ourselves and keeping our true supply and wealth from appearing.

Understanding God as All immediately reveals what was hidden in plain sight. What is revealed is all that we need and more than we imagine.

It is God when you hear, "I already provided what you need, just notice."

5. It's not God when you are intent on improving the situation your way.

Human ego is not God.

If you think about it, nothing ever turns out as you planned. In fact, when letting go and letting God, it turned out better than you could have ever thought.

Demanding the outcome you want is not of God.

The human sense of existence will never produce an answer that blesses all, as it always comes from ego and duality. Infinite Mind is constantly unfolding blessings beyond our comprehension because it is One.

It is God when you hear, "Surrender to being loved and cared for now."

- 6. It's not God when it requires any form of deceit or manipulation.

In our belief of being human, it's hard to imagine that things can't happen without our intervention.

We forget that nobody is really human, and that everybody is as much an expression of God as we are, and just as capable of being guided and directed by that awareness.

Trying to make it work is not God.

It is God when you hear, "Trust in Love."

- 7. It's not God when it claims that one person, sex, or race is better than another.

Claiming a sense of worthiness based on a privileged position through circumstances has nothing to do with God.

Within Love's eyes, there are no categories to place anyone at a different level.

Sometimes, it is our sense of personal human unworthiness that makes us claim that we are better than others.

Sometimes this claim is subtle, as in "I am glad I don't look that old" and sometimes it is horribly abusive, as in any kind of war.

In no case is it God. God knows no classes, states, or categories.

It is God when you hear, "All that exists expresses who I AM."

- 8. It's not God when it berates, undermines, depresses, or abuses anyone—including you.

The commandment, "Thou shall not kill," is not just referring to the human body, but also to the spirit.

For example, when someone says, "You can't do anything right, or you are not worth it, or you belong to me, or I can do that much better than you," they are killing the Spirit.

And that is not God speaking.

God as perfect Love expands and unfolds the Spirit. Imagine what it would feel like to be perfectly loved. Obviously there is no room at all for anything hateful in Love.

It is God when you hear, "I AM Love Loving Itself."

- 9. It's not God when you feel pushed or threatened.

If we agree with the worldview that there is not enough time, money, patience, love or any other suggestion of lack, then feeling pushed or threatened might feel normal.

However, God is Infinite All. This means there is no possibility of any kind of lack. God need not push or threaten, instead It guides by existing only as Love.

It is God when you hear, "Peace be still."

- 10. It's not God when it makes you feel apathetic or indifferent.

Sometimes we think it would be better if we "left well enough alone."

And yet some of the greatest evils of the human world have been caused by our indifference or looking the other way, or saying "I don't care, or what difference would that make?"

One of the "Devil's" greatest tools is our apathy to its claims.

You acting as the expression of Love will leave no room for apathy or indifference.

It is God when you hear, "Be active in Love."

- 11. It's not God if you are thinking, "what about me?"

This doesn't mean that we are not to be wise about what we need to do to take care of ourselves. It doesn't mean that we should give away all our light, leaving none for ourselves.

What it means is to not let our ego and self-centered needs guide what we say, think, or do.

There is no need to make the statement "what about me" when our intention is to live completely in each moment in the awareness of God.

That awareness brings all that we need. Me is not God. There is only I AM.

It is God when you hear, "Serve others in My name."

If we pay attention, we'll realize that there really is no "you" that is thinking.

It is either God or the belief of the Devil. We are either expressing God or we are allowing ourselves to be the tool of the Devil.

All it takes is the willingness to shift our perception to big R Reality, and the discipline to not focus on magnifying the outward material circumstances.

The time that it takes for what appears to be a change to occur may seem to vary. Remember, no matter what your sense perception tries to tell you, no matter what prison it attempts to send you to, it is always a lie about who you are and what is happening, when it does not reflect and express Infinite Good, Love.

Let's see how Sally is doing with Right Resistance.

Thirty-Four

Sally's Resistance

Sally's growing awareness that all the Right Thinking steps are embedded within each other prepared her for this next step, Right Resistance.

After reading about Right Resistance, Sally realized that the I Choose sheets and Quality Word lists were already helping her with Right Resistance. She was overcoming the resistance that kept her from being who she wanted to be.

However, one day nothing went right. She spilled soup all over the floor. Forgot to go to an appointment and realized she hadn't gone for a walk in the last three days.

That's when she noticed that the voice in her head that told her what a loser she had always been and always would be might not be telling her the truth.

Sally had always accepted that the voice in her head was herself talking to herself, which meant, of course, she listened. How could she not? It was loud. It spoke like her. And it told her things she had always believed.

Learning that it wasn't her voice, or God's voice, was a game-changer. Sally felt that it would be possible to heal all the situations and problems in her life.

A new hope arose in Sally. Perhaps it really was possible to change the story of her life.

Sally got serious about collecting quality words about herself. When she heard a negative version, she reversed it, found a quality word for it, and added it to her list.

She imagined herself as healthy and then asked herself how she would feel if she were healthy. After some practice and deep listening, she got the hang of narrowing all of her feelings down to one word. It was like packing a hundred feelings into a word.

Sally had two lists going.

One list was for reversing all the negative things she said or thought about herself. This list had words like diligent, to counter the belief she was lazy, and the word compassionate to dispute the judgment of herself and others that she often felt.

The second list was how she would feel if she were perfectly healthy. That list included quality words like relieved and joyous.

Sally figured she would keep the two lists going, not worrying about how long they were.

She had been listening and believing the negative for so long she knew it would take time to unravel. Besides, Sally wanted to get better at discovering, accepting, and living as her true Spiritual nature.

Here's what Sally wrote to continue her practice.

Overall Right Intent: *Get my health back.*
Right Intent: *To feel better.*
Right Premise: *I am already healthy and I feel great.*
Right Identity: *I am the expression of health.*
Right Resistance: *I resist ungodly temptations.*

Thirty-Five

Practical Resistance

This only takes a minute or two to fill out. But writing it out, repeatedly, helps to rewrite the story more effectively. Resist the urge to not do the assignments anymore.

Human personality, ego, worldview, does not want to go away. It will find many ways to stop you from cleaning up your old and limiting perceptions.

Don't fall for its tricks. Remember, anything that doesn't move you toward your true Spiritual nature is not your friend. Keep going!

This is our foundation. The next two steps, Practice and Action, will keep our house sturdy and safe.

Step Four: Right Resistance
My overall intent for reading this book:
My Right Intent:
My Right Premise:
My Right Identity:
My Right Resistance

- Continue noticing how you are self identifying, and how others see you.

- Keep your I Choose sheets going for anything that you are working on.

- Do your Quality Word list to replace the negative things you hear about yourself.

- Do a Quality Word list about how you would feel if what you chose as your Right Resistance were true.

- Choose at least one way that you will calm your thinking, quiet your mind and bring it into harmony with your intent. Do a meditation. Walk by yourself. Sit in nature. Listen to bird songs. Breathe.

Resistance Review

Before we head into the next week's Right Thinking step, take a moment and review what happened in the past week.

As always, don't skip this step. Remember, it's what we don't notice that drives our life without our consciously choosing it.

Reviewing the week helps ground the work into something tangible, and although our intents are not measurable, progress is. Even if the progress doesn't feel good, note that too. Everything is relevant for shifting our perceptions.

Things I noticed:

Ways I am stuck:

Things that have changed:

THIRTY-SIX

— · —

STEP FIVE - RIGHT REASONING

I t is a capital mistake to theorize before one has data. Insensibly one begins to twist facts to suit theories, instead of theories to suit facts.
— Arthur Conan Doyle

I bet you saw this chapter's heading "Right Reasoning" and realized that we have been doing this all along. And yes, you are right! We have been reasoning following a logical train of thought.

If this is that, then that is this, and then this is the outcome. Right? Yes, that sounds a bit confusing, so let's walk through what we have been doing and see if it makes more sense.

We started with the theory that what we perceive to be reality magnifies.

I call it a theory, but since no one has proved that it's not true, and we have many proofs it is, we choose that point of view as our beginning. Everything else flows from that point of view.

(If you want more on why I believe the theory is true, I write it out in detail in my book *Living In Grace: The Shift To Spiritual Perception.* Or read the first chapter of *Genesis.*)

Since it's true, it makes perfect sense to choose our point of view based on what we want to magnify, see, and experience in our lives. We are always choosing the best point of view that we can, because—well, why not?

We get what we believe, and we see what we believe. Therefore, it's a wise idea to believe the best scenario possible. I am sure you agree.

Then we explored the idea that emotions and feelings drive our perception and therefore, what we experience, so we added ways to get our state of mind in harmony with our point of view.

To review, here's an example of what this looks like:

We chose a perception that there is one divine Intelligence ruling all creation.

We know that there can only be one Creator, and we know that this Intelligence has to be all good or all bad, so we chose good because we realize that all bad would have long ago destroyed itself.

Next, we accepted that we are the expression, children, reflection of God, or Good, so our identity and experience can only comprise good.

We put this in terms that our human self can use practically. We set an Intent.

I didn't have to tell you to make it one that reflected all Good. You did that automatically. I knew you would. I'm not a mind reader, but I know that you wouldn't be reading this book if you didn't already want to express only good in your own way in the world.

After setting your Right Intent, you accepted that the intent is supported and guided by Divine Intelligence. That's your premise.

It's the same as saying, "I can do this because God is the only power, and that power is Love."

The next part is straightforward to reason out. Since there is only one God, one creator, one power, and you and I are the unique expression, reflection, action of that One power, we can state our Right Identity in those terms as a fact, as in "I am the expression, presence, of Love."

Next, we looked at what tries to tell us that none of this is true, and we resisted what it said. We called it a liar.

Interestingly, what comes up for most of us is that even though we have said that we are all the expression of the Divine, we think it might be true for every other person in the entire world, but not for us.

That is the human ego, personality, talking. You know what it's claiming, right? That we are God or gods. Wow. I know for sure that's not true. The world is most definitely not held in the palm of my hand. Or yours.

That is the best news ever. We are not God or gods. We are the action of One God. Or, as Mary Baker Eddy says, we are the compound idea of God.

If, and when, we allow ourselves to accept that somehow we escaped God's ever-expanding intelligent and all-encompassing Love and created ourselves and our lives outside of it; we are accepting a lie.

But it's tempting to believe it because that sure makes us unique, doesn't it?

However, if you figure out how that makes sense—how we can be outside of the One creation, let me know.

Otherwise, instead of agreeing with that lie about our identity, we don't agree. We use Right Resistance. We throw the lie out the door of our thinking.

I know, like a stalker, it comes back. Sometimes it pounds on the door or slips in a crack. It loves to remind us of all our mistakes—the stupid things we have said and done. As humans, we do all that, it's true.

As expressions of the Divine, we have done none of it, and that is the point of view and state of mind that we want to magnify.

And this is when Right Reasoning kicks in and we remember that anything that claims a power other than God is a lie.

There is only one liar, and it tells one lie, that there is a creator and power other than the one God, Good.

Accepting as a fact that we have power, that we created a situation, that we are bad, is agreeing with the liar. Let's not do that!

However, we have to let go of our human ego-self because the human ego is an idiot. I call myself an idiot at least once a day. I get upset over not being perfect or making mistakes.

But that doesn't mean that I can't face and replace that with the reminder that I, like you, am already the perfect expression of the Divine. I am not the human self or my personality.

Right Reasoning carries us away from the turmoil of humanness. It shelters us, takes us higher, brings us into the realm where we can see the light of Truth.

It is only the human ego that claims we are separate, that we are alone. The human ego that thinks people have to go through us to hear God's word. Not true. Everyone is a direct expression of God. We are equal and together as unique expressions of the Divine.

Yes, all of this takes practice, and yes, that's our next step. For now, just listen. Truth is always speaking directly to you.

What voice are you listening to?

Reason it out. Which one lifts you into the state of mind of heaven, and which one talks to the human personality?

That is Right Reasoning.

We all know this prayer. It's a perfect example of reasoning it out, especially when combined with Mary Baker Eddy's added definition.

Our Father which art in heaven,   Our Father-Mother God, all-harmonious, Hallowed be Thy name.   Adorable One. Thy kingdom come.   Thy kingdom is come; Thou art ever-present. Thy will be done in earth, as it is in heaven.   Enable us to know,—as in heaven, so on earth,—God is omnipotent, supreme. Give us this day our daily bread;   Give us grace for to-day; feed the famished affections; And forgive us our debts, as we forgive our debtors.   And Love is reflected in Love; And lead us not into temptation, but deliver us from evil;   And God leadeth us not into temptation, but delivereth us from sin, disease, and death. For Thine is the kingdom, and the power, and the glory, forever.   For God is infinite, all-power, all Life, Truth, Love, over all, and All.

Let's see how Sally does with this idea of Right Reasoning.

Thirty-Seven

Sally's Reasoning

When Sally read about Right Reasoning, she laughed. Wasn't this what she had been doing all along? *This Right Thinking was getting easier,* she thought. All she had to do was focus on how she reasoned for the next week and see how she could improve.

She liked the idea of "arguing" for the Right side of things. Sally decided to pretend that she was a defense attorney.

She would spend the week defending herself with logical reasoning against anything that tried to tell her she was a loser.

Halfway through the first day, Sally realized that she was going to be a very busy attorney. That voice in her head never stopped with the blaming.

It told her she was a loser in almost every way imaginable, to how she cleaned her house and how she ate. And it always had proof.

After all, all she had to do was look in the mirror, home, or relationships. *Who did that to themselves and their life,* that voice asked. It was you, it said, and Sally knew that was true.

The prosecuting attorney's claims of how she was guilty of being a loser was prolific. It claimed that everything wrong in her life was her fault, from the cold she caught last month to her cluttered home and neglected friends and family.

Because there was an element of truth in what the voice said, it was tempting for Sally to agree that she was a loser.

But she was unwilling to continue to live her life this way, so she claimed her innocence. She was not guilty.

But how could she be not guilty? What the voice claimed she had and had not done was correct.

That's when Sally realized that Right Reasoning couldn't start with the outcome of a problem, or even with the problem, because if she did, she would be stopped in her tracks. All around her was the evidence of her guilt.

Sally started to understand why it is necessary to begin with a point of view that negates all of the human picture.

She couldn't fix everything by staying in the human version of the problem. She had to step outside of it, rise above it, and begin with the point of view that she was the perfect expression of Infinite Mind.

Just because the human picture had become muddled and messed up didn't change the Truth, Sally reasoned. *If she started with Truth, the human situation would improve.*

Sally understood that this was the only permanent way out of the mess, so she decided to choose the Truth about her true Spiritual nature as her point of view.

She was determined to stand in that Truth to defend herself. She would not resort to arguing about the human problem.

Part of Sally didn't believe this would work. But since she had been trying all her life to become a better human, and not doing a great job of it, she asked herself, why not try it?

So she stood her ground against the prosecutor's claims. She claimed her innocence. She claimed her true spiritual nature. She told the prosecutor that the human story and the human picture wasn't the one that was true about her. She would not accept it.

Sally used the I Choose and Quality Words tools to Face and Replace everything. At first, it felt as if nothing changed, except she felt better about herself.

But as the week went on, Sally could see how she was gaining ground over the voice. There were even moments when she didn't hear it anymore, or it was so quiet she could ignore it.

Yes, Sally decided. *This might actually work.*

Here is Sally's blueprint for Right Thinking:

Overall Right Intent: *Get my health back.*
Right Intent: *To feel better.*
Right Premise: *I am already healthy and I feel great.*
Right Identity: *I am the expression of health.*
Right Resistance: *I resist ungodly temptations.*
Right Reasoning: *I am not the human picture.*

THIRTY-EIGHT

PRACTICAL REASONING

H ere's this week's assignments. All for you. Keep that in mind, just in case you feel like skipping this part.

This only takes a minute or two to fill out. But writing it out, repeatedly, helps to rewrite the story more effectively.

Step Five: Right Reasoning

My overall intent for reading this book:
My Right Intent:
My Right Premise:
My Right Identity:
My Right Resistance:
My Right Reasoning:

- Continue noticing how you are self identifying, and how others see you.

- Keep your I Choose sheets going for anything that you are working on.

- Continue your Quality Word list to replace the negative things you hear about yourself.

- Continue a Quality Word list about how you would feel if what you chose as your Right Reasoning were true.

- Choose at least one way that you will calm your thinking, quiet your mind and bring it into harmony with your intent. Do a meditation. Walk by yourself. Sit in nature. Listen to bird songs. Breathe.

Reasoning Review

Before we head into the next week's Right Thinking step, take a moment and review what happened in the past week.

Don't skip this step. Remember, it's what we don't notice that drives our life without our consciously choosing it.

Reviewing the week helps ground the work into something tangible, and although our intents are not measurable, progress is.

Even if the progress doesn't feel good, note that too. Everything is relevant for shifting our perceptions.

Things I noticed:

Ways I am stuck:

Things that have changed:

Thirty-Nine

Step Six - Right Practice

I am the tool with which God works. My virtue is to participate in this work, and I can do so if I keep the instrument which is given to me, namely my soul, in immaculate condition. — Leo Tolstoy

This step is an easy one. We've been talking about it all along. There is nothing new to do.

All we have to do is practice what we have already learned. And then practice some more. And enjoy the practice, because everything we love to do takes practice.

No one woke up one day, threw the perfect pot, danced like Baryshnikov, sang like Pavarotti, or knew things like Richard Feynman. No one. Not even them.

What does everyone have in common? Practice.

We are practicing to be life artists. As Henry David Thoreau said, *To affect the quality of the day, that is the highest of arts.*

We are practicing to overcome the belief that we are humans tied to material beliefs and conditions.

We are practicing to understand our true spiritual nature and live it to the best of our ability. We practice learning how to enjoy it and share it.

Whenever I think of practice, I think about the practice of ballet. Ballet is a practice that has been around for hundreds of years. Every day, ballet practitioners do a daily ballet class.

Every class begins with a barre routine that every ballet teacher follows. That means we could take ballet in Pennsylvania, and then in California or Paris, and do the same barre.

All over the world, the same set of steps in the same order. The only difference might be in the style or the twist the teacher adds to the practice.

Every discipline has this kind of practice.

What makes our daily practice different is that we get to set that routine for ourselves. So, what does your daily practice look like for you?

To design your own best practice, you need to know yourself and what you desire, and that's what we have been doing all along, isn't it?

To be life artists, we can't escape the need for practice to achieve awareness and wisdom. This practice is flexible, as it should be because this practice is knowing and understanding the Divine, which is the epitome of infinite ways to do something.

Of course, we intend to practice this in every moment, but we need to set times and studies and lessons to shift our point of view and state of mind until we live in it at all times.

We have to be willing to let go of what we have outgrown and no longer need. Whether represented by things or thoughts or habits, if it doesn't fit what we have become, let it go.

We don't keep the clothes we wore when we were ten, thinking we might wear them again someday.

Similarly, we need not keep outgrown ideas around thinking we might want to be that person again someday. Let them go.

Another type of practice is being good at what we want to do in our life.

If we desire to be a writer, we have to study writing, practice writing, practice reading, and practice listening to teachers about the art of writing. Practice expressing ourselves.

This is true, no matter what we desire to do with our days. Practice getting better at it. Do it your way, but practice.

Sometimes the practice may be sitting quietly every day in meditation. Or practice learning new technology.

Practice not agreeing with limitations imposed upon us through world, family, and friend's beliefs.

Even when these beliefs are meant well, and they often are, we still get to choose. Does it fit where we want to go and who we want to be?

Then we can practice being kind in our refusal to agree. We can do what needs to be done, but without spreading anger and grief.

When we study nature, we see how each element of nature is unique and yet fits together. Nature is diverse. Each bug, bird, animal, plant is living a life that serves a purpose and connects with every other living thing on our planet.

How many people live on earth? Each one of us is different, and yet we are the same. Even if you and I are doing the same job, we will bring our strengths and style to it.

Back to the ballet barre. Same barre. Everyone does it, intending to make every movement perfect. At the barre, everyone looks the same. The intent is to get to do the movements as correctly as possible. Each practice step is designed to strengthen muscles and make them flexible at the same time.

After the barre, it's time for action. The last half of the class is spent moving across the floor, putting into practice the barre's skills. Of course, each step in the second half of the class is also the same everywhere.

After that, a dancer gets to practice a choreographed dance. Why? To perform it. To share.

And then, each person takes the practice and expresses it in their unique way. The more they have practiced, the more they have eliminated what isn't needed, the more willing they are to be present, the more their unique self shines through.

I have used ballet as an example. Not only because I know it, but because it is one of the most rigid practices that I have ever taken part in.

You'd think that only rigidity would come out of that. And yet, that's not what happens. Individuality does. Even non-ballet dancers (like me) take that same ballet barre. Why? Because of the structure of the practice.

The point of all this is to give you an example of why it is vital to design your practice structure. It may change in the seasons of your life. In fact, I am sure that it will.

But we always have that still small voice within to guide us. As we get more and more skilled at Right Thinking and quiet the loud monkey mind voice in our head, we will become more able to listen to the quiet voice. The voice that brings us Angel Ideas.

All six steps bring us to the next Right Thinking step—Right Action.

In the meantime, think about your practice. What does it look like for you?

Remember, we are not practicing to get better at old habits. We are making new ones. That's Right Practice.

FORTY

— • —

QUALITY WORD PRACTICE

During the last few weeks, we have been using two tools to shift our thinking; I Choose sheets and Quality Word lists.

Once we finish an I Choose sheet, we are done—no need to look at it again. In fact, don't.

If you are still stuck, do another one. But looking through an old one is like picking up the garbage you just threw out and bringing it back into the house to study it.

Quality Words lists are a different story altogether. These we want to look at again. Quality words can act like our North star, keeping us focused on our true spiritual nature.

Quality words are taking things, turning them back into qualities of God—which they were in the first place. As a result, the original thing, situation, or idea will more accurately reflect its true spiritual nature too. Cool, right?

Look at your lists and see if you can narrow each list down to the top ten words. Now, here's what you do with them. If you have read my other books, you'll recognize this process, but it's always good to review it.

If this is new to you, you are in for a treat. After reviewing how to use your Quality Word list, we'll check in with Sally to see how she is doing.

How To Order Quality Word Lists

Using quality words, we will discover what we truly want. Often we'll find we already have it. We simply didn't recognize it because we were looking for the wrong thing.

All things are, in essence, composed of qualities.

When we translate things back into their qualities, a fantastic thing happens. We become conscious of what is already present for us. It may not look like we thought it would look like, but it will be what we wanted.

But first, we have to find out what our heart wants.

Quality Words will become a way of life once you experience the power of them. So, let's get started and make you an expert at using quality words to shift your life.

In this Right Thinking practice, you have made two lists.

- One list reversed the negative things you heard, or thought, about yourself. This list contains positive qualities. It is actually a list of what is true about your true spiritual nature.

- The second list is how you would feel if you were living your Right Thinking Intent.

Once you have both lists pared down to about ten Quality Words in each list, it's time to put them into order.

Yes, they are already in order. But they are in order based on how you thought about them. We need to put in them order based on how you feel about them.

Have you ever been at a place in your life where nothing happens towards what you want, no matter what you do? This is most likely because you have a quality or value block.

If we have two values that feel equal to us, our core-self will be confused about which one to provide.

Remember, our conversation about how state of mind overrides point of view? In the same way, what we feel overrides what we thought about as we made this list.

Yes, the heart rules the intellect—the feminine guides our masculine life.

This is not how it plays out most of the time in the worldview. We can see how well that works. It doesn't.

Doing this exercise will be a guide for your actions to follow your heart desires. It's one of the most powerful things we can do.

Remember, the order your lists end up in will not be the same order that your intellectual mind put them in while making them.

And you need someone to help you with this. You can't do it alone. But the person who helps you has to be in the same heart space that you are. If you can't find someone, let me know.

Once you find the person, both of you need to read the instructions listed below.

Once you understand the process, it becomes second nature, so take the time to let it sink in.

Quality Word lists not only work but are one of the most powerful and simple tools I know to shift lives.

Don't look at your list while your partner is working with you, as this will engage brain and logic. What you want to engage is your heart and inspiration.

Your partner will ask you the following question each time:

"Which is more important to you?" and will give you two words on the list to compare.

Your partner must not give you any other verbal or physical cues. Don't listen to anything except your inner voice. Respond with the answer it tells you. Don't argue with it.

If you cannot choose one as more important than the other, your partner should ask you, "Which one can you not live without?"

Notice that your mind tells you that if you choose one, you might not get the other. That fear comes from the point of view that there is never enough and that you don't deserve everything you want.

Since neither statement is true, notice these thoughts and move on. The truth is, once you are clear about what you desire to see, you will be able to see and receive all these qualities in a form appropriate for you.

Your partner must compare each word with every word until you have an ordered list. You will probably be surprised at the order if you have stayed with your heart and trusted your answers.

Here is how I do this.

(Don't worry, this is a step-by-step process. Easy. Don't let worry get in the way.)

Take a sheet of paper. Draw a line down the middle. Write your partner's original quality words on the left.

Put your finger on the first word on your partner's list. (This is so you don't lose your place.)

Ask the "which is more important" question by comparing the first word on the list to the second one. If they say the first word, move on to comparing the first word to the third word.

What if they say the second word is more important? Great. Cross it off and move it to the right side of the page.

Now compare the first word to the third word. If they say the first word is more important, move on.

What if they say the third word is more important than the first? Great. Cross it off.

But before you move it to the right side of the page, you have to find out if it is more important, or less important, than the word that is already over there.

So ask the "which is more important" question between those two words on the right.

Let's say the third word is more important than the second, so write it above the second word.

Go back to the left side of the list. Your finger is still on that first word. Compare it to the fourth word, and so on down the list until you have done the entire left side of the list.

If you have found more words that are more important than the first one, they will go to the right side after you compare them to that list, from the bottom up.

For example, you have two words on the right. The third word is first, and then the second. Now you have a new word. Compare it to the second. If it is more important, compare it to the third. If it is more important, put it at the top. If it isn't, it goes in the middle.

(Here's where you realize you need lots of spaces between the words on the right because you never know where the list is going.)

After you have completed comparing the first word all the way down the list on the left, you will have some crossed-out words on the left because they are now on the right in their right order.

Cross out the first word and add it at the bottom of the list on the right.

Draw a line under that list. You are finished with those words.

Go to the list on the left. Put your finger on the first uncrossed out word. Compare it with the next uncrossed out word below it.

Do the same thing with the words that you did before.

When you are done doing that with the new words, put a line under the list and start again on the left.

Usually, this takes two or three passes. But keep going until all the words are crossed out on the left and in order on the right.

Now you can move on to how to use your list.

How To Use Your Quality Word List

Now that you have a quality word list, how do you use it? Of course, you could ignore it and hope things change. But now that you have put so much work into the list, why not make the most of it?

Here are the four simple ways to use your list. Use it and get ready to experience more than you might imagine.

- 1. Use the qualities as a filter.

If something appears that you think might be what you are looking for and does not have at least the first four qualities—with the first one first and the rest following in order, it is not "it."

Think of the time you will save if you can eliminate quickly and easily what is not right for you.

For example, you discover that safety is first on your quality list for a means of transportation and the car you are looking at has a very low safety record, don't buy this car no matter how much you love it.

If you buy it, you will eventually be unhappy with it, and somehow you will unconsciously figure out how to get rid of it.

- 2. See the qualities everywhere.

See the qualities in everything, not just in what you're seeking. Notice that they're always with you in many forms.

You have always had, and always will have, each quality on your list if you practice looking and expect to see it.

A quality does not have to belong to you. It can appear anywhere. All of what you see is your world. The goal is to notice that the quality you're looking for already exists everywhere, and since you can see it—it exists for you—now.

- 3. Be grateful for each quality as you see it.

Be grateful for these qualities each time you see them, no matter where they occur. If the person you dislike most has one of these qualities, be grateful that you have seen this quality in your life.

Know that if it is "out there" it was first "within here" and therefore always available, and always part of your life.

- 4. Be and live these qualities yourself.

I know that you are discovering that having the "thing" you wanted is no longer as important. You have found that it already exists as thoughts—qualities.

As we express gratitude for this, we have shifted our perception towards our Right Intent. The result?

Sometimes we realize we don't need the thing we were asking to see, or it turns up in another package, or it appears in a way more excellent than we could have dreamed.

Whichever way this happens, it will more closely match your Right Intent which cannot help but produce in your world whatever you need at the moment. You have always had it.

None of us have ever been abandoned, nor could we ever be. Looking for qualities opens our eyes to what has always been and always will be ours.

That changes everything.

A Note About Your Quality Words

Can you say, "I am" in front of each word on your what-is-true-about-me list?

If not, think about changing them to the form that allows you to do so. Otherwise, these words may describe what you do, and in Right Thinking, we are aiming for who you are—your essence.

These can be the same words, just a different form.

If you like the word in the form that it is, keep it that way. As always, this is your practice, and doing it how it works the best for you is the way to do it.

FORTY-ONE

— · —

SALLY'S RIGHT PRACTICE

F ive steps into Right Thinking, Sally realizes that she is not only feeling better about herself, she is feeling happier. So much so, she slacks off and forgets about the sixth step.

After all, things are better. Besides, it's hard to keep going, especially since she has been doing this all by herself.

A few days go by before Sally notices that the voice in her head is loud again. Even more so.

She hasn't looked at her quality words, and she hasn't defended herself. She has left her mental door open. At first, she feels guilty. Then she gets angry at herself.

That voice is right. She is a loser. Sally lets herself fall into that belief for a moment, but recognizes almost immediately that it's not a voice that wants to help her.

It wants to stop her from remembering and living her true spiritual identity.

She knows what to do. She quickly walks herself back through the steps. It's easy. She's been writing them down every week. She finds her latest list and repeats it to herself.

When she gets to the sixth step of Right Practice, she realizes why Right Thinking has to be an ongoing practice.

She can't let herself lapse back into old beliefs. Moving away from and staying out of them will take time and dedication.

At first, that idea is depressing. She would have to practice Right Thinking her whole life.

Didn't she get time off? Didn't everyone deserve a break?

When she heard the still small voice say, "But this is the break," something shifted in Sally's thinking, and she realized that staying in Right Thinking was a vacation from the human mess and drama that wanted to claim her days.

It was harder not to practice, than it was to practice.

With that awareness, Sally felt as if the weight of the world had fallen off her shoulders. In a very real sense, that was exactly what had happened.

Here is Sally's blueprint for Right Thinking:

Overall Right Intent: *Get my health back.*
Right Intent: *To feel better.*
Right Premise: *I am already healthy and I feel great.*
Right Identity: *I am the expression of health.*
Right Resistance: *I resist ungodly temptations.*
Right Reasoning: *I am not the human picture.*
Right Practice: *I practice with my quality words.*

Forty-Two

Practical Practice

Here are this week's assignments. All for you. Keep that in mind, just in case you feel like skipping this part.

This only takes a minute or two to fill out. But writing it out, repeatedly, helps to rewrite the story more effectively.

Step Six: Right Practice

My overall intent for reading this book:

My Right Intent:
My Right Premise:
My Right Identity:
My Right Resistance:
My Right Reasoning:
My Right Practice:

- Continue noticing how you are self identifying, and how others see you.

- Keep your I Choose sheets going for anything that you are working on.

- Use your Quality Word lists to make decisions and shift perceptions.

- Choose at least one way that you will calm your thinking, quiet your mind and bring it into harmony with your intent. Do a meditation. Walk by yourself. Sit in nature. Listen to bird songs. Breathe.

Practice Review

Before we head into the next week's Right Thinking step, take a moment and review what happened in the past week.

It may seem like extra work, but it's not. Just keep the habit going, and you'll see how it all flows together.

Things I noticed:

Ways I am stuck:

Things that have changed:

FORTY-THREE

—·—

STEP SEVEN - RIGHT ACTION

I don't need time. What I need is a deadline. — Duke Ellington

Action. I love this step. But it's so easy to skip. For so many reasons. Resistance, apathy, fear, confusion, status quo. But without action, all that we have done up to now is talk.

We all know people who talk about concepts and ideas but don't live them. We are not those people. We choose to walk our talk.

Yes, we have been doing Right Action all along, because as with all the steps, they go together.

Each step circles around each other. They switch places like the do-Si-do in a square dance. The steps aren't a straight line. They are a tapestry, a spiral, an evolving unfoldment.

That doesn't change the fact that it's easier to study something by laying it out and looking at it step by step, which is what we have done with these Seven Steps To Right Thinking.

I have Right Action last in line because to take Right Action we have had to put ourselves in the right state of mind and point of view.

Otherwise, we might not end up where we meant to go. Or we might take action we regret, only because we didn't pause first. We could drive down the wrong road, navigate the wrong river, take the wrong bus...well, you get the idea.

If we take the wrong road, float down the wrong river, or ride the wrong bus, we can get off at any time. We all make mistakes.

The only error worth worrying about is the one we are afraid to admit and correct. It would be like saying, "Oops, I missed my exit, so I'll keep driving down this road."

That's not what we do unless we want to go exploring. Instead, we get off, check where we meant to go, and head that way. So when we take action that doesn't turn out the way we intended, we can try something else until we end up where we meant to go.

Or more accurately, where our Right Intent, Premise, and Identity have designed us to go.

I think it's easier to deal with the step of action by breaking it down into little pieces. We know them as goals and to-dos.

For example, if we intend to communicate our message with clarity, then what is a goal? That would depend on each person's unique expression of the Divine.

My goal and your goal may be different, even if we have the same intent. And goals can change with the year, the day, the hour, the minute.

I know mine have. I have the same Right Intent for what I perceive as my Life Mission, but changing seasons of life result in in different goals and different to-dos.

For example, my goal at one point was to publish a new book every month. I know people that do that. I broke it down into to-do steps.

But I quickly discovered that goal didn't suit me. It didn't fit into a bigger context of other plans I had for fulfilling my intent.

Something had to change. So I changed my goal and the to-do steps. I didn't change my intent.

I am continually adjusting my goals to support my Right Intents and expand my perception and ability to experience joy.

Take one of your intents. Check and make sure it's not a goal.

Please go through the next steps to clarify what that intent is and have it based on your Truth. Then set a goal based on all that. Yes, there can be many goals based on your intent, but start with one. Then break it down into to-do steps.

And I do mean, break it down—tiny steps.

I use several tools to do this, slips of paper, teux deux, kanban, a whiteboard, and a voice recording program.

I'm always tweaking what I am doing, attempting to match my actions with what keeps me in the Right Thinking process instead of falling into human personality quirks. It's a balancing act.

It takes time. It's a practice. So we might as well settle in and enjoy the process.

Your quality word list is going to guide you. These qualities are what is important to you. They are a representation of the essence of who you are.

Have you set an intent, goal, or to-do that doesn't fit your qualities?

Stop, check, and see. Don't pass go until you do. Adjust. Pay attention.

Remember the four ways to use your list? Review the "how to" in Chapter Eleven. Use them.

Doing this first will save heartbreak and time and keep you on your Right Intent track.

Let's see what Sally is up to now.

FORTY-FOUR

— · —

SALLY'S ACTION

After discovering the joy of practicing, Sally has become much more faithful about the Right Thinking steps.

However, reaching the step called Right Action both scared Sally and excited her.

Part of Sally wished that all she had to do was think about what she wanted using the Right Thinking steps.

After all, things had started to change even without doing much more than the homework assignments.

It would be so much easier to just imagine things getting better and not have to do anything.

On the other hand, Sally recognized that she was holding herself back from doing things she had always wanted to do.

And the more she practiced the Right Thinking steps, the more she felt like doing them.

Sally could feel ideas bubbling around inside of her. It was both terrifying and exhilarating to realize that she was finally going to do something about them.

Now that Sally could recognize the difference between resisting what isn't true and resisting what she wanted to do, the action part of herself was raring to go.

All she had to do was get past the old version of herself, the old perceptions, the old hangups. She had to keep telling the voice in her head to shut up, and she often pictured shoving it behind a door and locking it.

Being persistent in denying what it was telling her helped a great deal and doing the I Choose sheets and Quality Word lists helped make it all much better.

Getting out of her own way made things so much easier. Just wishing and wanting had not worked. Taking Right Action was the solution.

The other thing that Sally was experiencing was a renewed desire to do things she had long ago forgotten she liked to do. It was interesting to Sally that although these things didn't specifically relate to her intent to get her health back, they made her feel better.

So Sally resolved to take action on the things that were calling her to do. In the process, she was happier with everyone around her.

Sally stopped blaming them for how she felt or how she looked. She hadn't even realized she had been doing that.

Once she realized that she had been blaming others for where she was her in her life, Sally stopped by reminding herself who she was—a reflection of Love—which meant that the person who was annoying her was also a reflection of Love. That is Right Reasoning, Sally told herself.

The habit she worked on the most was the habit of feeling guilty or ashamed of how she had behaved, or what she hadn't done with her life, or how she had given up on her dreams.

That kind of thinking was not Right Thinking.

Sally realized that only by staying with Right Thinking could she clean up the messes she made and move happily forward in her life.

Sally took just one idea that had been bubbling up and made a goal and to-do list for it. It was easy now that she understood the difference between intent and a goal.

Yes, her intent remained to get her health back. She changed the wording, though. Now that she understood the process better, she realized what she wanted was to experience health. So that was her new intent.

Sally had always wanted to walk or run one of her town's charity events. So she made it a goal to walk in the next event and to finish. Someday she wanted to run it, but for now, this was a goal she knew she could accomplish.

Next, she made a list of action steps—things to do. Register for the walk was first on the list. Then she added stuff she would need. And how much she would walk every day to prepare.

As Sally finished up her seven weeks of Right Thinking, she realized that she could run through the seven steps in a flash, and in doing so, she could often heal a situation or problem quickly.

The day she and her husband started arguing, she silently walked herself through the Seven Steps.

This is what she said to herself.

I don't want to argue. My intent is to stop this argument. My premise is that Love is present here and now. We are both expressions of love and wisdom. I won't accept that he is wrong and I am right. We are both just trying to be happy. Yes, we are both expressions of love and wisdom.

With that, Sally reached out and touched his hand and smiled at him.

He sputtered to a stop and smiled back. And that was the end of the argument.

Yes, Sally decided. *Right Thinking does work.*

Here are Sally's seven steps for Right Thinking:

Overall Right Intent: Experience health.
Right Intent: *To feel better.*
Right Premise: *I am already healthy and I feel great.*
Right Identity: *I am the expression of health.*

Right Resistance: *I resist ungodly temptations.*
Right Reasoning: *I am not the human picture.*
Right Practice: *I practice with my quality words.*
Right Action: *I take action towards my dreams.*

FORTY-FIVE

—— · ——

PRACTICAL ACTION

A s you finish up these seven weeks, keep the practice going.
You will get better and better at it and probably run through the steps in a flash.

Still, sometimes it helps to take all this time to work through something.

Don't be surprised if it changes and heals more things than what you began with.

What appears as a problem is a symptom. Doing these seven steps reveals the underlying issue and shifts it, thereby resolving the problem.

Step Seven: Right Action

My overall intent for reading this book:
My Right Intent:
My Right Premise:
My Right Identity:
My Right Resistance:
My Right Reasoning:
My Right Practice:
My Right Action:

Yes, you could continue with these practice steps if you wish.

- Continue noticing how you are self identifying, and how others see you.

- Keep your I Choose sheets going for anything that you are working on.

- Use your Quality Word lists to make decisions and shift perceptions.

- Choose at least one way that you will calm your thinking, quiet your mind and bring it into harmony with your intent. Do a meditation. Walk by yourself. Sit in nature. Listen to bird songs. Breathe.

Action Review

Look back of these last seven weeks just one more time and answer these questions for yourself.

Things I noticed:

Ways I am stuck:

Things that have changed:

Forty-Six

— • —

Recap

If you follow your bliss, doors will open for you that wouldn't have opened for anyone else. — Joseph Campbell

If you have gotten this far, you have already experienced the results of Right Thinking. Healing of some kind has taken place in your life.

Perhaps it wasn't what you thought you wanted to heal. Maybe it doesn't feel the way you thought it would. But something has happened.

It had to. We have shifted our thinking towards infinite possibilities and away from the limited worldview. That will always, always change our experience.

All we have to do is to be willing to experience it.

Perception blindness is a real thing. It's what we have been striving to clear up. To open our eyes to see the perfection already present.

Sometimes that perception blindness is due to conscious choices. Other times it's because we are stuck in what we think is happening or should happen.

This summer, I watched a row of dahlias as they grew. I had been lazy and not taken the roots out of the ground for the winter, and didn't expect them to return. However, we had a mild winter, and some of them had survived.

At the end of the summer, the dahlias bloomed, except for one huge one that kept getting bigger and bigger. I had never seen such a huge dahlia. Was it using all its energy to grow big, and that's why there were no blooms?

I asked myself that question for a few weeks. Then one day, I asked myself if it was really a dahlia. Just because it was growing where I planted one didn't mean it was one.

With that question, I realized that not only was it not a dahlia; it was a tree. Yes, a tree. I had trimmed it as if it was a dahlia, so it was multi-branched, but it was a tree.

Because I wasn't expecting a tree to be there, and because in the beginning, the leaves resembled dahlia leaves, and it was a tree I had ever seen before, and because I wanted it to be a dahlia, it took months to see what was there all along.

I could tell you many stories about perception blindness. I am sure you could, too. We look for what we think the object or idea, looks like and not for its essence. And because of that, we don't see what is right in front of us.

Right in front of us is the perfection of the One Creator, the One creation. Right in front of us is the Truth of our Spiritual nature.

Blaming ourselves for not seeing it only makes it worse. Move forward. Look at what didn't work, only to move forward. Don't stay in the past. Learn from it and move forward.

Turn your attention to shifting out of perception blindness and into the light.

Then what appears to be broken or hurting or separated is more clearly seen in its Divine perfection. That's when we experience what we call healing.

Make an Intent to understand the Divine, to be Love in action. Be willing to let go of the human ego and personalities. They get in the way.

Like the tinman, the lion, the scarecrow, and Dorothy, we already have all we need. Use this thoughtful system of Right Thinking to find that out for yourself.

May our hearts be filled with the joy of Divine discovery. Strengthen us all to withstand that which ties us to the human beliefs of lack and limitation. May we all experience our true spiritual nature and light up the world with the awareness that we are One.

Here's a practice that may help.

Right Intent: *To live as the expression of the Divine.*
Right Premise: *I am the expression of the Divine.*
Right Identity: *I am Love Loving Itself.*
Right Reasoning: *Omnipotent God is Love.*
Right Resistance: *I resist anything that is not Love.*
Right Practice: *I consistently stay within the Truth.*
Right Action: *I do what Angel Ideas lead me to do.*

NOTE: Remember, if you would like a free workbook, you can find it here: https://perceptionu.com/the-library/workbooks/

Forty-Seven

Acknowledgements

M y heartfelt thanks to the *Seven Step To Right Thinking* class for being the beta testers for this book.

And for those wonderful members of the Beca Book Community who encourage me to keep writing.

Thank you especially to Jet Tucker, Jamie Lewis, and Diana Cormier for cleaning up all my errors in this book, and always being there when I need them to check up on me.

PERCEPTION MASTERY

FORTY-EIGHT

WHAT OTHERS SAY ...

Beca's *Perception Mastery* book is a gold mine of spiritual wisdom and invaluable methods to help you shift into higher levels of self-awareness. Beca designed this book to help you turn inward so that you can examine limiting beliefs in all areas of your life and shift your thinking to create and live your best life.

I enjoyed this book and all of Beca's books in *The Shift Series* because they are grounded in practical spirituality. Beca teaches effective, simple methods that have helped me shift my thinking and energetics to better align with the flow of universal abundance and create my life through my conscious intentions. We all have the ability to turn inward.

We have a choice in every moment, and when we slow down to listen to our soul, magic truly happens. If you are curious and willing, then read this book. —Tracy Wright Corvo

Let's face it. Humans tend to be creatures of habit. Why wouldn't we be, since we spend so much time dwelling on habits? And we know that what we focus on is pretty much what we get, right? That's what the *Perception Mastery* book is all about. Perception and habits. Beca

teaches us that "Perception produces reality, and what we perceive as reality magnifies."

If that is true, and I maintain that it is, the best thing we can do is perceive the best reality we can possibly imagine! And if habits are so ingrained in us, why not choose the best ones we can?

So, by shifting to the highest understanding we can imagine now by following simple principles and using some pretty nifty tools Beca teaches, not only are we learning to live our best lives, but by learning for ourselves, we are extending that benefit to the world.
—Jet Tucker

FORTY-NINE

— · —

INTRODUCTION

R eading is seeing by proxy. — Herbert Spencer

All the books in *The Shift Series* are the "children" of the first book in the series, *Living In Grace: The Shift To Spiritual Perception.* Each book addresses an idea brought forth in *Living In Grace* and expands upon it.

Like all the books in *The Shift Series, Perception Mastery* is a self-help book based on spiritual principles designed to support your personal spiritual practice.

Perception Mastery focuses directly on the rules of perception, which underlies all the concepts found in *Living In Grace.* Perhaps it should have been the first offshoot? Or maybe I needed to teach and coach for many years to understand how to set out the ideas more clearly and practically, which is why this book took so long to write.

It doesn't matter in what order you read *The Shift Series.* Following your internal guidance, you will find the one that will help you the most where you are in life.

However, each book has an intent, or more accurately, I have an intent for each book.

For *Perception Mastery*, it is to provide you, the reader, with tools that will:

- Give you a clearer understanding of your unique spiritual expression and how to live it.

- Help you master the experience of joy under all circumstances.

- Increase your ability to ask for and accept the overflowing abundance of Life's gifts.

- And as a result, experience a recognizable shift towards the life you want to live.

I know not every question or possibility is addressed in this book, but it is a sound foundation to build upon. Use it as a guide, a blueprint to practice mastering perception.

I trust that you have the inner wisdom and understanding to find what you need within these pages and will use it to expand your awareness of infinite possibilities for yourself and others.

Thank you for walking this spiritual path with me. — Beca!

Sometimes the shortest distance between two points is a winding path walked arm in arm. — Robert Brault

Fifty

— • —

Find a Friend

A man is known by the company his mind keeps. — Thomas Bailey Aldrich

To make this book even more fun and practical, perhaps you would like to do the steps with a friend or two because often it is helpful to do spiritual work within a community—however, not just any community, a community of like-minded souls.

Always choose your community of friends and confidants carefully. Make sure you all have each other's best interests in mind.

Not sure how to know if they are the right fit for you?

Ask yourself if you are a better person because you are together? Are you both kinder, more open, more confident, more joyful, more inclusive, more supportive of every living thing? Then you are on the right track.

Don't know anyone who does this for you yet? You will because like-minded souls find each other when the time is right. In the meantime, read and do these steps yourself, knowing you are not really alone.

If you need help, let me know. There might be a group going on that you can join, or I could be teaching a live class just as you begin this. You can find me at becalewis.com.

Take this time for deep thinking and the chance to rejuvenate your life. Don't wait. Get started.

Things will shift to bring you what you need and want if you are faithful to the practice and yourself. It always begins within. And with faith.

Not sure you have faith? You do. Or you wouldn't have opened this book. That's enough faith right there.

FIFTY-ONE

— · —

WHY BECOME A PERCEPTION MASTER

If life had a second edition, how I would correct the proofs. — John Clare

Perception is reality. How many times have we all said these words and maybe even believed them?

But are they true? And if they are, does it matter?

Yes, they are, and yes, it does. But too often, we misinterpret the words when we don't realize that we are the producers of our perception.

As perception masters, we learn to shift the reality we perceive rather than perceiving a reality presented to us.

Contrary to what we might wish to be true, there is only one thing we can actually "control." One thing only. Our perception, and therefore our reaction, and response, to people, places, things, and events.

Isn't that fantastic? Rather than trying to control everything, all we need to do is shift our perception?

As Mary Baker Eddy said, "It's not what you see, but how you see it." Or, as Henry David Thoreau said, "It's not what you look at that matters, it's what you see."

And when we learn how to see with the eyes of perception masters or prophets, like Buddha, Elias, Christ Jesus, or Mohammad, we will experience an entirely different world. Not because we made it change, but because we see and experience it as it already is. Perfect. Eternal. Glorious.

If this appeals to you, come with me on this journey as we shift our perceptions together. Because until we can fully rise above the perception that we are human, or even spiritual beings having a human experience, we will constantly be called upon to shift our perception, so we might as well become masters of it.

Will this perception shifting change anything? Absolutely. Because yes, *what we perceive to be reality magnifies*. So since (our) perception is (our) reality, let's shift our perception to the most glorious, loving, unlimited view of existence that we can muster up. As we get better at it, so will the world that we view.

Want to change the world? Start within. Start with perception, yours.

Be a shifter. Be a perception shifter. Be a perception master. Be a shift master. Then get out of the way and observe what is really going on. It's better than you think.

So let's hop to it and get this party started!

One more thing: Do these steps in your own timing.

When I teach this class, we do one step a week. In this book, Molly, our guide, is doing one every few days.

Take these steps faster, slower, whatever works for you. In fact, once you know them, you could take yourself through them within minutes. No matter which way you choose, the important thing is to do them.

And expect results. Oh, and have fun. Why not? It's a perception, after all.

FIFTY-TWO

MEET MOLLY

The landscape belongs to the man who looks at it. — Ralph Waldo Emerson

Molly is a made-up person. However, she became pretty real to me as I wrote this book. I think that's because she is a composite of all of us, and I recognized myself in her. As I think you will too.

Molly will work through each step of this book and share what she learns, which will help explain how each step of this process might play out in your life. Of course, not exactly.

But if we peek at what she thinks as she perfects her perception skills, it should help explain how to use the concepts and steps in real-life situations.

In a class, we talk about what we learn together, and that sharing helps remind us not only that we can do it, but we are not alone. So instead of classmates, we have Molly, a composite of all of us at different times in our lives. Although we are all beautifully diverse expressions of the Divine, we have much in common.

If you have a trusted friend doing this book with you, talk about what you learn together. You'll be pleasantly surprised to discover how much that helps.

No matter what, Molly's experience should help your experience. That's my intent anyway.

THE SEVEN STEPS TO SHIFT

FIFTY-THREE

— • —

STEP ONE: BE WILLING

He who would may reach the utmost height, but he must be eager to learn. — Buddha

This first step—Be Willing—is so important it could take up the entire book. And even though all the other steps might not need to be in the order that I present them, this one always must come first. All the time. Every time.

Because unless we are willing for something to change or shift, or become better. it can't.

Why? Because we are the ones holding the perception of a reality as a truth for us. And even though the entire universe could have changed, we won't notice unless we are willing to see the change.

Or we will experience the change through our personal paradigm filter, which means it will be a skewed view.

If you were wearing a pair of blue glasses, and I tried to tell you that the world is not only blue but beautiful shades of many colors, if you are not willing to take off the glasses, then the world will forever be only blue to you.

That nothing can happen unless we are willing is so clear that it's incredible how often we ignore it. And yet, we can see for ourselves that we can't, won't, don't, do anything unless we are willing to do it.

There is no way around this first step. But being willing cannot be forced on anyone or faked. It has to be voluntary, for both us and for those we wish were willing.

This book will help you open up the space for being willing. It will help you find the thoughts, ideas, and paradigms you have either not noticed, or noticed and didn't know how to change, so that you can either consciously choose to keep them or be willing to let them go.

Yes, we do things every day that we don't want to do. To do them, a part of us was willing. Discovering that reason will help us do things we don't do, even though we want to.

Imagine what it would be like to be consciously aware of whether or not we are willing. Imagine what it would be like if we realized we weren't willing to do something, and why we aren't willing, accept that we aren't willing, and be able to say no and mean it.

Or imagine what it would be like to be entirely in the willing mode to do what we want and experience the joy of the flow it would produce.

Learning how to recognize our unwillingness and improve our willingness is a practice. Although a straightforward concept, it involves a depth of awareness that most of us don't possess most of the time.

However, we can become skilled in this practice, and that's what we will do together.

Before we begin, why not prove this concept of willingness for yourself?

And even though, as in all things, we must begin within to shift our perception, let's start our discovery by looking outside ourselves and into our life.

Everyone has someone in their life that doesn't do what we want them to do. In fact, isn't a large part of life about trying to convince others to do something? Get our children to pick up their toys, be polite, don't slurp your food, hang out with the right people, pick the right school, fall in love with the right person.

What about what we want from our life partners, parents, our work colleagues? If they would only listen to us, everything would be so much better. Or on a broader scale. Politicians. What's wrong with them, anyway? Why don't they do want we want them to do? Why are they swayed by things we know are the wrong things?

How do we convince them? Some of us are more skilled at this than others, and all of us are terrible at it at times. And you know why? Because we can't change someone's mind, including our own, unless they, and we, are willing.

That's it. If someone is not willing, we have two choices.

1. We can stop trying to make happen what will never happen and is only causing us to beat our heads against a wall, hurting ourselves and others in the process.

2. Or we have to make space for them to become willing. And if they are not, let it go.

Make space. That is not the way we think about changing things. We usually push into change.

Instead, we will practice stepping back and making space for change.

And that begins where it must, within ourselves.

Are you willing to do that? Is there anything in your life that is causing you enough pain and frustration that you can say, *"Okay, I am willing. Nothing else has worked. Yes, I am willing."*

Isn't this the concept of organizations like AA? Nothing will change until the person suffers enough to be willing. Hits bottom.

But we don't have to get to suffering for this to work. You could suffer if you want to. Go ahead, go for it. But I'm tired of suffering—both my own and others. I would prefer that we all learn by following the light and angel ideas rather than experience suffering.

I, and you, may not be able to avoid some of this suffering. It will appear to come from the outside. Something outside our control. 2020 was the perfect example of this. All of us suffered—some more than others.

What we were willing to do with it made the difference and will make a difference as we move forward. It was the perfect lens for us to use to study our willingness. Our willingness to change. Our willingness to not react. Our willingness to help others.

So our first step in this seven-step shift of perception is to be willing, and the first thing we need to do to become artists at willingness is to discover what we are willing and unwilling to do and then decide what to do about it.

A cautionary note. The willingness I am talking about is not about human willpower. It's not about making something happen or creating it. That's not the willing meant here. This is a willingness for letting go and experiencing the intelligent, loving, creative force that is all around us, providing for us in every moment.

You don't have to believe this. You just have to be willing to find out if it is true.

That's the big picture.

The everyday picture is a little simpler. Are we willing to live differently, or get along with someone we don't like, or learn a new technology?

Are we willing to let it be okay that other people, even those we love, are not willing? Not willing to do what we want for them or think is best for them. Are we willing to let them be who and what they want to be?

In this way, we can still love them, listen, and understand, which may provide a safe space for them to be willing. Even so, we have to be willing that they might never get there.

A key point.

Often it is good not to be willing. I am not willing to intentionally hurt another or myself. I am not willing to sit on a hot stove. I am not willing to listen to people who only mean harm.

So, understanding our boundaries is a process of being willing, and that's a good thing.

Remember, we are not changing our human minds. We are releasing them so that we can see more. We are taking off those blue glasses. Ready! Go!

FIFTY-FOUR

THE TWO WORD KEY TO EVERYTHING

Sooner or later everyone sits down to a banquet of consequences. — Robert Louis Stevenson

How many times have you tried to change someone, or even yourself, and failed miserably?

Without knowing a single thing about what happened or what you were trying to do, I know why it probably didn't work as well as you wanted it to.

One day, I decided I wanted to stop getting in my way. I wasn't doing anything overt. However, I could feel myself not letting things happen. Very subtle. But it was becoming quite annoying. I wanted to experience more of what we all know, that the universe moves towards us, and the Infinite loves to provide us with what we want and desire.

I asked myself, "If that's true, why does everything stay about the same?" After all, we live in an ever-expanding universe filled with more riches than we can ever imagine. Why don't all of us consistently experience an overabundance of wealth in all its forms?

The answer is simple. The solution is also simple, but not easy.

We have to break the habit of consciously and unconsciously saying no to what is being offered. We have to stop the habit of walking away from the open hand, bearing gifts.

Why do we do this? Perhaps we think we're not worthy. Or we believe we can do it ourselves, thank you very much. Or we are self-contained. Or we are afraid that having what we want will bring us responsibilities that we don't think we can handle. Or we are trapped in our habits.

For sure, our perceptions have made us prisoners of what we believe.

We allow enough abundance into our lives to keep us comfortable in whatever manner we expect or are used to. But against more than that, we erect a barrier. Yes, invisible most of the time, but still a barrier.

When I am paying attention, I can feel the barriers I've put up. Observing my habits, I realize I have lots of them hanging out in the tiny crevices of my life, ready to be called into action if I should need them. They willingly spring into action if there is too much supply of wealth in my life.

So I took to heart, once again—because I, like you, have done this countless times in my life—the first step of any shift. I decided to be willing. Really willing. Consciously willing. Willing to say yes. Willing to break old habits.

It's easy to say we are willing. But are we?

Inside, unconsciously, are we shutting down our energy? Are we blocking help? Are we saying, "that's too much for me to handle?"

To change anything at all, from life to light bulbs, we have to be willing. And when we are willing—well, stand back because things will flow.

The universe moves towards us and pools at our feet, providing what we need long before asking for it. We stand on the abundant earth that has been given to us. We walk through its air, drink its water, glory in its beauty. Can not the Intelligence that provides all this provide for its loved ones? It can. It does. Say yes.

Say yes to what Life wants to give you.

Be willing to do what it takes to receive it. Be willing to ask for help. Be willing to step forward into your gifts. The gift always contains a way to use it. Would an intelligent divine Mind design Life any other way?

Be willing is the key to what works and what doesn't. We can't help anyone if they are not willing, including ourselves. It's the first step to making any shift or change in our lives. Be willing. Everything flows from that one point.

My dance teacher at UCLA used to say, "Expand, take up space." It's the same thing. Be willing to be who you are, and surrender to abundance.

Be willing—the two-word key to everything.

FIFTY-FIVE

BE A SHIFTER

By giving up the need to know, we can begin to know in a whole new way. — Shinzen Young

As you know, in the fantasy world, a shifter is someone who can be many things. Some of them are dragons (I have a dragon or two in my fantasy books). Others can be anything at all, from a bird to a fish to a different being altogether. My favorite fantasy shifter is Odo from Deep Space Nine.

However, to be a shifter in our world, we have to become perception masters. And to do that, we must first be willing to accept that each of us contains within our essence all that we need—as does the person we love the most and the person we like the least.

We all have unlimited possibilities to shift to who we want to be, which is who we were designed to be.

To become more willing, sometimes it helps to imagine ourselves as trees, the sky, a light beam, or—the list is endless. If you have read my *Imagination Mastery* book, you are already doing this kind of thing. If not, this is an excellent time to begin.

What good does it do? It shifts us out of the limited human view of ourselves, which is minuscule compared to who we truly are, and imagination expands that paradigm.

Keep that in mind as we go forward. And remember, although you are becoming a perception master for yourself, it will help others too. As Michael Jackson said, start with the man in the mirror.

I'm gonna make a change For once in my life It's gonna feel real good Gonna make a difference Gonna make it right

No message could have been any clearer If you want to make the world a better place Take a look at yourself and then make the change
— Michael Jackson, *Man In The Mirror*

Fifty-Six

Practical Willing

The one who is truly wise sees the consequences of his actions. —
Babylonian Talmud

Molly's friend Sally gave her the book *Perception Mastery* and
suggested she read it. Molly said thanks. and then put the book away,
thinking that the last thing she needed to read was a woo-woo book
about shifting perception.

She had some genuine issues to deal with, and no amount of
perception blah-blah would fix it. Besides, having the time and
bandwidth for learning new things was for young people, not for
people like her.

Molly couldn't decide if her problems were too big or too small to
do anything about them. She should be grateful. She had a place to
live, a husband, grown kids, even the makings of a garden.

Sure, she felt overworked and unappreciated, but didn't everyone?
She didn't like her job, but they needed the money. And Molly
realized that if she was going to be honest with herself, she also didn't

enjoy being stuck in the house all day. So the job gave her a place to go.

The year of working from home and not going to the office almost made her crazy. Although Molly was grateful she kept her job when others lost theirs, she was bored. Still, it was a job.

The more Molly allowed herself to think about it, the more she believed it would be wrong to want more. She had work. They had money to buy groceries. Her children called once in a while. Her husband wasn't mean, and sometimes he did things to help around the house. What were her problems, anyway?

However, one day, while dusting, she ran across the book again. Flipping through the pages, Molly noticed that there were steps to being a perception master, whatever that was.

Still not understanding why she needed to shift her perception for anything to happen, she decided it couldn't hurt.

It was only later that she realized that choice was the point of the first step. She had become willing just a tiny bit. Enough to read the book and try out the exercises.

What Molly discovered as she did the exercises both shocked her and made her mad. Who she was mad at, she wasn't sure. But as her list grew of what she was not willing to do, she was astonished.

It was harder for her to make a list of what she was willing to do. Then she realized that her life mirrored back to her what she had been and was willing to do.

It was simple things, like shopping for groceries every day, dusting the house, doing a job that bored her. She was also willing to ignore the state of the house and garden. She was willing to wear clothes that didn't fit her and listen to news that depressed her.

Once she got started, Molly couldn't stop. Both lists grew. She tried not to judge them. She had to ask herself every day if she was willing only to notice, not judge. Sometimes she was. Often she wasn't.

Finally, she asked herself the question she might have asked at first. *Was she willing to be happy?*

When she realized her answer was no, she sat down on the bedroom floor and cried. How could she not be willing to be happy?

And then she realized she cried because she did want to be happy. Of course, she did. That meant she was willing. It was a revelation, and with that conscious choice to be willing to be happy, something changed for Molly.

If this was what perception mastery was about, she wanted more of it. She was willing.

Fifty-Seven

Molly and Being Willing

The one who is truly wise sees the consequences of his actions. —
Babylonian Talmud

Molly's friend Sally gave her the book *Perception Mastery* and
suggested she read it. Molly said thanks. and then put the book away,
thinking that the last thing she needed to read was a woo-woo book
about shifting perception.

She had some genuine issues to deal with, and no amount of
perception blah-blah would fix it. Besides, having the time and
bandwidth for learning new things was for young people, not for
people like her.

Molly couldn't decide if her problems were too big or too small to
do anything about them. She should be grateful. She had a place to
live, a husband, grown kids, even the makings of a garden.

Sure, she felt overworked and unappreciated, but didn't everyone?
She didn't like her job, but they needed the money. And Molly
realized that if she was going to be honest with herself, she also didn't

enjoy being stuck in the house all day. So the job gave her a place to go.

The year of working from home and not going to the office almost made her crazy. Although Molly was grateful she kept her job when others lost theirs, she was bored. Still, it was a job.

The more Molly allowed herself to think about it, the more she believed it would be wrong to want more. She had work. They had money to buy groceries. Her children called once in a while. Her husband wasn't mean, and sometimes he did things to help around the house. What were her problems, anyway?

However, one day, while dusting, she ran across the book again. Flipping through the pages, Molly noticed that there were steps to being a perception master, whatever that was.

Still not understanding why she needed to shift her perception for anything to happen, she decided it couldn't hurt.

It was only later that she realized that choice was the point of the first step. She had become willing just a tiny bit. Enough to read the book and try out the exercises.

What Molly discovered as she did the exercises both shocked her and made her mad. Who she was mad at, she wasn't sure. But as her list grew of what she was not willing to do, she was astonished.

It was harder for her to make a list of what she was willing to do. Then she realized that her life mirrored back to her what she had been and was willing to do.

It was simple things, like shopping for groceries every day, dusting the house, doing a job that bored her. She was also willing to ignore the state of the house and garden. She was willing to wear clothes that didn't fit her and listen to news that depressed her.

Once she got started, Molly couldn't stop. Both lists grew. She tried not to judge them. She had to ask herself every day if she was willing only to notice, not judge. Sometimes she was. Often she wasn't.

Finally, she asked herself the question she might have asked at first. *Was she willing to be happy?*

When she realized her answer was no, she sat down on the bedroom floor and cried. How could she not be willing to be happy?

And then she realized she cried because she did want to be happy. Of course, she did. That meant she was willing. It was a revelation, and with that conscious choice to be willing to be happy, something changed for Molly.

If this was what perception mastery was about, she wanted more of it. She was willing.

FIFTY-EIGHT

— • —

STEP TWO: BECOME AWARE

*N*othing remains as it was. If you know this, you can begin again, *with pure joy in the uprooting.* — Judith Minty

I know we would all like to think that we are aware, but you know that most of the time we are not. How could we be? If we were aware of all that is happening at all times, we probably couldn't function.

To enable us to live in the swarm of information that is our world, we have selective awareness, which is good. It keeps us focused. Our brains filter out what is unnecessary.

The problem is, if we aren't constantly checking, we get stuck in the paradigm we've created. Unless we actively choose to become aware of something other than what we currently know and believe, we stay stuck in an unyielding loop.

To experience the life we want to live, we must constantly be willing to see differently—to shift our perception. And to do that, we must become aware of what constitutes our current life and belief system.

Awareness is vital to our well-being because a lack of awareness keeps us at one end of a point of view in a distorted, conditioned mind, which is out of balance and at odds with the other end.

To release ourselves from the paradigms and belief systems that may have kept us safe at one point but now stop our progress, we have to be willing to become aware of our current physical, emotional, and mental states to uncover hidden thoughts and habits.

You will notice, as we walk this perception-shifting path together, that all these steps intertwine. Perception mastery is not a straight line. It curves and spirals, rises and falls.

However, these steps do have an obvious order. Take these first two. If we are going to be willing, we have to be aware of what we are willing to do or not do.

As we do this work, it's essential to remember that we all express our true spiritual nature differently. One is not better than another, just as one color in nature is not better than another. Contrary to what many of us have been taught to believe, we are not in competition with each other. Just as in all nature, cooperation is our natural state.

Yes, we all have different preferences and different desires, but they are designed to blend together, to live in harmony with each other. Therefore, it is essential that we become aware of our actual preferences and desires, not what we think they are or were told they are.

Yes, we are allowed to make choices that benefit us. Not only allowed. It is necessary. We can choose for ourselves, not blindly following previously set paradigms and perceptions. As perception masters, we make mindful, conscious choices.

As in all things in life, we practice if we want to become skilled at something. Now, as we practice being willing, we add in the skill of becoming aware. As we do so, we discover that there are things we should not be willing to do. Or things that others do we should not be willing to let happen.

So besides being willing to do, we also have to be willing not to do. But how aware are you of what you are not willing to do?

"Beca," you might say. "You have lost your mind. I am not willing to do lots of things, and I am perfectly well aware of them."

Hum. Are you? Are we? And do you know the underlying reason you are not willing?

Because we all do things we tell ourselves that we are not willing to do, but we do anyway. All. The. Time.

And you know that we all are unwilling to do things we know we "should" be willing to do.

So what are we missing?

The why of it.

Why are you willing? Why are you not willing? What is the "voice in your head" telling you about your choices that keep you from moving forward or letting go?

In the practical awareness section, you'll be doing something very simple but extremely powerful. It's a perception tool I call "I Choose sheets."

If you have done them before-—since this is one tool I always talk about—welcome back. If not, don't worry. They are easy to understand. I'll tell you how to use them in the Practical Awareness section.

Stick with me here for a second as we talk about what this tool can do for you. Using an I Choose sheet not only begins the process of becoming aware but also grounds it into action.

When we become aware of what stops us from doing what we think we want to do, one of three things will happen:

1. Either... Having all the blocks removed, we are energized, excited, and are taking action steps towards what we are willing to do,

2. Or—nothing happens. At all. This is when you grab your handy paper and pen and start another I Choose sheet based on what you have learned. Or you could continue the one you are working on. Either way, keep going until the hidden block reveals its sneaky little self, releasing you from its hold,

3. Or—you discover, perhaps to your surprise, that you don't want to do it. Maybe you don't have the time, and you realize that something else is more important. Or it was something you used to want to do, but that desire belonged to a different you. One from a different time and place. Or it was something that others have told you one way or another that you wanted it.

Pausing here.

Our entire culture is designed to make us want or need something unnecessary. Buy this. Think that. Do it this way.

Becoming aware of our willingness and why we are willing—or not—is a critical step on our perception shifting path.

But sometimes, we don't pause long enough to listen.

I made that mistake as I was writing this book. I saw something. It spoke my language. It had a deadline. It had a bargain price. I bought it. Then I read more and realized they were selling fear. I hadn't noticed that. Two minutes after buying it, I canceled it. I heard my internal voice and listened to it.

Yes, it was a pain to cancel. But I was willing to do it, anyway.

We all make mistakes. But we'll make fewer ones, correct them more quickly, and learn what we need to know from them when we are willing to become aware.

Discovering that you don't want something you thought you did is time for a celebration. You've made space. You have given yourself a gift of time in your life. Now you have room for something with a better or a more current why.

Become aware of your choices. And be willing to choose it and see if it is still what you want.

Yes, this is an ongoing process. That's life for you! We might as well get to living it and celebrate the adventure.

Fifty-Nine

Choose Consciously

I choose, therefore I am. — Amit Goswami

Did you know there's a voice in your head constantly telling you why you can't do something? This voice is called many things: the monkey voice, the ego, the shadow—whatever you call it, it's imperative to know and understand one thing. That voice is not your voice. I know it sounds like you, and it says things you think you might say to yourself, but it's not.

So, why is it there?

That's like asking why do we believe we are human. Who knows? At this point, it's all someone's story, believe them or not, it doesn't change anything.

Here's what we do know and does change things. The voice in our head runs the paradigm we think we must live within, and unless we know what it is saying to us, we are stuck in its prison. It drives the car we call our life. It has us choosing things we may or may not want anymore, or perhaps never wanted.

However, we do have free will, so let's put that freedom to work.

Let's find out what that voice is saying and then replace it with what we consciously choose. Being willing, becoming aware, and consciously choosing breaks open our current paradigm. It shifts our perception. And as a result, the world we experience shifts to match our new perception.

Remember, perception is reality. "What we perceive to be reality magnifies."

Therefore, since we can make conscious choices, let's shift our perception to the best version of what I call big R Reality we can get to right now. Which for me, and perhaps for you, is a gloriously Loving One Intelligent Reality because that's the one I want to experience.

Now that we know what we would consciously choose, let's do an I Choose sheet. Doing this is so simple it might seem ineffective. However, I promise you it works if you do it.

Here we go:

Get out a tablet of paper and a pen. Notice I didn't say get your computer. I love writing on my computer. But I Choose sheets work much better when they are handwritten. Besides, when you finish with one, you can burn it. Very satisfying.

Begin by stating what you want as a choice.

How do you know what you want? Remember the question you answered at the top of this chapter? What are you willing to do? Choose that.

After that, there are just two steps to learn.

- First, pause, listen for the voice in your head telling you why you can't have it or why it won't work.

I guarantee you that the voice is there. Don't worry. It can't hurt to hear it now. In fact, you want to listen to what it's been telling you all along, and you have been accepting as true.

Once you hear that voice telling you why you can't have what you are willing to do, don't write what that voice says. Please don't give it any power by agreeing with it.

- Next, choose and write the opposite of what it's saying. I call this "face and replace."

Face what it says, and replace it with what you consciously choose.

Let's head over to see how Molly does an I Choose sheet so you can see how it works.

SIXTY

MOLLY AND BECOMING AWARE

The world is changed not by the self-regarding, but by men and women prepared to make fools of themselves. — P. D. James

Molly decided that the one thing she was willing to do was to be happy. And she was ready to take action towards that intent.

Choosing happiness was more complex than she thought it would be. Did she have a right to be happy? What was happy, anyway? But she knew that the point of this practice was to find answers to questions like this. That she was willing was a big step forward.

As for what Molly thought she wanted, and now realized that she was unwilling to do, was the idea that she would someday have a small farm with lots of animals.

That was a dream she had as a child. Now she realized she was not willing to do the work to pursue it. She could barely muster up the desire to keep a garden alive. It was a relief to let that idea go and focus on doing what made her happy now.

Molly discovered something else that she realized was important. Although she had a few projects she had been planning to do in the next month, Molly realized that if she wanted to become a perception master and discover what made her happy, she needed to put the projects aside for a few weeks and do this work first.

Molly hoped that by practicing the seven steps, she would find a better way to do the projects, or perhaps she would discover they weren't necessary. Either way, she accepted that she only had so much time, and instead of being upset about that, Molly chose to take the time to understand how to shift her perception.

Molly knew it was a skill that would come in handy for almost anything. If, in the process, she discovered more about her true spiritual nature, well, that would be glorious. If it only made her life a bit better, and she felt a little happier, it would be worth it.

Here's the beginning of Molly's I Choose sheet. Follow this format precisely for yourself. Your voice may say entirely different things. It knows you well.

Notice that often the voice repeats itself. Stay strong. Deny what it says. It will give up.

You choose. You listen (face). And choose again (replace).
- Molly writes: I choose to be happy.

She hears the voice say: "You don't know how to be happy."
- Molly writes: I choose to know how to be happy.

She hears the voice say: "No one is happy."
- Molly writes: I choose to be happy.

She hears the voice say: "You have no right to be happy."
- Molly writes: I choose to know that I do have a right to be happy.

She hears the voice say: "You don't know what happiness is."
- Molly writes: I choose to understand what makes me happy.

She hears the voice say: "People will be mad if you are happy."
- Molly writes: I choose to have people around me who love that I am happy,

She hears the voice say: "The world is a sad, lonely, and frightening place."
- Molly writes: I choose to experience a happy world, filled with friends, and a safe place to thrive.

She hears the voice say: "You have no friends."
- Molly writes: I choose to have friends.

She hears the voice say: "Your husband doesn't want you to change."
- Molly writes: I choose to know my husband wants me to be happy.

Okay—you get the idea. You can see that Molly could go on with this I Choose sheet for many, many pages. That's a good thing. We all have multiple hidden beliefs that run our life.

Being aware of them, choosing consciously to face and replace them, works so well it may feel like magic. And yet, it can be scary. Our human self, ego, is going to fade away, and it doesn't want to. It's okay to be afraid. But don't let that fear stop you. It's the path towards freedom from the voice running your life.

Feel the fear, and do it anyway.

Molly keeps on writing for days. Watching the twists and turns of where this takes her becomes more exciting than worrying about what will happen. And to her surprise and delight, Molly realizes happiness has been there all along, just waiting for her to clear out the clutter of old beliefs and perceptions.

Molly keeps writing more I Choose sheets before moving on to the next step, Understanding Signs and Symbols.

Here are Molly's answers to the Practical Becoming Aware questions.

*What did you become most aware of?
That I have a hard time knowing what I want.
*What did you choose to be willing to do?
I chose to be willing to be open to doing a different kind of work.
*Why?
Because I am tired of being confused and unhappy about it.
*What action did you take to do it?
I am making a list of things I like to do.
*What are you not willing to do?
Complain about my work.
*Why?
Because complaining makes nothing better and distracts me from happiness.
*What action did you take to stop doing it?
I stopped that voice as soon as I heard the complaining.

SIXTY-ONE

PRACTICAL AWARENESS

Live the actual moment. Only this moment is life. — Thich Nhat Hanh

Before we move deeper into awareness, look back at your willingness answers in the last chapter.

These don't have to be long answers—just a note to yourself is sufficient.

Now, narrow down your answers to the one you want to focus on today.

What one thing are you willing to do and take action on?

This answer will be the basis for your first I Choose sheet.

But first, let's do a Becoming Aware exercise. This exercise can be very enlightening, so try it. Make notes to yourself about what you find.

Notice:

What's in your house: In a drawer. In a closet. What someone is saying. What you do with your time. What you don't do with your time. How you think about something. How you do something. What you listen to. What you believe.

Look where you normally don't look. Listen where you normally don't listen.

Make a list of what you most want to become aware of during this exercise.

Ask yourself why.

And, as always, avoid judgment, shaming, and regret. That was then. This is now. Let's get on with it without the unneeded and unnecessary baggage that no Loving Creator would ever ask us to carry.

Get the lesson. Say thanks. Move on.

And, here's an exciting part! You will, I promise, discover that you already have many things that you think you want. Already present. Perhaps wrapped in a package that you, until this moment, didn't recognize.

Don't worry if you haven't experienced this yet. We'll do more exercises later in this book to help open your awareness even more to what is already present.

Here's the most fantastic thing. No matter how much abundance, love, grace, opportunities, etc., you have now, there is always more waiting to be seen when you are ready.

And now that you have a few ideas to work with, you can consciously choose and discover a why or two.

Tying It Together: Becoming Aware

(Check back to see how Molly answered these questions if you need to prime the pump.)

Write the answers to these questions:

- What did you become most aware of?

- What did you choose to be willing to do? Why?

- What action did you take to do it?

- What are you not willing to do? Why?

- What action did you take to stop doing it?

Make an I Choose sheet about at least one of these questions. We'll learn more about I Choose sheets later in this book and this way you'll have some to use when we get there.

SIXTY-TWO

— • —

STEP THREE: UNDERSTAND SIGNS AND SYMBOLS

M atter is matter only to the material state of consciousness, but once we rise to a mental state of consciousness, matter is not matter, but mind. — Joel S. Goldsmith

Why this step? Because the outside, visible world is the projection of the internal and nonvisible inner world of our point of view and state of mind. We learn either the essence of the Truth they are revealing or the lie they are telling through signs and symbols.

They are the mirror that reflects back to us what we believe to be true. Then we can adjust our perception to clean up the view, just as we would adjust our clothes or hair or check our teeth in the bathroom mirror. Doing so changes the reflection because we have changed ourselves.

Obviously, we must know how to discern the difference between "good" and "bad" signs because signs and symbols make up every part of life—from traffic to nature. Understanding the difference between signs and symbols of what is True and the reversal of what is True is crucial.

Often we wait for something to "tell" us what to do. We ask for a sign to direct us. We don't realize that in doing so, we still can only see what we have become willing to see based on our current paradigm.

I used to choose to do things I knew might not be that good for me, thinking it was necessary to learn from them. Then I became aware that it was a programming that was entirely unnecessary and potentially quite dangerous. We don't need to walk dangerous paths or choose stupid things to learn what we need to know.

We have other ways to learn, much safer and more enjoyable. When we are willing to become aware, signs and symbols will assist us in learning with more grace.

We can rest easy trusting that we are constantly being guided. There are always signs. However, we often miss them because we thought these signs would look, or feel, different.

Or we don't like the one we got, so we ignore it.

Or we misinterpret it.

Ignoring—or misinterpreting—is both a habit and mis-perception. In the next chapter, we'll delve into the depths of perception. But for now, we need to recognize that no one sees anything the same. We all interpret what we experience or see from our personal, trained, educated, and accepted paradigm, or perspective.

In addition, in our belief in humanness, we have minimal and constricted views of the world. We see fewer colors than birds, smell fewer smells than dogs, notice much less than an ant.

To make it worse, we are constantly comparing, regretting, reviewing the past, and being afraid of the future.

Humans, what are we going to do about them?

Here's what we are going to do. We are going to remember that we are actually not human and forgive ourselves when we forget.

We are in Truth the essence of all that the Divine expresses, which includes all those amazing miraculous things that the natural world encompasses.

We use mirrors of all kinds to discover, uncover, and reveal the universe's true nature and of ourselves. We pay attention to signs and symbols.

But we don't want to get stuck in the sign or symbol. Signs and symbols are not anchors. They are guideposts on our path. Signs and symbols are not places to build a house or belief system to live in forever, forgetting that there is so much more.

If we believe them to be real rather than only signs and symbols, we will be locked into the accumulation of things rather than be free to be the full expressions of boundless life.

Evil acts are often committed after a sign or symbol "tells" someone they are doing the right thing. As a fiction writer, I often have the antagonist believe that the signs and symbols are aligning for them to do something evil.

We want to avoid making a sign or symbol conform to what we want to see and hear—because they will.

We interpret everything from our personal internal point of view. This is why we must be increasingly more willing to become aware of what we believe to be reality. And then consciously choose the reality that most aligns to our current highest understanding of good—which evolves as we break open old paradigms and belief systems.

We must develop the habit of always beginning anything with an intent to do the "next right thing" and base it on a foundation of Love, compassion, kindness, and harmony for all creation. That way, we will not be misled as often or recognize much faster when we have been.

Be willing to become aware of the signs and symbols surrounding you. As you do this, you might begin to notice, or strengthen your awareness, that there is a loving, intelligent force that underlies everything.

Be willing for this to be true. Look for signs and symbols that this is true.

Yes, I know that by doing so, we are building a perception, paradigm, belief system. But this one produces good for all beings. Yes, I believe this to be our true, what I call, big r Reality. And yes, I have to continually go back to being willing, becoming aware, and seeing the signs and symbols that support this Truth.

But since we know that *what we perceive to be reality magnifies*, I want to magnify this Reality, and it is so much easier to stay on this path when we walk it together.

SIXTY-THREE

TURNING THINGS INTO THOUGHTS

The truth is you are already what you are seeking. — Adyashanti

To interpret signs and symbols correctly, we need to learn and apply the skill of turning things back into their true nature—thoughts.

Yes, I know we often say this the other way around, turn thoughts into things. But going that direction is when things can go horribly wrong. Our thoughts and perceptions are not always, in fact, almost always, not the best ones to project into the world. We think we know what's best for us, but we don't, because we begin with our biases and assumptions about what we want.

Suppose we stop thinking of ourselves as a creator, a manifestor, a demonstrator and instead realize that we are the expression of an Intelligent, Loving Creator. We can give up the farce of trying to control everything and make things happen when we understand and accept that.

Instead, we are learning to get out of the way by willingly shifting our perception to becoming aware of the Intelligent One Creator. Understanding that signs and symbols surround us, we see Its handiwork. With this shift, we thrive abundantly in our lives.

We want to learn to discern what things are actually composed of—Mind's thoughts, God's thoughts, the Divine Mysteries' thoughts.

It's time to use my other favorite tool for becoming a perception master: Quality Word lists. If you have done them before, you know how powerful this tool is. If you haven't, you are in for a treat because turning things back into the essence of what they are—thoughts—well, it's the pathway to freedom, my friends.

SIXTY-FOUR

HOW TO DO QUALITY WORD LISTS

An excerpt from my book *Living In Grace: The Shift To Spiritual Perception.*

Pick anything that you're thinking about or desiring to see and list its qualities. For example, let's say that you were thinking about a car. You want the idea, or quality, of transportation. So how would you like that transportation to look? You might say that its qualities include safety, effortlessness, speed, security, luxury, grace, convenience, and so on.

You have probably phrased this request as something you want or need. However, if you use the words need or want, they imply that you're lacking something. It is a statement of separation. As an expression or reflection of the Infinite One Loving Mind, how could you lack? However, when you believe you are lacking, you are.

What we perceive to be reality magnifies, so if we perceive lack, we receive lack. An unlimited Reality cannot lack; therefore, neither can you.

Since everything has already been created, we are asking ourselves to wake up to what has already been provided.

Steps to making qualities lists.

Remember, we are not interested in things here. Since things are in essence composed of qualities, we translate back into qualities the things of which we desire to become conscious.

- Step 1: Take a moment and list 8–10 qualities of something you want to "see." Use one word to express each quality. If you are using sentences, you have not come to the heart or essence of it.

- Step 2: There are two kinds of qualities lists: You can either list the qualities of the thing itself, or you can list the qualities of how you will feel when you have it.

For example, let's go back to the idea of buying a car. Your quality list for the thing—or car—might contain ideas such as red, fast, inexpensive, safe, etc.

If you choose to do a qualities list of how you will feel when you drive this car, it might read "wealthy, secure, free, joyful, etc."

If you wish, do both lists. Otherwise, do the list that makes the most sense to you. What you choose to see does not matter. It can be as important as having a home or as simple as setting the table for dinner. It is being conscious of the qualities of these "things" that make a difference.

Now that you have a quality word list, let's learn how to put them in order before learning how to use it.

SIXTY-FIVE

—·—

HOW TO ORDER QUALITY WORD LISTS

We denizens of Earth have a common vice: We take what we're offered, whether we need it or not. You can get into a lot of trouble that way. — Robert Sheckley

Once you have a list pared down to about ten Quality Words, it's time to put them into order.

Yes, they are already in order. But they are in order based on how you thought about them. We need to put the qualities in order based on how you feel about them.

Have you ever been at a place in your life where nothing happens towards what you want, no matter what you do? This is most likely because you have a quality or value block.

If we have two values that feel equal to us, our core self will be confused about which one to provide.

Remember our conversation about how state of mind overrides point of view? In the same way, what we feel overrides what we thought about as we made this list. Yes, the heart rules the intellect—the feminine guides our masculine life.

This is not how it plays out most of the time in the worldview. We can see how well that works. It doesn't.

Doing this exercise will be a guide for your actions to follow your heart's desires. It's one of the most powerful things we can do.

It's important to remember that the order your lists end up in will not be the same order that your intellectual mind put them in a while making them.

And you need someone to help you with this. You can't do it alone. But the person who helps you has to be in the same heart space that you are. If you can't find someone, let me know.

Once you find the person, both of you need to read the instructions listed below.

Once you understand the process, it becomes second nature, so take the time to let it sink in.

Quality Word lists not only work but are one of the most powerful and simple tools I know to shift lives.

Note: Don't look at your list while your partner is working with you, as this will engage brain and logic. What you want to engage are your heart and inspiration.

Your partner will ask you the following question each time:

"Which is more important to you?" and will give you two words on the list to compare.

Your partner must not give you any other verbal or physical cues. Don't listen to anything except your inner voice. Respond with the answer it tells you. Don't argue with it.

If you cannot choose one as more important than the other, your partner should ask you, "Which one can you not live without?"

Notice that your mind tells you that if you choose one, you might not get the other. That fear comes from the point of view that there is never enough and that you don't deserve everything you want.

Since neither statement is true, notice these thoughts and move on. The truth is, once you are clear about what you desire to see, you will be able to see and receive all these qualities in a form appropriate for you at this time.

Your partner must compare each word with every word until you have an ordered list. The order will probably surprise you if you have stayed with your heart and trusted your answers.

Here is how I do this.

(Don't worry. This is a step-by-step process. Easy. Don't let worry get in the way.)

Take a sheet of paper. Draw a line down the middle. Write your partner's original quality words on the left.

>Put your finger on the first word on your partner's list. (This is so you don't lose your place.)

Ask the "which is more important" question by comparing the first word on the list to the second one. If they say the first word, move on to comparing the first word to the third word.

What if they say the second word is more important? Great. Cross it off and move it to the right side of the page.

Now compare the first word to the third word. If they say the first word is more important, move on.

What if they say the third word is more important than the first? Great. Cross it off.

But before you move it to the right side of the page, you have to find out if it is more important or less important than the word that is already over there.

So ask the "which is more important" question between those two words on the right.

Let's say the third word is more important than the second, so write it above the second word.

Go back to the left side of the list. Your finger is still on that first word. Compare it to the fourth word, and so on down the list until you have done the entire left side of the list.

If you have found more words that are more important than the first one, they will go to the right side after you compare them to that list, from the bottom up.

For example, you have two words on the right. The third word is first, and then the second. Now you have a new word. Compare it to the second. If it is more important, compare it to the third. If it is more important, put it at the top. If it isn't, it goes in the middle.

(Here's where you realize you need lots of spaces between the words on the right because you never know where the list is going.)

After you have completed comparing the first word all the way down the list on the left, you will have some crossed-out words on the left because they are now on the right in their right order.

Cross out the first word and add it at the bottom of the list on the right.

Draw a line under that list. You are finished with those words.

>Go to the list on the left. Put your finger on the first uncrossed out word. Compare it with the next uncrossed-out word below it.

Do the same thing with the words that you did before.

When you are done doing that with the new words, put a line under the list and start again on the left.

Usually, this takes two or three passes. But keep going until all the words are crossed out on the left and in order on the right.

Now you can move on to how to use your list.

Sixty-Six

How To Use Quality Word Lists

I know the secret of life: If you want to have loving feelings, do loving things. — Anne Lamott

Now that you have a quality word list, how do you use it? Of course, you could ignore it and hope things change. But now that you have put so much work into the list, why not make the most of it?

Here are the four simple ways to use your list. Walk your qualities through these steps and experience the world as it is—a spiritual universe.

• 1. Use the qualities as a filter.

If something appears that you think might be what you are looking for and does not have at least the first four qualities—with the first one first and the rest following in order, it is not "it."

Think of the time you will save if you can quickly eliminate what is not right for you. For example, you discover that safety is first on your quality list for a means of transportation, and the car you are looking at has a deficient safety record, don't buy this car no matter how much you love it.

If you buy it, you will eventually be unhappy with it, and somehow you will unconsciously figure out how to get rid of it.

• 2. See the qualities everywhere.

See the qualities in everything, not just in what you're seeking. Notice that they're always with you in many forms.

You have always had, and always will have, each quality on your list if you practice looking and expect to see it.

A quality does not have to belong to you. It can appear anywhere. All of what you see is your world. The goal is to notice that the quality you're looking for already exists everywhere, and since you can see it—it exists for you—now.

• 3. Be grateful for each quality as you see it.

Be grateful for these qualities each time you see them, no matter where they occur. If the person you dislike most has one of these qualities, be thankful that you have seen this quality in your life.

Know that if it is "out there," it was first "within here," and therefore always available and part of your life.

• 4. Be and live these qualities yourself.

This is the walk as one step as you walk your talk.

It's not as hard as one might think. If you wanted the quality and saw it somewhere in the world, you already possess it.

Remember, we can't see what we don't already know or imagine.

So embrace the quality, find ways to live it, and become whatever you wish to experience.

Perhaps you will discover that having the "thing" you wanted is no longer as important because you found that it already exists as thoughts—qualities.

Or perhaps you discover that you already have the "thing" you wanted. You didn't realize it because it didn't look the way you expected.

Using the four steps opens our eyes to what has always been and always will be ours. That changes everything. It's the shift to a spiritual perception.

Sixty-Seven

Molly and Understanding Signs and Symbols

An error in the premise must appear in the conclusion. — Mary
Baker Eddy

Molly decided to take the Perception Mastery steps at a pace that
would allow her to spend more time contemplating each one. Every
morning she reviewed Practical Willingness and Practical Awareness.

These two steps had forced her to pay more attention to her
thought processes, and that has been both comforting and difficult.
Comforting because she could see that doing those two steps was
changing her perception of herself and the world. Difficult because
not all the things she noticed made her feel good about herself.

But Molly understood that allowing the voice in her head to
constantly criticize her and make her feel guilty was defiantly not
making her happy.

Because Molly realized that allowing those negative thoughts
about herself would not produce her desired results, she started using

I Choose sheets to face and replace them. That meant she had a few I Choose sheets going at one time.

Molly also decided to ask herself these two questions every day:

1. What one thing are you willing to do and take action on? Why?

2. What is the one thing you thought you wanted to do and then discovered you are not willing to do it? Why?

Sometimes the answers were simple, like making a phone call she had been putting off and deciding she was unwilling to wear clothes that didn't fit anymore.

Other things were more personal. Molly found herself willing to do something her husband asked her to do that she would typically resent doing. And she discovered she was not willing to eat something she knew wasn't good for her.

The more aware Molly became about what she was willing to do and not willing to do, the more aware she became, resulting in being more willing. It was definitely a circle. The more willing, the more aware. The more aware, the more willing.

Molly was beginning to wonder what she had gotten herself into, but she kept going, grateful for every hint of progress and positive changes in her life.

Eventually, Molly decided she was ready to add in the step of Understanding Signs and Symbols. But she wasn't clear about what it meant. Did it mean that the world she saw outside was what she believed?

Yes, she knew Wayne Dyer had said, "We see what we believe," but she had put that aside, not thinking about what it meant if it were true.

Now she was ready to figure it out. Did it mean that she created what she was seeing? Or did it mean that she filtered through her point of view what she was seeing?

Reasoning that it would be impossible for her to be the creator of the ant she saw on the kitchen sink, let alone the sun in the sky, she knew she was not the creator of the world. Then it made sense that what she saw was filtered through her personal paradigm.

That's when being a perception master became a little bit more exciting for Molly. If all she had to do was bust open her paradigms, be willing to consciously choose and expect the highest understanding of good she had in each moment, and she was willing to do that.

Molly reasoned that if she interpreted all things through that perception, life would have to get better because she would see more of the good that was already present.

This is what Molly has done so far:

- She decided to be willing to be happy.

- She decided to be willing not to be willing to do things that didn't make her happy.

- She decided to be willing to become aware and be willing to consciously choose to face and replace thoughts that didn't support her highest understanding of good at each moment.

For this step, Molly started a list of all the signs she could see. This list included the obvious, like human-made signs, and the less obvious—to her—ones found within nature.

Then she began a list of things that could be symbols of something else. Along the way, she realized that signs and symbols are the same things. A stop sign is a sign to stop, but it is also a symbol of protection or safety.

The sun could symbolize unconditional love for all creations, and the ant was a symbol of diligence.

Molly decided that she'd be willing to become aware of a symbol each day and interpret it as a sign of perfection, goodness, love, and kindness and see what happened from there. She'd watch for signs that pointed her towards that path and signs that attempted to pull her off it.

Like a sign at a crossroads, everything that happened during the day could point her towards unhappiness or happiness.

If she found she was traveling down the wrong road, she was willing to change her mind and go back the other way. When she ran her choices through the filter, or perception, that "all things work together for good to them that love good," it was easier to see if the sign or symbol was pointing her down the right road, or it was a distraction.

Using an I Choose sheet that began with "I Choose to see the good already present" was eye-opening. Molly noticed how often she looked at what was not working rather than what was.

That night when her husband told her he couldn't go on the vacation she had been looking forward to because he had to work, she wanted to either yell at him for disappointing her or cry because that he didn't care about her feelings.

Instead, she paused and asked herself if she was willing to be happy, anyway. *Yes,* she mumbled to herself and then chose to see what had just happened as a sign that he was also choosing to be happy and that it wasn't personal.

That day Molly ran across a quote from Andy Rooney, and she took it as a sign to be grateful for what she had, which brought her back to happiness.

For most of life, nothing wonderful happens. If you don't enjoy getting up and working and finishing your work and sitting down to a meal with family or friends, then the chances are you're not going to be very happy. If someone bases his happiness or unhappiness on major events like a great job, huge amounts of money, a flawlessly happy marriage, or a trip to Paris, that person isn't going to be happy much of the time. If, on the other hand, happiness depends on a good breakfast, flowers in the yard, a drink or a nap, then we are more likely to live with quite a bit of happiness. — Andy Rooney

After that, Molly felt prepared to try making a Quality Word list. Since she was choosing to be happy, she asked herself what happiness felt like to her. If she was happy, how would she feel? It was harder to do than she thought it would be.

Molly thought that since happiness was a quality, it was something she understood. Didn't everyone understand what it meant to be happy? Apparently not, was her conclusion. She had words, but she didn't know if they were her words for how she would feel if she were happy or just what other people said about happiness.

Instead of rushing this list, she made notes to herself during the day when she had a moment of feeling happy. She also noticed when other people seemed happy and tried to experience what they were feeling. She even asked herself if her husband was happy. For now, she was not ready to ask him directly. It would mean she would need to share the work that she was doing for herself, and Molly worried sharing it would uproot the new seeds of understanding that she was gaining.

For Molly, this whole idea of turning something she wanted back to qualities was a revelation. And she decided to enjoy the process instead of rushing it. Molly thought that if she moved on to the next step in perception mastery, perhaps it would help her with what she was doing with her unfinished quality word list and strengthen her growing understanding.

Sixty-Eight

Practical Signs And Symbols

To see ourselves as others see us is a most salutary gift. Hardly less important is the capacity to see others as they see themselves. ——
Aldous Huxley

As you look for Signs and Symbols, try sinking into the awareness that there is a Loving Intelligence behind all that is both visible and invisible. Yes, "human" awareness teaches and leads us through sensations, and signs and symbols. Interpreting signs and symbols correctly will lead us back into an awareness of that Loving Intelligence.

Everything in nature speaks to this truth. Spend even a few minutes a day becoming aware of the immensity and beauty of what you see, even if it is only a glimpse of the sky and clouds through the buildings of a city.

The leaves of a single tree speak to the recurring abundance and the cycle of continuing life. A bee shows us the joy of what we might call work, but what a bee knows is living the essence of its purpose.

Even human-made signs point us back to a Loving Intelligence. Stop signs remind us we are part of a community. Guard rails tell us that someone cares about our safety.

The signs and symbols that direct our lives surround us. All we have to do is become aware of those who tell the truth and those who don't.

Tying It Together: Understanding Signs And Symbols

- What signs or symbols have you noticed using the skill you have already practiced in becoming aware?

- What did you learn from them?

Now back to the first step:
- How willing are you to make changes based on what you learned from being aware of signs and symbols?

These three steps are intertwined. From here on, you'll notice more and more that they live together. Become aware of signs and symbols and then be willing to take action based on what you have learned.
- Use an I Choose sheet on something you've discovered.

- Make a Quality Word list for something you want to experience. Like Molly, perhaps you don't finish it before the next step, but get started.

- When you have finished your Quality Wordlist list, get help to put them in order, and then follow the four steps to use them.

-

Here are some things the lying voice in your head might say to you:

"There are too many choices, so I can't decide."
Say no to this lie. Pick one.
"If you pick the qualities now, you might get them wrong."
Say no to this lie. No matter what you choose, you'll be right.
"There are more critical things to do."
Say no to this lie. What's more important than finding out how you really feel?
"You don't understand enough to do this."
Say no to this lie. Of course, you do. You are the expression of an Intelligent One Mind.

Okay, this list could go on and on. Maybe make a list of the lies that come to you so you'll recognize them in the future.

You can see how I Choose sheets and Quality Word lists go hand in hand. Sometimes the Quality Word list comes first. Sometimes the I Choose sheet. But be sure to use them both and notice how quickly things change for the better.

Note: Sometimes, the change doesn't feel like it's for the better. Sometimes things have to be cleaned out first. Don't worry. Keep going, and trust that it all is well.

Sixty-Nine

—— ◦ ——

Step Four: Perception Rules

*Y*ou'll see it when you believe it — Wayne Dyer

Now that we are becoming willing, aware, and noticing signs and symbols, we can focus on the heart of our shift—perception.

I love the double entendre of this step. Yes, Perception Rules, and yes, there are perception rules.

Think of your perception as a master algorithm. We know how algorithms work on the Internet. We search for something, and then we immediately see ads for it showing up everywhere.

What we see on the Internet is determined by the algorithm that has been deciding what we want to see, based on our previous actions and choices, and filtering out the rest.

Our lives are like that. Everything that has happened to us, from the moment we opened our eyes to the bright lights of this world, is set into an algorithm, paradigm, belief system that delivers what we see and experience and filters out the rest. It's not evil. It's just the way it is. And often, it's for our own good. But it also keeps us stuck. The algorithm doesn't change on its own. We have to shift it.

That perception rules is a law in the physical universe, and we can not overturn or negate. Perception produces reality, and *what we perceive to be reality magnifies.* That's how it works. We see what we believe. We might as well use it to our advantage and consciously choose what we believe.

Now that we know that perception rules, let's do a deep dive into what that means because, without understanding this step, we can get stuck in our past beliefs and experiences.

It's obvious, isn't it, that to shift anything in our life we have to shift what we believe? However, the first question to ask ourselves is not "how do I shift my perception," "but am I willing to do it?" This willingness step is one we have to check consistently.

The good news is that we have already begun the how of shifting. We have been willing to becoming aware of what we already believe. We continue to clarify that awareness by paying attention to the signs and symbols which mirror back to us what we believe.

Now for the critical step—consciously choosing a perception or a belief system that improves our life experience. Because once again, *what we perceive to be reality magnifies*. We see what we believe.

Shifting perception is not working at something to make it happen. Instead, it's allowing it to come into our experience.

If you have ever looked at a Magic Eye picture, you have experienced the result of letting go. I keep the book *Beyond 3D* near my computer and look at one page a day. After doing this for a long time, I already know what the picture will be. But if I **try** to see that picture, I can't. To see it, I have to stop trying, let go, and let it reveal itself.

If we hold that point of view that we are the creators of our existence, not only will we find it impossible one day to sustain it, but we get in the way. Even if you don't believe that a loving, divine intelligence has already created everything, why not imagine that it's true and build that as a consciously chosen point of view?

Since perception produces reality, why not choose a point of view that there is a Divine Intelligence that lovingly creates and provides at all times for all of life? Why not let go and let life become joyous and easy?

However, we know by choosing any point of view doesn't mean the results are instantaneous. Actually, they are, but we rarely experience it because that dang algorithm filters the results out—most of the time. Sometimes all things align, and there is what we often call a magical event when actually it was a moment when all our perceptions of the universe's physicality dissolve and we see that all along it's been a spiritual universe.

So why doesn't this "magical event" happen all the time? Why the delay? Because there is not just one mode of perception, there are two modes: state of mind and point of view.

Our point of view is what we believe and want to be true. Point of view perception is what we intentionally or unintentionally use as the building blocks of our lives. We see and hear and experience points of view all the time. Sometimes we get angry at others' points of view and even our own.

Points of view are constantly on display. From the way the person at the store check-out treats you, your neighbor's garden, your friend's opinions, the people in the news opinions, what you say to your friends, what you say to yourself about the state of the world.

Noticing our point of view is imperative. How can we shift something if we don't know about it? Often we adopt the point of view of our parents, friends, politicians, community leaders, and influencers without noticing or deciding if that's really what we want to experience in life.

Points of view become ruts and habits if not consistently examined. Too often, we become prisoners of our beliefs.

The intention of the steps of Perception Mastery is to assist us in stepping out of our ruts by stretching our point of view into something that better aligns with the concept of an infinite Intelligence, a loving God, an abundant life.

This shift will open our self-imposed cell doors and change our lives for the better. Improving a point of view affects everyone equally and lovingly and is the work and practice of a lifetime.

And yet, there is a critical piece of perception that determines the outcome of that shift. Because we remember, there are two modes of perception, and they have to agree with each other.

If we desire a permanent change, we also have to shift our state of mind perception.

And what is a state of mind perception? State of mind refers to our emotions and feelings. It's what we feel to be true—either as a form of joy or fear.

Guess which mode of perception runs the show? You're right. It's our state of mind perception.

We can believe that abundance is the law of the universe all we want, but if our internal emotions and feelings reside in either fear or doubt that it is true, at least for us, our experience of life will more closely match that state of mind rather than our point of view.

To effectively and permanently shift our lives, it is critical to align the two modes of perceptions.

If we can get our state of mind perception into harmony with our point of view perception, we are in sync or in flow with the universe. Until our emotions and feelings—our state of mind—is the same as what we believe—our point of view—it will be hard to make changes. And if we somehow succeed, it will be difficult, and the change will not be permanent.

It's like driving with our brakes on. Or trying to switch channels on the TV when the batteries of the remote are dead.

Here's how perception works: Our point of view produces what we experience in life. We verify what we believe through our senses and then agree that what we see and experience is reality. With this agreement, our personal reality reproduces itself again and again. Every reproduction creates a stronger belief.

That experience, belief, perception produces an emotion, which becomes our state of mind. That state of mind strengthens our faith in our point of view, and the cycle continues.

We want to build a cycle of infinite possibilities, not a closed cycle of that's how it always has been.

Just because we decide that our point of view perception is that there is consistent, unbiased abundance, it won't change our experience very much until our state of mind agrees with it.

This works both ways, of course, for the "good" and the "bad." It explains why we get better and better at something, from growing gardens to making money. It also explains how we get stuck in ruts and can't get out.

So, let's make sure we strengthen what we want to experience, not the reverse.

Nothing we experience is how it really is, anyway. Everything we experience is the out-picturing of our personal highest understanding of Truth. We are seeing our point of view and calling it reality.

When our perceptions aren't in harmony, what we accomplish won't be as satisfying or as long-lasting. Remember, by doing this work, we are not making anything happen. We are getting out of the way.

The question is, how do we shift our state of mind?

First, by noticing, becoming aware of our emotions and feelings, not judging them. Just noticing. For example, when we pay our bills, our state of mind might be that abundance is life, but what if we are fearful that there won't be enough now or in the future?

Take yourself through the first three steps. Ask yourself: *Am I willing? What are my emotions about money? What are the signs and symbols that give me clues about my perception of money, wealth, abundance?*

The intent is to bring our emotions and feelings into alignment with our point of view.

We often ignore the ways we already know to shift our state of mind because we think we don't have the time. But, once we understand that state of mind drives our point of view, it's clear that it comes first.

I came home one day from a visit with a loved one feeling that all had gone well. I enjoyed every minute and thought that we had enjoyed the time together. Then I got a phone call and discovered that I had failed at providing what they wanted from their point of view. They said they never wanted to see me again.

At first, I was shocked. Then I was angry, then depressed, then sad, and then angry again. No amount of believing that Love is the governing force of the Universe was going to bring my experience into harmony.

So I chose a few ways I knew to calm my state of mind. I read a fiction book first. Reading a good book always takes me out into another world. Then I turned to a book that helped remind me about the reality I have chosen as my point of view.

Calmer, I spent a few minutes in meditation, then did some breathwork. Calmer still, I decided I needed to talk to someone who would understand what happened and give me some insight into what to do next. The person I called understood, listened, and gave me some excellent feedback. She also made me laugh, and that lightened the experience. After that, I was calm enough to go to a yoga class and thoroughly enjoyed it.

Yes, it took a few days before I was entirely in harmony again, and then I took action in that calm state by writing a note of apology. I had to wait a few days to do it because I kept wanting to explain myself since I didn't see that I had done anything wrong. But in this case, that would not have produced the outcome I desired, a return to harmony within myself about unconditional love, and hopefully provide some peace to the person who was so angry at me.

I never had to mail the letter. The person called and apologized and asked if we could start again.

Yes, I still had to work out my state of mind to let it all go, but I knew the steps to take, and it didn't take long before I felt free from the upset.

There were other things I could have done to bring my state of mind back into harmony. I could have gone for a walk, sat by a tree, worked in the garden, listened to music, done an I Choose sheet, a Quality word list... the ways to bring harmony to our state of mind are endless.

But when we think doing these things are a waste of time, we don't do them. Instead, it's where we must begin.

SEVENTY

YOU CAN'T SOLVE AN ILLUSION

The great acts of love are done by those who are habitually performing small acts of kindness. — Victor Hugo

Once in a while, it hits me. Life is simple. But then I forget and make it complicated again.

But, in those brief shining moments of clarity, I remember that what we experience is all perception. That's why life is simple. The answer to everything lies in the premise that all we have to do is shift our perception.

The problem is we forget this simple fact.

My sister sent me a math riddle that appeared freaky and impossible. I couldn't figure it out. Then I reminded myself to "Shift your perception and begin with a different premise." When I did that, the answer was obvious.

The riddle intended to confuse. It started with a logical premise and one that was easy to accept. But in that premise, there was no answer—ever—because the premise began with an error.

When I shifted my premise, the answer was immediately clear.

The worldview is precisely like that. It begins with a premise that appears logical, a premise that we can easily accept. In fact, our five senses tell us it's true.

Within that premise, we search and search for answers. We read books, talk to friends, get counseling, let go of desires, and remind ourselves to have faith. But none of these methods provide an answer that works for long if they begin with a premise that is an illusion.

There will never, ever be a correct answer to an illusion.

When we begin with the correct premise, the answer is straightforward.

I was working on some writing that required me to copy what I had written in one document and paste it to another. I copied and pasted and saw nothing. In the past, I would have assumed that I didn't copy and paste correctly. I would have spent some time in confusion and irritation at the problem.

That time I paused. I started with the premise that I had copied and pasted correctly. I highlighted the area on the page that I had pasted into and chose black for the text. "Magically," it appeared. It was always there. I had pasted white text to a white page, so it was invisible to my eyes.

During a rescue attempt in the first Star Trek episode, "The Menagerie," the crew tries to blast through a mountain with their phasers. Nothing happens, so they keep firing away. Nothing changes. They give up and attempt many other means of rescue, none of which is successful.

Finally, Spock and Captain Kirk realize that the Talosians, the planet's inhabitants, are masters at creating illusions. After that discovery, Kirk and Spock begin again with the correct premise that their phasers work.

With no extra effort, the illusion of the untouched mountain dissolved, revealing the hole in the mountain that had been there all along.

It's that simple. The premise determines what we perceive as the outcome. What premise do we begin with when attempting to discover an answer or dissolve a problem?

If we begin with the premise that the worldview is correct and that our senses report the truth, we will never see the Truth and what is already present.

It takes a lot less work when we begin with the correct premise and let it reveal the answer than trying to make something work inside of an illusion.

The great teacher Christ Jesus has told us all, "Ye shall know the Truth, and the Truth shall make you free." Hum. Doesn't that sound like the idea if we begin with the Truth—the correct premise—that it dissolves the prison of the worldview without effort?

The effort belongs to the shift of perception. The effort in letting go of false premises. The effort belongs to giving up personal preferences and ego.

Once we make that shift, the work is over, and the provisions we need for our life stand revealed.

Of course, that shift is an ongoing process and practice. Yet, it is one with guaranteed results and so much more satisfying than chasing illusions.

Seventy-One

Perception Is Fluid

We now know that memories are not fixed or frozen, like Proust's jars of preserves in a larder, but are transformed, disassembled, reassembled, and recategorized with every act of recollection. — Oliver Sacks

I handed Bill the information that Joe wanted. A few days later, I asked Joe if Bill had given it to him. When Joe replied that he hadn't, I said I would find it for him.

Thinking that Bill might have put the information on his desk, I turned to go into his office. However, the door to Bill's office wasn't there! It had disappeared.

Confused, I walked over to the wall where the door should have been and stared at it. Blank.

"I thought there was a door to Bill's office right here," I said to Joe.

"Nope, the office door has never been there," was his reply.

I knew I had seen the office right where that wall currently resided, but since it obviously wasn't there now, I decided to pretend that it existed but, perhaps in another realm, and somehow not in this one.

I know, I read too much science fiction, but it was more satisfying than thinking I had not seen it when I knew I had. I knew the answer to where the office door was would reveal itself, eventually.

The mystery solved itself a few days later. Walking to a class, I turned and saw the open door to the office right where I had I thought it was.

At first, I allowed myself to pretend for a moment that I had stepped back into the realm where the office door existed.

Not so. Instead, I realized that there was another wall in front of the one where I had looked before. Yes, it was in the exact direction that I thought it was, but not in the same space.

Here's the point. Perception is fluid. It changes based on who we are, what we were thinking, what we are noticing, and what we believe is real.

Nobody sees the same thing the same way. Actually, we don't even remember things the same way we experienced them either. Perception is fluid.

And since it is, here's the critical question.

Why do we fight so hard to maintain how we think things once were, or how we want something, and people, to be?

Will power, stubbornness, decisions build on hurt feelings, divisions, wars, and sadness are all planted in perceptions that can be shifted at any moment.

I love the idea of free will. However, I think we have misinterpreted it and wasted its true power on wanting things how we want them to be instead of using it to shift our perception about every event, every idea, every concept, and every desire.

Because we have free will, we can choose our perception. We can choose one that is limited and restrained, or we can choose one that is expanded and open.

Have you read the book *Pollyanna* lately? In this book, Pollyanna chooses a perception of good about every event that comes into her experience. She is a master of shifting to a perception that brings good to everyone whose life touches hers. She sugarcoats nothing. She simply sees it differently.

How many things do we fight for that could quickly be resolved by shifting our perception about it to see the good? How many years do we waste wishing for something that we could easily have if we shifted our perception about how it will happen or how it will look?

With free will, we can choose whether we most want to be happy or if we want most to be right. With free will, we can choose to accept a dualist reality where some people win, and some lose, or we can choose, and act from, the perception that omnipresent Good is the only power.

Guess what. We get the one we choose.

This isn't about right and wrong. It's about choice, about fluid perception, about what kind of life we want to live.

There is no need to hang onto hurt feelings or painful experiences. Facing them, recognizing that the perceptions that trap us are false memories, and replacing them with a revised and more spiritually healthy perception improves everyone's life.

Seriously.

I was right about where the door was, except I was wrong about where the wall was that housed that door. Instead of arguing or even thinking I had imagined that door, I simply waited to see if it showed up again. It did.

Perception is fluid. Perception is not a creator; it simply shows us what we believe to be true.

So, why not choose a perception that omnipresent Good is all that is going on. If we do that together, we just might remove all the obstacles that keep us from seeing that Good IS all that is going on.

The two most powerful things we can do with our free will are to be willing to let Good direct our path and to set our feet on a path to action directed by the quiet voice within that is All-Good.

Do you have something better to do with your time than shift your perception, be willing to listen to the guidance of the Divine, and then take action? Didn't think so. Let's shift together; it's easier that way!

SEVENTY-TWO

BROKEN PERCEPTIONS

Perhaps one has to be very old before one learns how to be amused rather than shocked. — Pearl S. Buck

You've heard the joke about the beautiful redhead that goes into her doctor's office and complains that everything hurts. Okay, here's the rest of the joke, and then I promise to make a point.

"Impossible!" says the doctor, "Show me."

The redhead took her finger, pushed on her left shoulder, and screamed, and then she pushed her elbow and screamed even more. She pushed her knee and screamed; likewise, she pushed her ankle and screamed. Everywhere she touched made her scream.

The doctor said, "You're not really a redhead, are you?"

"Well, no," she said, "I'm actually a blonde.'

"I thought so," the doctor said. "Your finger is broken!"

Don't you love how symbolic this joke is?

Not the "blonde" part, the "only one thing broken" part.

In our lives, we all do precisely what Miss Blonde did. We touch everything, from money to love, with a broken perception, and it all hurts. It feels as if everything is going wrong when all that needs to be "doctored" is our perception.

We can tell we have a broken finger by the pain we feel, and we can tell a broken perception in the same way.

It is not necessarily a physical pain. Although that can be a symptom, it is also emotional pain. We all have both kinds of pains sometimes.

One symptom of a broken perception is the anger that is being expressed these days throughout the world. There is anger over how others think or live, or act, or what they believe in, or even just what they look like.

In our own lives, we feel frustrated by the car in front of us. We snap at loved ones. Life feels limited, and happiness seeps out of our days.

All of this pain is because of a broken perception. If we have a broken finger, we take the time to heal it.

However, broken perceptions often remain throughout a lifetime, causing pain whenever it touches something.

We all know what an unbroken finger looks like, but what about an unbroken perception? What does it look like? With an intact finger, all its parts line up perfectly. Everything functions together as one. It works in the same way in an unbroken perception.

Let's take the unbroken perception or point of view that God, Spirit, the infinite intelligence of Mind, has Love as its base concept, essence, and principle. Most of us would agree that this is true about God. We also agree that God is omnipresent, omnipotent, omniscient, and omniaction. Therefore, all that can go on is Love.

So, where does the anger we spoke about come into play? We can see that to feel anger, we have to break away from the point of view that all is Love. We may say that it is true, but we don't experience that it is. Our state of mind perception is not in agreement with our point of view perception.

How do we fix this broken perception? Here's a simple way to do so. We face the damaged perception, uncover the lie that it is stating, and replace it with what is true. Yes, it's that simple.

Going back to our example of anger at someone with whom we disagree. We face the fact that we don't. Then we replace it with an unbroken perception. We call this technique "face and replace."

The replace part could go something like this:

"Because all I see and know is filled with Love, and a visible representation of Love, then there is no place for anything but Love in my thinking and experience. Because we are all One within this Love, there is no other person for me to be angry with. It's my misperception and I willingly give it up to experience the harmony of Love's presence."

As this unbroken perception replaces the broken one, what we experience in our world shifts. *What we perceive as reality magnifies,* so a broken perception produces a broken experience. A whole perception produces a whole experience, one without pain and judgment because there is no place for pain or judgment in infinite Love.

We can see how a broken perception touching any part of our life would be painful, and the unbroken perception of the Principle of Love in action would dissolve that pain.

Unlike broken fingers, broken perceptions are deliberately contagious.

It is essential to know this so that we stop spreading them. We'll know when our perception is whole and complete because our life experiences will be harmonious and joyful.

We will feel loved ourselves, and we will experience unconditional love for everyone else. This is undoubtedly worth the effort it takes to heal a broken perception.

Let's see what Molly is up to, and then go to some practical things for you to do.

SEVENTY-THREE

MOLLY AND PERCEPTION RULES

Finish every day and be done with it. You have done what you could; some blunders and absurdities no doubt crept in; forget them as soon as you can. Tomorrow is a new day; you shall begin it serenely and with too high a spirit to be encumbered with your old nonsense. — Ralph Waldo Emerson

In the past, if her husband had disappointed her, Molly would have added that disappointment to her list of resentments about how life wasn't fair.

This time, she chose to put her disappointment aside. Instead, she decided to use her vacation as an opportunity to make choices every day based on what she wanted to do that would increase her happiness. Since she was off work for the week, she could design each day how she wanted it to be.

Getting to that decision was tough. Molly had many reasons why she didn't want to get over her disappointment. But when she realized she was building a prison of beliefs for herself, Molly decided she would use whatever tools she had to break out.

Molly started her prison break by walking herself through the perception mastery steps.

First, she knew she had to let go of how she had wanted their vacation to be and become willing to not be angry at her husband. That opened up the space to be willing to let each day be a discovery of things she wanted to do.

Molly also decided that she was not willing to ruin her time off with disappointments, regrets, and anger.

To do this, Molly realized she had to become more aware of what she liked and didn't like. Once she began to pay attention, she discovered that finding the answers was easier than she thought it would be.

Molly noticed her thoughts more often and acted on the impulses that moved her toward happiness. She did her best to reject the ideas that didn't move her towards joy. Sometimes the signs were clear, like her favorite movie was playing. Other times, she had to pay more attention.

Molly also decided to use the week to discover what she liked and didn't like about her job—and why. She started a list. Molly treated it as a research scientist, not taking what she wrote personally.

As the list grew, Molly added the step of Perception Rules. As she did this work, she got a clearer idea of who she was and how it fit and didn't fit the work she was doing. Molly noticed the opinions and beliefs that weren't hers but had accepted as hers. She noticed ideas she had carried forward from childhood that no longer fit the woman she had become.

Learning that her state of mind was affecting the outcome of her point of view was a revelation. If she approached every day of her work with dread, nothing was going to make it better.

Molly wrote what she wanted her point of view to be about work. Not the work she was doing now. Not her current job. The idea of work.

She stuck with her original point of view that she wanted to be happy and consciously chose this as her perspective about work.

Molly wrote: *"Work provides a way to express my unique gifts, and expressing my gifts makes me happy."*

To get her state of mind into harmony with this point of view, she made a quality word list of how she would feel if she expressed her unique gifts. She didn't worry about whether she knew what her unique gifts were. All she wanted to know was how she would feel if she understood and lived them.

When she finished, Molly asked her best friend to put her quality word list in order for her. She didn't tell her friend anything about what the list was or what she was doing. She just showed her the instructions for doing it.

When they finished, Molly had her quality words in order and was ready to use her list. Since her friend was curious about what she was doing, Molly gave her the *Perception Mastery* book and said, "If you like this, perhaps we can do it together because I'll be starting this over again once I got through it this time."

In the meantime, Molly took the top word on her list, "fulfilled," and began the practice of using it the four ways. When she asked herself, "What am I doing right now that makes me feel fulfilled," it helped her see how many things felt good to her. Even doing the housework and gardening gave her a sense of fulfillment.

Then she noticed when she didn't feel fulfilled and asked herself why. She didn't judge what she discovered. She simply noted it to herself.

Molly also carved out time, three times a day, to do something that quieted her mind. At first, she felt guilty about doing it. Then she realized that was the voice in her head trying to keep her in an old way of being. One she didn't want anymore.

Molly discovered she liked a routine she could count on, but one she could change if she felt the desire to do it differently that day. Once Molly realized that made her happy, she added it to her list of how she wanted to design her days.

Now, over halfway through the seven steps, Molly noticed the changes in herself. It hadn't been easy, but that didn't mean she wasn't enjoying herself. And she noticed little things in her life moving more in harmony. Molly didn't care if it had always been that way or not. What counted was she was experiencing it now.

Here is Molly's quality word list in order on how she would feel if she was expressing her unique gifts. It surprised her that the quality word happy was at the bottom of her list since that was what she had chosen first, but then she realized if she felt all the things on her list in order, she would be happy.

Fulfilled, Satisfied, Joyous, Grateful, Humble, Aware, Useful, Peaceful, Energized, Happy

SEVENTY-FOUR

PRACTICAL PERCEPTION RULES

Better keep yourself clean and bright; you are the window through which you must see the world. — George Bernard Shaw

To practice this step, why not look at something that disappoints you and find out why. It doesn't matter what you choose, because it will open a portal into many other parts of your life. It's all connected.

So whatever comes to mind, go with it, at least begin with it. This could be anything from your parents, children, friends, work, house, car, garden, or clothes. It doesn't have to be significant. It could be the chair in the living room, the way your hair looked this morning. Just pick something.

Tying It Together: Perception Rules

Here's an example of how to tie together what you have learned so far using the idea of feeling disappointed.

- Ask yourself, "Am I willing for this to not disappoint me?"

- Then, become aware of why you are or are not willing.

- Notice how you feel, the signs in your body or your life that point out your disappointment.

- What perception, belief, has brought you to this disappointment?

- Are you willing to shift that perception?

- To what? Write it out.

- How would you feel if you were not disappointed?

- Make a quality list.

- Put that quality word list in order (don't forget you need help with this part.) (Chapter Four)

- Use it. Take the first word through all four steps. If you can do this with each word, go down the list in order. (Chapter Four)

- Notice if your state of mind agrees with this state of mind.

- Make an I Choose sheet to choose that state of mind.

- Take personal quiet time every day to bring them into harmony.

A few examples of things to do during that time: Meditate, walk alone, visit nature, conscious breathwork, study, listening, mindful reading,

Of course, you don't have to use the idea of disappointment. If another idea comes up for you, use that!

The good news is that as you, and I, and all the people joining us, make conscious shifts towards an enlightened point of view and state of mind, our perception shifts become easier and more effective.

SEVENTY-FIVE

— · —

STEP FIVE: CHOOSE SPIRITUAL PERCEPTION

We do not want churches because they will teach us to quarrel about God. — Chief Joseph

The practice of shifting perception is an ongoing process, but it is a joyful one—most of the time.

Noticing the story we have chosen to live within is tricky. We have to notice, but we can't get sucked into it at the same time. We need to remind ourselves that it's a rewrite of our story. Every story needs a rewrite. It's not personal.

Sometimes the best we can do at the moment is make the story better. That's not a bad thing. There is no need to feel guilt or regret at what we didn't do right or didn't know before.

Progression is the key. As we adjust, rewrite, and consciously choose, we move towards the opening of light that reveals that big r Reality is not a game or a story.

Until now, we could use all the steps we have learned to shift our lives, no matter what version of the worldview we chose. But now we have arrived at the step where we consciously choose a spiritual perception because this is where the difference truly happens.

And we are ready because we have been practicing a spiritual perception all along. However, in this step, we will actively choose to make it the foundation of our life.

What is a spiritual perception?

It is a dividing line between doing everything with the sole intent and purpose of making our physical life better, or doing it with the intent and purpose to know and live as our true spiritual nature. It's where we consciously choose to see all that we call physical as it is—spiritual—and let that perception shift our world and daily life into the Infinite.

This is not about what we each call God. Or what religion or church we belong to or tenets we hold dear. It's not about separation, making some beliefs right and some wrong. It's about a choice between seeing the world as material or seeing it as spiritual. Not divisive—unified.

Probably, if you have gotten this far in this book, you have already chosen a spiritual perception, or at least have a strong desire for it. All along, we have been making that choice. Every time we choose the highest understanding of good in each moment, we choose a spiritual perception—a spiritual point of view.

This step makes it more real. It grounds the choice into our belief systems. This is where we step up to the plate and say, "Yes, the multiverse is spiritual."

What does that mean practically and in each of our lives? Let's find out.

Of course, we must begin with the awareness that what we perceive to be reality magnifies. We know this doesn't mean we are Life's creator. It means we are reflectors and expressers.

This is a critical awareness. It means that when something good happens—we didn't create it, manifest it, pray it into existence, or demonstrate it. It was already present. We shifted our perception and our actions to allow ourselves to experience it.

Thankfully, it also means that when something terrible happens, we didn't do that either.

The funny thing is, we barely take credit for the good we do and berate ourselves for the wrong things we do. That doesn't sound to me what a loving Father-Mother-One-Creator called Love would do to us or want us to do to ourselves.

Or saying it simply, which is probably the best kind of perception to choose, "Whatever is not Good, Kind, Loving, and Harmonious is not True."

We want this to be an accurate statement. But every day is filled with what appears to be alternative facts.

Yet, what has become more apparent in every field of study is that our perception filters what we see and experience.

If I could wave a magic wand and wipe away the filter, film, veil, paradigm, and beliefs of what appears as a material world in all its inconsistency and pinging between opposites—we would see and experience only Love and Harmony.

As William Blake said, "If the doors of perception were cleansed every thing would appear to man as it is, Infinite. For man has closed himself up, till he sees all things thro' narrow chinks of his cavern."

Our perceptions are like clouds. The sun is always present. As we dissolve and shift those clouds and perceptions, the sun, the Truth, appears where it has always been.

And here's where the symbol of the sun comes in handy. We don't specifically see the sun. We see the rays of light, which have to pass through—or onto—an object to be seen.

We are those rays of light (expresser) and objects (reflector). As with all symbols, the analogy isn't entirely accurate when they remain within human perception, but they move the clouds away.

I figure the parting of the waves of the Red Sea and parting of cloud stories in the scriptures are the same attempt to tell us to shift our perception and see what is already True.

Perception does rule. And because it does in our human belief system, we need to know the rules of perception. But one day, if we get to the place of awareness of only the Divine, that rule vanishes. And even now, once in a while, the clouds of our mist-perceptions part, and we experience we are part of the Divine Loving Intelligence.

The Bible says it this way: *For now we see through a glass, darkly; but then face to face: now I know in part; but then shall I know even as also I am known.* — Corinthians 13:12 KJV

I imagine, like me, you yearn for that day. That's why this work means so much. It gives us a path to walk that parts the clouds, providing a glimpse of our true spiritual nature.

To get there, we consistently practice shifting our perception to a spiritual point of view using tools and techniques that work. We are students and practitioners of shifting our perceptions to more closely match the Truth of our being.

We are willing to. We are aware of what we have accepted as true. We use signs and symbols provided for us to understand our conscious and unconscious choices.

We know that shifting perception is the only way to change our lives permanently.

What is your point of view? Make it the best, highest, broadest, closest to the Divine, Great Mystery, One Awareness, Intelligent Love that you can in each moment.

Then practice bringing your thoughts, feelings, and actions into harmony with it. Anything that clouds your vision of your point of view, you can say no to.

In my book *Living In Grace*, I ask, "What if this is a game?" If you think that might be true in this small r reality, you might enjoy the book, *The Simulation Hypothesis* by *Rizwan Virk*.

However, game or no game, it does not negate that there is One Intelligence called Love. But it reminds us of the importance of perception and not "logging on" to any game that is not removing the clouds.

Doomscrolling will never take us out of the game or provide a perception that offers a life of satisfaction and joy.

Choose your side: peace and harmony or confusion and division.

Don't let the noise of the unreal world distract you from knowing the Truth of One Awareness, Divinity, Infinite Intelligence that is Love—and then acting from that Truth. This is not a passive decision. It is an active and ongoing practice.

And as we have discovered, it's easier together, since that is the truth of Creation, anyway. We are One.

That voice that claims you are not a ray of Divinity expressing Love and Creativity is lying to you. Maybe it thinks it's doing you a favor. But as we become more aware, we can thank it for helping and send it on its way. Or at least make it sit in the corner and be quiet.

Use your imagination here. Let it take you into the realm of the Infinite. Let yourself feel what that feels like. Only a moment of that sunlight of Love can shift anything to its native harmony.

Every time we choose a "better" perception, our world shifts. Let's decide not to be blind to that immediate shift. Celebrate every sign or symbol that something has changed for the better. Not just for you as a person. The world. Everyone in it. The universe. Everyone and everything in it.

We used to believe that we are within our bodies. You know we are not. Just because we rarely experience this doesn't mean it is not true. Send your imagination out into the vastness of unlimited Intelligent Love.

Let it be true that as you do that, you are no longer the being in the body, but you are the being of the Divine.

Imagine that!

SEVENTY-SIX

THE DREAM AND THE DREAMER ARE ONE

I think 99 times and find nothing. I stop thinking, swim in silence, and the truth comes to me. — Albert Einstein

Here are three stories that tell a tale of dreams.

1. One morning, I woke up and said this to myself, "Today is the day I am going to go next door and tell our neighbor to stop letting his dog come into our carport and use it for a toilet."

Good idea, except we didn't have a carport, nor was there a dog that lived next door.

2. A Satellite Company had sent our information to a credit collection agency claiming that we had not returned their two receivers. This was despite the fact we had delivery proof and were assured that all was okay after calling at least five times (on that issue alone). They claimed we had taken the card out of one of them, so we owed the entire $150.00 for the receiver.

Having experienced these kinds of issues with them the entire time we had their service, my first reaction was anger at the injustice of the

337

accusation and the fact that I had to defend myself against something we had not done.

3. It was just one more thing in our rental home that didn't work right. Turning the knob for the heater in the living room didn't make one bit of difference. I turned it up. It didn't get warmer. I turned it down, and it didn't get cooler. For weeks I fiddled with it and then decided I would call the landlord in the morning.

The following day, on the way to the phone to make the call, I walked past the knob and realized that I had been fiddling with the wrong knob for two weeks.

What makes it even sillier is I had already worked the correct knobs for over a month. It's just one day I forgot there were two.

What do these three stories have in common? I was dreaming.

In the first story, it is obvious it was just a dream. And like a dream, it is equally apparent that the dreamer—me—and the dream were one.

Okay, you may think, "But two of these stories weren't dreams. They really happened."

Yes, they did—but where did they happen? They happened in the human dream.

And once again, the dreamer and the dream were one. It was my state of mind perception and my point of view perception that "created" them.

In the incident with the Satellite Company, I was already caught up in a belief of injustice. Not just about the Satellite Company but "out there" in the world.

Aren't we all daily bombarded with reports of poverty, mistreatment, wars, crimes, and man's inhumanity to man?

This bombardment enforces the point of view perception that there is another power than Divine Love, and it's doing a great job of taking over.

This builds a state of mind perception of fear, doubt, and outrage. These two modes of perception perpetuate each other.

The story about the knobs illustrates what happens when we live in a state of mind and point of view perception that things don't work as they should.

When we only pay attention to what doesn't work, we become blind to what does.

Did you notice one more thing these three stories have in common? In each one, an outside force—a dog, a satellite company, a heater knob, made a mess in our life.

Seen symbolically, the dream about the dog made it clear to me it was time to say to myself, "Stop allowing negative thoughts to invade your life."

Playing in the dream of mortal human existence is sometimes pleasant. It's when the dream turns "bad" that we think that it just might be time to wake up.

Let's all wake up from the human worldview without waiting for things to turn nasty.

To do so, we must start from the point of view and state of mind perception that there is only One Divine Power, not two. To experience the truth of this statement, we must maintain this perception no matter how real the dream of a separate power appears to be.

A wrong statement, or perception, does not change the truth about Truth, and a correct perception does not create the Truth. It reveals it.

The Truth is, there is just One power, and it is Good.

It's time to wake up and live this Truth. It has to start somewhere. It might as well be you and me.

SEVENTY-SEVEN

A SAMPLE SPIRITUAL PERCEPTION

Of course, we all can choose the spiritual perception that works for us. But, I thought I would include mine as a template. You are welcome to use it or tweak it to fit your personal preference.

From *Living In Grace: The Shift To Spiritual Perception*

When we choose the path of Spirituality, our point of view from that point forward must be that of big r Reality. There is no room for standing on both sides of the issue.

Let's be clear about what we mean by Reality. Reality is Heaven here and now. Reality is the Truth that what appears to be material is really Spiritual. Reality is One—of everything. There is no separation or duality. Reality is the reflection, the thought, and the creation of One Mind. The Reality is, there was never a separate material creation.

Much of the time, we have to argue attorney-style with our small-i (ego) so that it will step aside and yield to Truth. Here is the premise we are going to ask our small-i to agree to in order to walk the Spiritual path of Grace.

The Shift premise.

> There is a Higher Power. That Higher Power is Mind.
> There is only One Mind. That Mind is Infinite
> Intelligence. That Mind is Perfect Love. That Mind is
> the only Cause and Creator. That Mind is God and Its
> idea = I AM.

If you read the above and thought "religion," stop! It doesn't matter if you resisted this premise because it reminded you of religion, or if you loved it because it reminded you of religion. This is not a religious premise. Please don't place unlimited abundance within the codes and rules of religious belief. All religions have this premise at their core, but they have mostly strayed from it in order to maintain their reason for being.

If you resist knowing and accepting that there is a Higher Power, God, then perhaps you are not yet ready to live from an unlimited viewpoint, and it's still more comfortable for you to stay with your current life than to let go of limiting ideas. If so, That's okay. If you are willing at least to just look at the possibility, read on.

The most important part of this shift is to desire to know and act from the understanding of what is True—and what is True is all is God. We could also use the word Good since Good and God were originally the same word. Substitute the word Good for God if it helps you to avoid any preconceived notions about God. However, when I am using the word Good instead of God, it is not the good that is the opposite of evil, which is a limited and dualistic approach. Good in this context means Perfect One.

If you are ready for an unlimited viewpoint, you know and accept that there is a Higher Power, or at least you are willing to look at the possibility. You can call this Higher Power any name you wish, as long as it contains the understanding that there is only One, an

Infinite Loving Intelligence. To make this point clear, I will discuss it from the standpoint that God, Higher Power, is Mind.

You can call God the One Taste, One Engineer, Love, Good, whatever registers within as True for you.

Is there a God? As a teenager, I briefly questioned this. My first taste of religion had been one where questioning was not allowed. This presented me with ideas from which I could draw no logical conclusions. It suggested that we could never understand God and were not allowed to try. It told me that I could never be good, that guilt was part of my being. I could not accept these teachings, so in tossing out the religion I also tossed out my understanding that there is a Higher Power.

This didn't last long. Simple things told me there was Something much more, in day-to-day life, guiding others and me.

It was an internal knowing. It was the blast of joy that came from seeing the clouds one day as I started down the stairs at my dorm. I glanced up and saw the sky through a skylight. It was awareness of the simple beauty of what I was looking at, and of the incredible Intelligence of what must have created it. It was the awareness that even though I thought I was painting a picture, or choreographing a dance, something higher than my human self was guiding me. I knew without question, as you do, that there is a Higher Power. There was something greater than my human self. I just didn't know how to make use of that knowledge. I wanted to know more about this Higher Power. After much reading, thinking, and listening, I understood that One Mind is the only answer.

Only an Infinite Intelligent Mind could hold the world and the infinity of being in Its thought. Could there be two minds running the world? No. Even two human minds can never agree totally on everything.

It has to be One Mind, an Infinite Intelligence.

The next step in this premise is that there is only One Cause and Creator. Since there is only One Mind, there can be just one Cause, one Creator. Since there is only One power, there is no other power to create something. This means there is nothing that we did or didn't do that could remove us from the State of Grace, or from being the reflection of One Loving Mind. We can breathe a sigh of relief! All we need to do is yield to the State of Grace to become conscious of the Truth of One.

The radical view that we'll soon begin to live from is that there is only One Mind, One Cause, One Creator, and It is Intelligent Infinite Love. This means that perfection, joy, and good are the Truth about who we are. The Truth is not some goal to achieve or someplace to go. When we make this kingdom of God—One Mind, Love—the starting point, all other needs are met. Heaven is here, at hand, and ours now, because it is Truth. We can live on Main Street and still be living in Heaven because there is only One Creation, God's, and that One is Spiritual. This is our Spiritual point of view.

Love's Promise—The Spiritual Laws of Grace.

1. *But, seek ye first the kingdom of God, and his righteousness; and all these things shall be added unto thee.* —Matthew 6:33, Bible

2. *Ask, and it shall be given you; seek, and ye shall find; knock, and it shall be opened unto you.* —Matthew 7:7, Bible

3. *And it shall come to pass, that before they call, I will answer.* —Isaiah 65:24, Bible

Seventy-Eight

Molly and Spiritual Perception

I wanted to change the world. But I found that the only thing one can be sure of changing is oneself. — Aldous Huxley

Molly approached this step with quite a bit of trepidation. *What is spiritual perception*, she asked herself. Was it what she had learned in the church that she grew up in?

If so, Molly wasn't sure she wanted that one because it included a god that punished and destroyed. To be fair, she wasn't exactly sure if that was actually the basis of her parents' church, but the people in it seemed to think so.

Because although they claimed they based their church on love, she didn't think they believed that. She had seen too much hate and prejudice for people who had different beliefs than they did. If God was unconditional love, then where was theirs?

On the other hand, Molly realized they might not know that their point of view and state of mind didn't match. Still, she wanted no part of a perception that didn't begin with a point of view that there was only One Intelligence, and it was Love. Molly knew she didn't understand how that could be true, and her belief that it was true was as tiny as a mustard seed.

But Molly reasoned that if it were true that perception is reality, that was the reality she wanted.

To make it easy to remember, she chose One Intelligent Love as the basis of her spiritual perception. She then took the quality words "unconditional love" and practiced using them as the basis of her actions, using the four steps of using quality words as her guide.

Molly paid attention and noticed when and if she saw unconditional love and was grateful for seeing it and expanding her perception of what it looked like.

She asked herself to notice how she felt about people, places, and things. Did she have unconditional love for them? If not, why not?

Molly realized she had to look beyond the physical to discover something to love. Was she grateful for what she saw? Did it align with her spiritual perception of unconditional love? If it didn't, she decided it couldn't be true.

Since she wanted to be happy in her work, Molly asked herself to find a way to love each aspect of everything she did unconditionally. As she did so, she discovered something that felt very important to her.

She could love something but not like it and choose not to do it. She could love that her work provided income and safety, but not like that she felt stifled in it. Because she had love for herself, she could choose something that better matched her individuality.

As Molly discovered more about what she was willing to do or accept and what she was not willing to do or accept, she remained grateful for what she was finding. Even when she noticed her prejudices, both personal and directed towards others, she remained grateful for the awareness.

She did her best to have unconditional love for herself, too, reasoning that if she was going to stick with the spiritual perception of One Intelligence and It as Love, she had to include herself. She was not separate, as her ego and personality consistently claimed.

Molly found there was joy in the perception mastery practice because it was a path to walk. Even if she didn't like some of what she found, Molly knew she was dissolving beliefs that stood in her way of being happy.

She began to think of the work as a cleaning out of her mental home. It was a mess at first, but that was okay. She knew it was necessary—too much clutter, both in her thinking and in her house.

The quote by Antoine de Saint-Exupery, "He who would travel happily must travel light," became her guide. She would travel light, both mentally and physically. Letting go would become something she enjoyed instead of something she feared.

Molly decided to follow the spiritual perception that she was the expressor and reflector of One Intelligent Love, and observe how her thinking, actions, and life aligned or didn't align with that perception.

SEVENTY-NINE

PRACTICAL SPIRITUAL PERCEPTION

How wonderful it is that nobody need wait a single moment before starting to improve the world. — Anne Frank

It's time to choose your spiritual perception. I have given you mine, and Molly has given you hers. You are welcome to use them or tweak them to make them your own.

The vital part of this exercise is that you choose one. You can adjust what you choose as you practice using your spiritual perception as the basis of your days. Just make sure that your spiritual perception is the best one you can imagine today.

Use your own spiritual beliefs to choose the words that resonate with you. Let go of prejudices and other people's opinions and how others live their lives, and decide what is Truth for you.

Tying It Together: Spiritual Perception

- Write out your current highest understanding of your

spiritual perception.

- Be willing for your spiritual perception to be true.

- Become aware of the times when you act as if you don't believe it.

- Understand that the world shows us what we believe, which gives us the opportunity to bring our actions back to our spiritual point of view.

- Don't forget to spend the time you need to bring your state of mind into harmony with your point of view. Imagination comes in handy here. If you would like to strengthen and expand your imagination, you could try my book *Imagination Mastery*. It goes hand in hand with *Perception Mastery*.

- Use the face and replace tools of I Choose sheets and Quality Word lists to help align your point of view and state of mind.

This step of choosing a spiritual perception can feel fantastic. Allow yourself to believe.

Make your spiritual perception the best idea of life that you can imagine. As you let go of old beliefs and patterns, allow yourself to continue expanding your spiritual perception to be precisely right for you.

If you want real control, drop the illusion of control; and let life live you. It does anyway. — Bryon Katie

(If you would like a daily prompt to notice simple things about life that might shift your perception about them, I have a free daily email, only a few sentences long, called *The Daily Nudge* which you can find at becalewis.com

EIGHTY

— · —

STEP SIX: WALK AS ONE

Sometimes our light goes out, but is blown again into instant flame by an encounter with another human being. — Albert Schweitzer

What does walk-as-one mean? It could mean "walk your talk," and it certainly includes that idea, but walk as one prompts us to ask ourselves, what one?

It includes:

- Walk as one with our chosen spiritual perception.

- Walk as one with our state of mind and point of view.

- Walk as one with the Divine.

- Walk as one with our community, our family, ourselves.

Walk as one begins with listening to the wise, still small voice within—often called intuition or gut feelings—and then taking the action it suggests and encourages us to do.

Walk as one is living as our unique spiritual blessings and sharing them with others.

This step often gets overlooked or given lip service but is not actually taken. It can be the step where we get stuck because we aren't living our spiritual point of view. Talking about it, maybe. But not living it.

Putting our point of view and state of mind into appropriate action "proves" that we believe what we say. It's a practice. But we don't need special equipment, or special times in the day to practice. The opportunity is always present.

Walk as one is about relationships. All relationships. The relationship with ourselves and with other people, places, and things. It's about what we want for ourselves and what we wish for others. Walk as one is considering how our actions affect others.

When we walk as one, we acknowledge our kinship with all living things.

Walk as one always contains action. Always.

When we walk as one, we take action to provide what others need when we can. When we see something wrong, we speak up. Without action, all that we believe in is only words. Pretty words sometimes, but useless without helpful action.

Talking about kindness and doing nothing kind or nothing to stop unkindness is worse than useless.

The Bible tells us this, "For as the body without the spirit is dead, so faith without works is dead also." — James 2:26

It also tells us we can know the tree by the fruit it produces. No amount of lovely words makes up for treating others with contempt or disrespect. That tree is rotten, no matter how beautiful it looks on the outside.

When our actions do not match our point of view or state of mind, we fool ourselves. And it's important to remember that some people hold a point of view and state of mind that is not about harmony, love, community, unselfishness, and kindness. They have chosen the

351

opposite. And some of them are incredibly proficient at speaking words that mislead. Pay attention.

Liars and pretty words have fooled us all at one time or another. It's a dangerous resemblance and often hard to detect. I found release from one such person when I became fully aware of how they made me feel and how they separated me from my loved ones, and the expression of myself. I had noticed the fruit of the tree.

Ask yourself, "What is their intent? Do they advocate walking as one? What one? Is it about the unity and equality of all things?"

Try not to get lost in the "how" of all of this. I don't have the answers. I don't think anyone does. There are more things that we don't know than what we do.

But you and I do know that perception produces reality, and because of that, we choose the best reality we can imagine.

Do I make mistakes? Absolutely. I can get lost in criticism, resentment, self-pity, discouragement, anger, too. But as I practice, I notice more quickly when I have fallen off the path, and I am grateful for the tools and support around me that help me get back on.

Walk as one is the opposite of the belief that we can attract what we want by thinking about it with no action required. It would be lovely if this were true. Or would it?

Everyone would stay home expecting the thing they want to show up at their door. There would be no community or sharing of gifts. There would be no proof that our faith is genuine.

Not taking action on what the still small voice leads us to do is faith without works. And it is a waste of the unique gifts and talents we have been given that are meant to support, encourage, and inspire others within our chosen community. Without action, we are robbed of the joy of working and learning together. Yes, action is always required.

But it is not about how significant the action is that we take. Every step, no matter how small, is equally important. Each of us does what our gifts and talents enable us to do. Walk as one is a tapestry of threads, each one necessary for the fabric of lives to be complete.

Most of the time, we don't know the impact of our actions. But if we intend to bless and support others in their life, then we don't need to worry if it worked out okay.

We only have to watch the cycle of nature to see that Life is reciprocal. We give and we receive. But often, it is not a direct response. When we go to the store, hand the clerk money, we immediately receive what we paid for.

But Life is often not that direct, nor should we expect it to be so. Life is more of a cycle, a spiral. But it always spins back to us. Sometimes we miss what we have received because our point of view might be that what we do never works, or people don't take care of us, or... well, this list could go on and on, and I cover this point more thoroughly in the book *The Four Essential Questions*.

In truth, Life returns to us much more than we give because It is Love loving Itself after all. What a fantastic point of view to adopt and practice bringing our state of mind into harmony with it. Imagine how much good you and I would accept in our life if we were fully walking as one. Knowing and living that point of view, we would never hoard what we receive. We'd let it go, knowing there is always more.

In this Earth game, we must overcome the belief of lack and at the same time be in harmonious and balanced relationships.

There is nothing we can do, think, or say that is not about a relationship. Truth is practical; therefore, our expression of Truth will be practical and useful.

When we apply and use the Truth in every relationship we have, including our bodies, supply, work, and loved ones—we walk as one.

How glorious is that?

EIGHTY-ONE

IS SPIRIT CALLING YOUR NAME?

Attitude follows action far more often than action follows attitude. We change our mood as a result of how we act. If you want to feel a certain way, begin by acting as if you do. On the other hand, if you truly want to accomplish something, waiting for the mood to strike is ineffective. — Seth Godin

We were at the local corn fest and had arrived just in time to hear the raffle announcer say, "Coleen Springer, you have won the bike."

It was a cute little bike. I am sure Coleen would have loved it. They kept calling her name, and when she didn't answer, they said they would draw again.

So, Coleen, or a parent, spent the time and money to purchase a raffle ticket, had hoped she would win the bike, and yet they were not present for the drawing.

Do we do the same? Do we practice, study the science and spirit of God, and yet decide to take time off, hoping we won't miss our name being called?

Yes, that's what we do. We get distracted by the out-picture we call our lives. The claims that it is more fun to do something else mislead us. Or the lie that we have studied enough.

Moments go by, days go by, years go by, and how often has our name been called without our knowing it? Called for gifts of the heart. Called to pick up the supplies we asked for. Called to do a good deed, called to stop danger, or called to correct the illusion that danger has occurred.

There are other ways we can miss Spirit's calling other than being not present. One way is to ignore it. We do that all the time, too.

Once, while out jogging, I heard my name being called and actually did what it requested for me to do.

You are probably thinking, "Oh my, how glorious, it must have been something very important."

No, it wasn't. In fact, Spirit's calling is almost always about being faithful to the small details of life, and when we prove we are present and listening, we hear the message more often, clearer, and yes, sometimes it is something "important" to do.

In this case, it was something very simple. I was jogging in the early dawn and saw a clump of marigolds lying in the road. Something or someone had pulled them out of the garden.

I heard the voice, "Replant them."

I ignore it and kept running. I heard the voice again, "Replant them."

That time I turned around, grabbed the flowers, found the hole they came out of, replanted them, said a few words of encouragement to them, and then continued down the road. It took less than a minute to do this.

It is very doubtful anyone saw me, and the homeowner probably never knew what I had done. Yet, I am the one who benefited. I saw those flowers every time I jogged by, happily growing as if it never happened. Most of all, I benefited because I heard the call and I answered it.

Spirit is calling with these messages: "Stop following the lies of the worldview. Don't be afraid; follow my voice. Hold hands with your neighbor and walk this way. Do good without expectation of return. Be diligent, stay in Truth, don't get distracted. The time is now, not later."

The consequences of not being present are far more serious than not receiving the bike meant for you. It is a dangerous decision to take time off from living the whole truth of God at all times or to ignore the voice of Spirit that is calling you.

The reward is much greater than a bike. Yes, it is work, but there is no other work as worth doing. It is the experience of heaven on earth now. It is the awareness of grace in your life now. It is the awakening to your true spiritual nature, the Am in I Am.

Your name is always being called. Be sure you are prepared and present to hear and act on it.

EIGHTY-TWO

—·—

MOLLY AND WALK AS ONE

You get treated in life the way you teach people to treat you. — Wayne Dyer

One day, Molly ran across something written fifty years ago by Oldham and Hackman about the characteristics of work that produced satisfaction and fulfillment. The five questions meshed perfectly with the practice she was doing using the four steps of quality words with her list of how she would feel if she was fulfilled in her work.

She found an article by *Seth Godin* that broke the article down into five factors:

1. Task significance: Does the work you do create meaning or impact?

2. Task identity: Do you feel ownership (emotionally) in the work you're doing?

3. Autonomy: Do you have the freedom to make choices?

4. Skill variety: Is the task monotonous?

5. Feedback: Are you in a place where you can safely and easily get feedback and use it to improve?

The answer for Molly was no to every question except the question, "is the task monotonous?"

Yes, her work was boring. But not only at work, but the work she did at home. However, now that she had become more aware that her beliefs played a significant role in how she experienced life, Molly wondered if it was her job and home life's fault or how she approached it?

So she went back to the steps of perception mastery.

She asked herself if she was willing to do work that created meaning and impact. Molly realized it was partially the work, but mostly her feelings about it that made it feel unimportant. Washing dishes didn't create meaning or impact unless she used it to express her gift of order.

Molly asked herself to be more aware of how her attitude affected her work, the people she worked with, and, of course, her husband. If she was always unhappy, how did she make others feel?

By paying attention to the reactions of others to her presence and what they said to her helped her recognize the signs and symbols all around her.

Molly reminded herself of the perception rule that *what she perceived as reality magnified*. Could she change her perception, her point of view and state of mind, about work and her husband?

Yes, she decided. She was willing to choose a spiritually based perception for her work, husband, and other relationships.

Which meant she had to act as if it were true. *Geez,* she muttered to herself, *that might be the hard part.* But, once again, Molly was willing.

All week her husband had been going to work while she stayed home. At first, it had been hard to let go of the resentment that he had not taken her on the vacation she had wanted. But as the days wore on, and she followed the perception mastery steps, without even noticing it, her resentment had faded away.

It was then that Molly realized she had begun to walk as one with her point of view and state of mind. Yes, it was only baby steps, but it was making a difference in how she felt about herself, her work, her husband, and the other people in her life.

And that night, when her husband helped her with the dishes instead of heading off to do his own thing, she said "thank you" and meant it. Instead of letting resentment fester beneath the surface, she faced it and replaced it with how she wanted to feel.

Molly took her list of quality words and wrote a sentence with them. Molly didn't worry about the order, only about her intent to walk as one with her point of view and state of mind.

Writing the quality words this way helped her remember what was important to her, so she memorized her sentence and repeated it as an affirmation to herself as often as possible during the day.

Molly's sentence:

"Expressing gratitude brings fulfillment, happiness, and peace. Being useful, I am energized, satisfied, and joyous. When I am aware, I am humbled by the presence of Love."

EIGHTY-THREE

—∙—

PRACTICAL WALK AS ONE

A learning experience is one of those things that says, "You know that thing you just did? Don't do that." — Douglas Adams

You've learned many practical ways to walk as one. All that remains is doing them.

It doesn't matter how big an issue you face or how small, you can walk it through these steps.

Tying It Together: Walk As One

Want to change your hairstyle? Thinking about moving? Need a new idea for a book you're writing? Does a relationship need to be addressed? The seven steps can go quickly or take days, weeks, or even months.

However, sometimes the first step gives you the answer you seek. "Am I willing to change my hairstyle?" You ask yourself.

"No," you answer. Done. That's it.

However, if you want to know why you don't want to change your hairstyle because you know it would probably be a good idea, the next step would be to become aware of why you are unwilling.

Ask yourself: *What is my perception about this? Is my state of mind in harmony with my point of view?*

One way to begin is to do an I Choose sheet.

Write something like this, "I want a new hairstyle."

Check Chapter Three to remind yourself how to complete this. It may surprise you that the reasons behind this unwillingness carry into multiple areas of your life.

Perhaps, in the end, you remain unwilling, but you will know why you are unwilling, which makes all the difference. Doing the I Choose sheet helped you become aware while removing old beliefs and providing clarity.

The other tool you could use here is a Quality Word list. How would you feel if you had a new hairstyle?

Once you have them in order, take the first word through the four ways to use a list. Then go down the list one word at a time. You can review the steps in Chapter Sixty-Four, but here's the synopsis.

1. As a filter.

2. As an awareness and signs and symbols check.

3. As a gratitude practice.

4. As a walk as one practice—as you live as those qualities yourself.

It doesn't matter how big or small the question you are asking is, or the item you are working with. A new dining room table or a significant business transaction may seem miles apart. But they are all connected. And it is always about relationships—with ourselves and the people, places, and things that make up our experience of the world.

- Remember to stop at least once a day and pause in silence without an agenda. Be aware of the noise, but let it go. Listen within, with no expectations, desires, wants, or needs.

- Once you have walked yourself through these steps, write a sentence with all your quality words and use it as an affirmation. Not about something you want, but a statement of fact.

I know you can guess the last step; we've already included it in this step. But there is always more to learn about gratitude, isn't there? Ready to be grateful? Let's go do it!

Where there is love there is life. — Mahatma Gandhi

Eighty-Four

Step Seven: Celebrate With Gratitude

In the external scheme of things, shining moments are as brief as the twinkling of an eye, yet such twinklings are what eternity is made of—moments when we human beings can say, "I love you," "I'm proud of you," "I forgive you," "I'm grateful for you." That's what eternity is made of: invisible imperishable good stuff. — Fred Rogers

Celebrate with gratitude is an interesting play on words. Because we would think that if we were celebrating, we were grateful, or if we are grateful, we are celebrating.

But that's not always the case.

Many celebrations have nothing to do with gratitude. And sometimes we feel grateful and aren't happy about it. Yes, everyone knows the value of feeling grateful, but how often do we consciously practice, sinking deep into the feeling and not the words?

To truly celebrate with gratitude, we have to be paying attention. Of course, that's what we have been doing all along—paying attention—and then shifting the story to a better one.

It seems simple enough. And it is. The idea of it is simple. It's the execution of it that takes practice—having a system for that practice. Thankfully, we have one, the seven steps of Perception Mastery.

Here's how we walked those steps:

First, we chose to be willing.

Then we chose to become aware of what we, consciously and unconsciously, were thinking and doing.

To help us become more willing and aware, we paid attention to signs and symbols and interpreted them correctly—to the best of our current ability.

Then we began to study and understand how perception rules. We diligently adjusted our perceptions to match what we want to experience. Not just for ourselves, but for others, too.

In this book, we have walked the path of spiritual perception together. We have increased our willingness to shift, listen, and take action based on the point of view that there is an Infinite power and that One power is Love in action.

With all that in place, it was easy to walk our talk. Well, maybe not easy. But easier to be willing to do it.

It has become easier to walk away from anything that doesn't bless ourselves and others. Easier to choose to always begin with the still small voice within ourselves.

We have learned how to—and continue in—the correct identification of ourselves. We have practiced ways to silence any voices and ideas that debase who we are or someone else is.

Why? Because we know that voice lies. That's its nature, not ours.

So, of course, we are willing to celebrate because we have a proven path to walk on and dependable people to walk with us.

And we are aware that Love loving Itself is the Reality we want to live within. And we know how to dispel any illusion saying otherwise. Or at least we know it can be done—and we are willing to do it.

We celebrate with gratitude that there is a path to follow.

We celebrate with gratitude that like-minded souls walk that path with us, making it safe and comfortable.

We celebrate that the process is the point. That Life isn't about competition—it's about cooperation. We celebrate that we know that Life is not about how much stuff we acquire. It's about living as our true spiritual essence.

We celebrate because we know that we have never left the Truth of harmony. We celebrate because we know our path is to shift our perceptions to see what is already and has always been present. We celebrate because we are opening our hearts and minds to enable ourselves to see.

As we walk the ever-expanding circle of our increasing awareness, we celebrate with gratitude—for what we now know, understand, and have put into practice.

Our gratitude is unending for the awareness that as we shift to spiritual perception and focus on our highest understanding of an infinite unconditional Love, what is untrue is revealed. We are grateful that we know all untruths can be dissolved by facing and replacing them with the point of view and state of mind that we are all One within Divine Love.

We remind ourselves that the purpose of becoming perception masters is not to change the outside picture but to know and experience and be the activity of Infinite Intelligent Love.

We are grateful that in doing so, what appears as an outside picture will shift to reveal that what we need and want is already present.

EIGHTY-FIVE

YOU CAN REWRITE THE STORIES OF YOUR LIFE

Before you speak, let your words pass through three gates: Is it true? Is it necessary? Is it kind? —Rumi

Core values, family history, worldview agreements, and personal habits all come together to produce a movie we call our life.

If these ideas come together to form a pretty picture, then life is good; when they don't, then life is not so good. In the not-so-good times, we stand in the middle of this movie, like characters on the screen, and try to change it.

We try to adjust the picture on the screen, forgetting it is a projection. We forget that the movie and the movie viewer are one. It is a projection of our point of view and belief systems.

This is not a whimsical idea. This is a fact.

In the book *Biocentrism* we read, "Moreover, if one accepts that the external world occurs only in Mind, in consciousness, and that it's the interior of one's brain that's cognized 'out there' at this moment, then, of course, everything is connected with everything else."

This means it is absolutely possible to change our lives. Why? Because our lives are the out-picturing (but not the creation) of what we believe and perceive to be true.

It also means that there is only one way to make a change: to shift our perception from within.

But what if we want more than just a better life? What if we want to be what we really are? What if we want to experience ourselves as the outcome or idea of the infinite Mind or omnipotent Light? What then?

To do this, we must re-think reality and reset our perception. We must stop identifying ourselves as human. We must stop believing what the five senses tell us and listen instead to the quiet voice within.

We stop acting as if the movie and script are real. We stop wanting the story to get better and want instead to let go and live as the idea of God.

This is a radical thought and decision. It demands a root change. It follows the biblical word "repent," which means turn around and walk the other way.

We turn away from the movie playing in our heads, which results in what we call our lives.

We turn away from identifying ourselves as human and reset our thinking and perception.

It demands that we let go of how we want it to be, think it is, and then follow through with action and commitment to Truth.

This radical shift demands that we turn away from trying to fix things and people. We turn away from our story. Instead, we turn to the fact that what exists in our lives, and who we think we are, is one and the same, and be grateful for this spiritual fact.

This is not a halfway decision. It is a complete shift. Yes, it may appear to take time to reset habits and beliefs, but that too is only set within our agreement of what is true.

It may appear that others need to change first. Again, not true. What appears as they, or that, is really our own perception. There is no way to separate the thinker from what it is thinking.

Our responsibility is not to create, control, or make happen. Our responsibility is to stop separating ourselves from the ever-present infinite intelligent flow or force we call God.

Our responsibility is to let go and be what we are, which in turn resets what we experience as our lives.

As we do this, we can expect more beauty, peace, abundance, grace, happiness, love. We can expect all the fruits of good to be more present in and as our lives.

Not because we worked at becoming good and wise humans, but because we gave up the story.

We consistently listen and follow the still, small voice within. We pay attention to the symbols that prove the presence of God. We continually reset our perceptions to match our current, highest, and best understanding of the Divine.

And then, because we have refocused the projector, the movie we call our life must conform.

This surely is something to celebrate with gratitude.

Let's check on Molly one last time and see how she is doing with these seven steps and the practice of gratitude. And then onto a review in the Practical Gratitude section.

Eighty-Six

Molly and Gratitude

The most important things in life aren't things. — Anthony J. D'Angelo

We are not the same persons this year as last; nor are those we love. It is a happy chance if we, changing, continue to love a changed person. — William Somerset Maugham

Molly believed that this step would be the easiest of all of them. After all, who doesn't know how to be grateful?

Apparently not her. To Molly's dismay, she discovered she wasn't willing to be grateful for many things. Resentment and anger simmered just below the surface about so many things that gratitude was not something she wanted to feel. After all, she had a right to those feelings, didn't she?

Molly decided she did. So she sat down in her favorite chair with a pen and paper and followed the Perception Mastery steps to let herself be angry and resentful. She was willing, aware, and saw all the signs that pointed to why she was right to feel that way.

Then she got to perception rules. That's where things fell apart.

Molly had begun to understand that her perception was "creating" her outside world, revealing to her precisely what she wanted to see. Her beliefs and perceptions filtered through everything to support the story she told about her life. She wrote the story and continued to support it by not facing and replacing it as needed.

If she wanted to experience the world through the perception that it was unfair, hard, unloving, and full of work she didn't like to do and people she didn't want to see, then that was what she would get.

The question was, would that make her happy and fulfilled? If it did, then she could continue with that same perception. But Molly knew it wouldn't.

Begrudgingly, Molly moved onto the next step, choosing a spiritual perception. She stuck with the one she had been working with, *One Intelligence and It is unconditional Love* because Molly didn't think she was in the right frame of mind to make up another one. That meant she was back to the last step, celebrating with gratitude.

No, she was still not wholly willing to be grateful. She could feel herself clinging to the story she had been telling herself about life, but Molly decided she could be grateful that she was now aware of what she was doing. She could be grateful that the choice was hers to make. She could be grateful to herself for getting started on this fresh path.

It surprised Molly to discover that letting in just those few drops of gratitude started melting away her resentment. It was still there, so she turned her attention to being grateful for simple things, like the sunrise, the wind in the trees, her favorite ice cream in the freezer.

The more she practiced being grateful, the easier it became, and Molly was grateful, knowing that eventually her anger and resentment would fade away. But in the meantime, she wouldn't be mad at herself for having those feelings.

By the end of Molly's week off, she realized she was looking forward to going back to work. She made a list for herself of why she was happy about it. Some things on the list surprised her. Others didn't. She still wasn't sure she wanted to stay at that job, but Molly knew she would know what to do next as she practiced the seven steps.

The anger at her husband because of their ruined vacation plans had dissolved without her even noticing. Instead, she found herself thanking him for what he did that made her happy. Although he still did things she resented, they had become less important to her. It was a small step, but it made her happy to be grateful rather than angry.

Although only a few weeks had gone by since Molly had begun this practice, she could feel and see the difference in how she was experiencing life. There was a sense of relief in her heart when she fully realized that what she could change was herself. And how to change herself was to shift her perception and that she knew she could do.

People are like stained glass windows: they sparkle and shine when the sun is out, but when the darkness sets in, their true beauty is revealed only if there is a light within. — Elisabeth Kubler-Ross

Eighty-Seven

Practical Gratitude

It does not do to dwell on dreams and forget to live. — J. K. Rowling

You realize that our mistrust of the future makes it hard to give up the past. — Chuck Palahniuk

Dear reader, you made it!

Doing these seven steps was like one of those outdoor circuit training paths, wasn't it? You know the ones: Stop here and do a pull-up. Stop here for lunges.

The Perception Mastery path stopped for willingness, awareness, noticing signs and symbols, understanding perception rules, choosing a spiritual reality, walking as one, and gratitude.

We are stronger, more flexible, and more joyful for taking this trip around the circuit and will become more so as we go around the path over and over again. Unlike the paths stuck on the one plane of the dimension called the Earth Game—this path spirals up and out into infinite possibilities.

You have tools to use along this path. Now that you have arrived at gratitude, why not do another I Choose sheet about something you want to expand or be grateful for?

Then perhaps make a Quality Word list of how you would feel if you were always in gratitude. Once they are in order (remember you can't do this yourself, you need someone outside you to ask the questions). Go back to Chapter Three to remind yourself how to do that and then go to Chapter Four to review the four steps for using these quality words.

Yes, you'll end up in gratitude again since it is part of step two. Gratitude is always part of any path to happiness.

- Write a sentence using those quality words, and let it help guide you into that perception, both as a point of view and a state of mind. Say it in front of a mirror. Go ahead. Do it.

Remember that *what we perceive to be reality magnifies.*
Or we could say it this way:

- The multiverse is composed of infinite possibilities.

- We narrow down the Infinite Possibilities by what we observe.

- What we observe is what we believe to be true.

- Changing our perception and beliefs changes what we observe, which then reveals a different possibility.

Every day, we have multiple opportunities to shift our perceptions. Remember, there are infinite possibilities, so there is no point in getting stuck in a perception that does not serve you, the ones you love, or the world.

We can choose to let life get better. We can choose to perceive life as good, harmonious, and abundant for everyone all the time. Yes, that means we are constantly shifting our perceptions. But why not do it? No matter how wonderful life is now, we are just getting started with the possibilities of expressing our unique spiritual gifts.

Keep up your practice. Go back through the book. It's always here for you. Make use of it!

Life is a celebration of Itself. We have joined together in that celebration, and I am profoundly grateful for you. Each person walking this path makes it easier for all of us. Thank you!

There are only four questions of value in life, Don Octavio. What is sacred? Of what is the spirit made? What is worth living for, and what is worth dying for? The answer to each is the same: only love. — Don Juan

EIGHTY-EIGHT

AUTHOR NOTES

I hope you found this book useful. I know these seven steps work—if we use them. Sometimes even I forget. I'll find myself in some kind of crisis, or confusion, and then remember that I have steps to take to get myself out of them.

This path—the seven steps to shift—is the first path I designed while teaching my first Shift Class in 1992, and I, and countless others, have used them since. I know they work.

So don't let them sit unattended in this book. Practice them. Let these steps help shift your life to the one you want to experience. That's the point of this shift series of books, after all—to make a difference.

Every shift of perception towards the point of view that we are all part of one glorious Loving Intelligent One moves us closer to that day when we see clearly who we, and all beings, are in Truth.

Thank you again for walking this path with me. If you feel moved to, please share this book and perhaps write an honest review so others can decide if this is for them. A few sentences is all it takes.

And, if you like this book, you might like other books in . You can find them on my website at becalewis.com, and everywhere you buy and read books, including your library.

Thank you for reading, and shifting with me. ~Beca

BLOOMING YOUR LIFE

· ♥ · ♥ · ♥ · ♥ · ♥ ·

EIGHTY-NINE

— · —

HAPPINESS IS ...

*T*he world is a looking glass and gives back to every man the reflection of his own face. — William Makepeace Thackeray

In order to be utterly happy, the only thing necessary is to refrain from comparing this moment with other moments in the past, which I often did not fully enjoy because I was comparing them with other moments of the future. — Andre Gide

NINETY

— • —

PREFACE

To be a Flower, is profound Responsibility. — Emily Dickinson

This book began as a blog post in 2008. Then it became a 7-Day Shift email course. And then, like a tree, it grew into a talk that I gave at various functions. After that, it branched out into an online video course, then a class, and now a book.

As with the blog, course, and classes, I have an intention. I want to help you design your days and life to match who you are, discover what you need to thrive, explore the possibilities of happiness, and apply what you learn.

In our classes, we agree to fully take part in a community garden of like-minded souls so that every member feels the support and encouragement of walking with a group of people on the same path with everyone's best interests in mind.

I know that reading a book may not feel the same to you. But if you wish to, you can imagine that you are in this community and feel its support as you read through this book. Think of all the people doing the same thing as you. Each of you is making life better for the next person, even if you never meet them.

However, perhaps you can find a friend or two to study this book with together, and you will make the same agreement to support each other.

Or maybe I'll see you in class one day, or on one of my online courses, or perhaps you'll join our at perceptionu.com

However, even if you feel you are doing this by yourself, let me assure you that you aren't. I know that all the support you need will be present for you in a multitude of ways if you expect to see it.

In addition, there are communities of life-gardeners that you may not know now, but as you do this work for yourself, you will become one of them.

My desire for you is that your life blooms with happiness now and into your future.

But to bloom happiness, we must have the desire to be happy. We have to decide to cultivate the intent and passion for our life to bloom.

Even if you don't feel that way now, stick with me for a bit, and let's see if we can't unearth that desire. It's there, I promise.

And if you already feel it, let's expand that intent and desire together. Let's be willing to bloom profusely as ourselves—each of us as an individual bloom, but always connected and needing each other in this garden of life.

Darwin called it "an abominable mystery" — he wrote: *Look into a flower, and what do you see? Into the very heart of nature's double nature — that is, the contending energies of creation and dissolution, the spiraling toward complex form and the tidal pull away from it. Apollo and Dionysus were names the Greeks gave to these two faces of nature, and nowhere in nature is their contest as plain or as poignant as it is in the beauty of a flower and its rapid passing. There, the achievement of order against all odds and its blithe abandonment. There, the perfection of art and the blind flux of nature. There, somehow, both transcendence and necessity. Could that be it — right there, in a flower — the meaning of life?*

Welcome to the garden! — Beca

PS: Please be sure to do the *Practical Blooming* section at the end of each chapter. Otherwise, this book is only partially valuable to you. It would be like looking at a catalog of seeds and plants but never planting the garden.

If, as you read this, you discover you would like to pursue more of the ideas in this book, try another book in *The Shift Series*. Each one has a different focus, but the same premise. The mother tree book is *Living In Grace*. The rest of the series are the branches.

Section One: Preparation

NINETY-ONE

— · —

BLOOM WHERE

O ur mind is a garden, our thoughts are the seeds, you can grow flowers or you can grow weeds. — Rita Ghatourey

We've all heard the saying, "bloom where you're planted." There's truth in this. Because sometimes, maybe often, we find ourselves somewhere we would rather not be. And if the choice is between being miserable or happy, then for heaven's sake, let's be happy. Let's choose not to droop or languish and instead do our best to bloom.

However, wouldn't it be better to plant ourselves where we would bloom best?

I love the process of gardening. And over the years, I have learned that some plants don't grow well where I put them. Sometimes—don't tell anyone—I swear I hear them begging me to move them somewhere else.

So even though when I first plant them, I pay attention to what the plants' needs are, sun or shade, for example, sometimes I need to move them anyway because they aren't thriving. There are other factors at work. Perhaps, like people, they don't like the area, or the neighbor is too noisy, or they want a different view.

I moved a plant once that looked so bedraggled I was afraid to move it, thinking that the transfer might kill it. But I did it anyway because it kept asking me to. I moved it from the backyard, a nice shady spot, to the front yard, also a nice shady spot, and within hours it perked up and, by the end of the day, looked better than it had ever looked. It thrived there. And every time I check on it, I swear it says thank you.

So yes, if I can see plants in this way, I can certainly see us humans as plants. But as human plants, we have many more abilities than a plant does.

Well, perhaps plants have more abilities than we think, but that's for another day. If you are interested in the intelligence of the plant kingdom, I have listed a few books on it at the end of this book in the Resources section.

But I know you are here for you, so let's find out where you will thrive the most. It doesn't mean you will pick up and move yourself, although you might. It just means you will give yourself more choices that enable you to thrive as intended by the Master Gardener.

NINETY-TWO

—— · ——

WHY HAPPY

*A*ct as if what you do makes a difference. It does. — William James

This book is about taking steps to experience happiness, and who doesn't want to be happy?

I really should warn you that this is a trick question because although you are likely to answer, "everybody wants to be happy," but you may be consciously or unconsciously thinking that you don't have the right to be happy.

Even if you believe that you have the right to be happy, and it would be a good idea to be happy, do you know what happiness is for you?

Many of us have been trained not to be happy. I remember my friends and I being careful not to be laughing when we came home because we might get the evil eye for being too happy.

Perhaps we agree that we have the right to pursue happiness, but not the right to experience happiness, so we have never stopped to think, "Hum, when am I happy? What makes me happy?"

Often we believe that if we choose to be happy, it means that we will pick ourselves first, and then others will be unhappy because of our choice.

Sometimes we think something will make us happy, and yet, either it doesn't or has an outcome we didn't expect, like this brief story about the cat and the mice that I heard long ago.

A cat died and went to heaven. God met her at the gates and said, "You have been a good cat all these years. Anything you want is yours for the asking."

The cat thought for a minute and then said, "All my life I lived on a farm and slept on hard wooden floors. I would like a few real fluffy pillows to sleep on."

God said, "Say no more." Instantly, the cat had three huge fluffy pillows.

A few days later, six mice were killed in an accident, and they all went to heaven together. God met the mice at the gates with the same offer that He made to the cat.

The mice said, "Well, we have had to run all of our lives: from cats, dogs, and even people with brooms! If we could just have some little roller skates, we would not have to run again."

God answered, "It is done." All the mice had beautiful little roller skates.

About a week later, God checked on the cat. He found her sound asleep on her fluffy pillow. God gently awakened the cat and asked, "Is everything okay? How have you been doing? Are you happy?"

The cat replied, "Oh, it is wonderful! I have never been so happy in my life. The pillow is so fluffy, and those little Meals on Wheels you have been sending over are delicious!"

Obviously, the cat was thrilled, but the mice probably had to show up at the pearly gates again. And I bet the next time they didn't ask for roller skates.

We all have learned lessons the hard way, but it's not necessary or required. We often have to let go of ideas that no longer serve us and instead choose ones that do.

In this book, we will explore reasons for being happy, discover what happiness feels like for you, and most of all celebrate the fact that we each must be happy before the other people we love, and who love us, can be their happiest.

Ninety-Three

—·—

Leading Happiness

The supreme accomplishment is to blur the line between work and play. — Arnold J. Toynbee

We milled around, waiting for the class to begin. All of us strangers except to say "hello." The teacher enters, turns down the lights, starts the music, and we are no longer strangers—we are one in happiness.

An hour flies by, and I think of nothing but enjoying myself with the rest of the class, with the grandmother from Russia who doesn't speak a word of English but has a massive smile on her face, and the teenager beside me bouncing with delight. We are all ages, all ranges of ability, all together, all laughing, all thoroughly enjoying each other and ourselves.

How does this kind of joy happen?

It begins with the teacher who leads us into it.

I have taken this kind of class from three different teachers. One marks the steps, one teaches it as if it was an exercise class, and the other dances her heart out, leading the class with joy and the pure happiness of moving to the music. It's easy to know which class I choose to attend.

Taking the class are people of all ages, from eighteen to eighty, which provides an inclusiveness that gives us all permission to be ourselves. No one is trying to compete with another. Instead, all the ways of doing it are accepted and celebrated because we are doing it and not talking about doing it.

The only ones who don't seem to enjoy themselves are the ones who can't bring themselves to participate fully. They are too busy judging either themselves or others,

The community keeps me going. If I were doing these classes at home, I would be bored and walk away. Instead, the community carries me forward long past when I would have stopped on my own. When someone doesn't show up for a few sessions, people notice and ask where they are, and if they don't get a suitable answer, someone follows up to make sure everything is okay.

All this happens because the teacher fully and completely expresses herself with joy and passion. She is adventurous and curious. Often during class, she will lead us into a different way to do the same move, exploring various ways to have fun.

However, there is another crucial point. The teacher is expressing herself with skill. She knows what she is doing. She picks the right music, plays it at the right sound level, and says the right things.

We are all teachers and leaders, whether or not we like it!

Perhaps we don't have the label of "teacher," but by living our lives, we are setting an example and leading the way. So, why not do it with skill and fully express ourselves with joy?

It's easy, really. It just takes a shift of perception.

If we approach a task—say grocery shopping—with the idea that it is a chore, it takes time away from something else, there's not enough money to get what we want, we feel overwhelmed with other things that we must do, it's crowded, the timing is terrible, it's hard to get to, oh my... I could go on and on, which I know we all sometimes do, then what we will experience is a waste of time.

However, we can shift our thoughts and perceptions to something like this:

"What a blessing it is that there is a place for me to find what I need.

"How grateful I am that others have worked to provide this place for me.

"It's lovely that I will be able to participate for this brief time with a community of shoppers who, like me, are being provided for in this way.

"I am grateful for the exchange of money for substance. All timing belongs to the Divine, whose timing is always perfect.

"What a gift that I can experience this abundance of supply and share that experience with others."

Yes, I could go on and on in this way too, and my experience at the grocery store will be far from unpleasant, with the bonus that I contribute to others having a joyful time at the store too.

As I thought over why that teacher is so successful, I came up with seven ideas that we can apply to our own lives and lift others and ourselves into the atmosphere of Love.

- Fill your heart with joy and express it openly.

- Be adventurous and curious.

- Gather a community (family, club, tribe) that supports and encourages each other.

- Make it possible for many kinds of people to find your community.

- Find a way for members to be wholly involved in their own style.

- Enjoy each other for what they are, not for what we wish they were.

- Commit to being more and more skillful at what you bring to the community.

We can see how these ideas can be applied to our home or business life, and in doing so, we are actively shifting the worldview and its activities from lack and greed to abundance and sharing.

Actually, we will fulfil the promise that we are the "light of the world," and each day will be the one "the Lord hath made."

All of this happens with no effort on our part other than letting go of what we want people, places, and things to be like, and relaxing into the guidance, creativity, and joy of Love.

NINETY-FOUR

— • —

HAPPINESS: A SHIFT OF PERCEPTION

I have learned over the years that when one's mind is made up, this diminishes fear. Knowing what must be done does away with fear.
— Rosa Parks

Do you want to know something that will make things both easier and harder at the same time?

Here it is.

Everything we experience results from our personal private perception, not a "set in stone reality," but perception. This idea has been around long enough and studied long enough for all of us to agree that it's true. And if you need more proof, perhaps this book will help.

I'll talk more about perception as we move through the book, but to get us started, let's agree that life and how we experience it—is all perception.

And since that's true, let's review how perception works.

Perception is a filter. It only allows into our thinking, and therefore into our lives, exactly *what we perceive to be reality,* not what I perceive for you, but what you perceive to be a reality for you.

Common sense and practicality are essential to me. Thinking that we have a right to be happy, yet experiencing unhappiness, makes no sense. So because I know it is all perception—as do you—I have made it my life's study and work to shift perceptions to what is True (capital T).

The outcome of this perception shift is happiness. As Eleanor Roosevelt said: *Happiness is not a goal, it is a by-product.*

In this book I hope to help you plant the garden of your own life, which will continue to bloom long after you plant it.

Not only that, your happiness will "naturalize" itself, just like the daffodils I planted one fall. They were beautiful the first year, but they continue to spread without effort on my part, becoming more and more beautiful and abundant each year.

This can be your own personal self-started and well-grounded economic stimulus plan that can never be uprooted.

Renee, a composite of all of us, will be your guide throughout this book. I hope she answers a few questions you might have that I could answer if we were in a class together or if you are part of our *Perception Circle* Community.

But if you have questions that don't get answered, please find me and ask. I'll do my best to help.

If you are ready to bloom, it's time to begin—with questions, of course, because answering questions about yourself to yourself is an excellent way of knowing yourself, so don't skip the practical questions at the end of each chapter—starting with this one!

PS There is a workbook attached to this course. I'll ask the questions in this book, but if you don't enjoy writing in your book or you are reading this on an eReader, you might enjoy using a workbook. Of course, you could always use your own paper. Whatever works for you! You can find the workbook link in the resource chapter of this book.

NINETY-FIVE

— • —

PRACTICAL BLOOMING: PREPARATION

Answer these questions from your heart and not your head. Be honest with yourself. Take your time! If you can't be honest with yourself, who will be honest with you? Besides, it is the only way to bloom your life perfectly and consistently.

Don't forget, if you want a workbook, you can find the link to it in the resource chapter of this book.

Otherwise, be sure to write the answers down somewhere.

Because happiness is an innate quality for any being, given that it is part of the harmony and joy that is the omnipresent Divine, we don't have to create it.

Instead, we move and remove anything that is blocking both our view and experience of happiness.

Let's do it!

1. Do I want to be happy? Yes — Not Sure — No
2. Do I feel I have a right to be happy? Yes — Not Sure — No
3. Is there anyone I think would be unhappy if I were happy? Yes — Not Sure — No
4. Who?
5. Are there specific times they would be unhappy if I were happy? Yes — Not Sure — No

6. What are those times?

7. Is there anyone I think would be happier if I were happy? Yes — Not Sure — No

8. Who?

9. This is when I am the happiest.

10. This is what makes me happy.

NINETY-SIX

— · —

RENEE: PREPARATION

*I*f *I hadn't believed it, I wouldn't have seen it.* — Yogi Berra

Renee read those words of Yogi Berra and wondered if it was that easy or perhaps it was that hard. If she shifted her beliefs, she would see what she wanted to see? Live the life she dreamed of living?

That's it? That's how it works? Renee asked herself. *Does that mean that all I have to do is shift my beliefs—or more accurately—my perceptions?*

To Renee, this sounded like magical thinking. If you think something, it comes true.

Right, Renee said to herself. *This sounds as if I am not required to do anything except sit around and imagine or daydream.*

That didn't feel right to her. She wanted to do something with herself, not sit on her couch and practice shifting perceptions so her world would change.

Besides, if that was how it happened, the implications of that were horrible. *If we think something, we create it?* Renee asked herself. Does that mean I create all the evil in the world then? What about God? Is there one? And why would a loving God create all the war and disease and hatred that has been part of the life on earth experience?

Renee recognized this as a dark night of the soul question—a question that Renee hoped would be answered soon, because she realized that these questions had been eating away at her all her life.

She wants to be a kind, generous and loving person. She wants the Universe to be loving and generous to all life forms. And she often asked herself why it doesn't always work that way? Was it her fault?

And although she likes her life and puts those kinds of questions aside in order to get by, they haunt her sometimes when she accidentally hears the news.

Renee understands that getting by is not thriving. She and the world are not thriving.

What she wants to do is thrive. Renee wonders if she changes her perceptions and beliefs and finds her perfect environment—whatever that is—will the world change too?

If the answer is yes, then again, is it her fault that it isn't like that now?

She prays the answer is "no, it isn't."

But then, if it isn't her fault, whose fault is it? Is it anyone's fault? But most of all, Renee wants to know what she can possibly do about it. Can she, and the world, thrive? And if so. How?

Answering the *Practical Blooming Preparation Questions* woke Renee up when she realized she had never thought about most of them before.

Was she happy? Maybe. Did she believe she had a right to be happy? Maybe.

In fact, Renee marked all the yes, no, maybe questions as not sure. She wasn't. But now she wanted to know why she wasn't sure. Shouldn't she know?

Renee decided that if reading the book and answering the questions would bring her clarity, she would fully commit to doing it. And she hoped by the end she would be able to honestly answer *yes*.

In the meantime, Renee started answering the last two questions.

When am I happy?

To find the answer, she needed to pay attention to herself and her feelings during the day.

What makes me happy?

Renee thought she knew some things that made her happy, as long as they didn't have to be profound or important.

As she started making a list, she realized she was happy doing it, so that was her first thing on the list.

It made her happy to discover what made her happy.

SECTION TWO: SEVEN HAPPINESS STEPS

Ninety-Seven

Step One: Prepare To Grow

·♥·♥·♥·♥·♥·

NINETY-EIGHT

— • —

DECIDE TO BE HAPPY

Normal day, let me be aware of the treasure you are. Let me learn from you, love you, bless you before you depart. Let me not pass you by in quest of some rare and perfect tomorrow. — Mary Jean Irion

Abraham Lincoln said, *Most folks are as happy as they make up their minds to be.* This is a perception-shifting statement, isn't it?

If we want to be happy, we have to decide to be happy.

But the problem is, how do we make up our minds to be happy?

The United States Constitution says we have the right to *pursue* happiness. It doesn't say we have the right to *be* happy.

And that is often the problem. The worldview has trained us to believe that we don't have the right to be happy. As if our being happy means we rob someone else of their happiness. Or what right do we have to be happy when there is so much suffering in the world?

Not being happy will not solve the world's problems and, in many ways, contributes to them. And happiness, like love, is unlimited. Not only do we have a right to be happy, but we also have an obligation to find it for ourselves, which will help others find happiness.

Imagine that. If everyone were happy, greed and all the sins that branch out from it would vanish. So let's go to a higher power than the Constitution and claim our right to be happy.

But since we often believe that we don't have a right to be happy, being happy may feel wrong.

However, as we plant ourselves in a new version of our lives, we can shift that belief of not having a right to be happy. We will know with absolute certainty that not only do we have a right to happiness, but that happiness is a quality that is innate in each one of us, and we can and will find it and live it.

There are many causes and reasons for unhappiness, but in the end, there is only one way to be happy. Decide to be.

This is the good news, isn't it?

Because when we learn how to choose and accept happiness, we will eliminate all those reasons and causes of unhappiness. This means there's no time like the present to be happy, so let's get started!

We are ready for the first step: *Prepare To Grow.*

And the question is, "How do I prepare to grow?"

Just as in any successful garden, we begin by preparing the soil of our lives. Our perceptions.

That's what we are doing when we decide to be happy. We are going to shift our beliefs and perceptions.

Which makes it imperative that we understand how perception works to ensure that our perceptions work for us, not against us.

NINETY-NINE

PERCEPTION SHIFTS

*E*verything has been figured out, except how to live. — Jean-Paul Sartre

As we have agreed, everything begins with perception. Perception is the medium in which we plant ourselves.

I know you have heard, and maybe even said, the phrase, "It's all perception."

It sounds great, but what does that mean? And if we agree it *is* all perception, then the obvious next step is to ask ourselves if we act as if that is true?

Because if that statement is true, then life gets very easy, doesn't it? It would mean that to be happy and bloom in our lives, all we have to do is shift our perception. It would mean the end of trying to make things happen outside of ourselves. Instead, we would spend time shifting our perception to what we want and how we want to live.

Well, it is true. It is all perception. That's the good news.

Because it means we know exactly where to begin anything, we begin by shifting our perceptions. We will find our belief systems and perceptions within ourselves and shift them to ones that help us and others bloom in our lives.

How easy is that? Easy.

But only if we are willing to make these kinds of shifts. This, my friends, is the first key to shifting perception. Any perception.

Be Willing

Being willing is always the first step to doing anything, including consciously choosing new perceptions and beliefs and letting go of those that do not align with our true selves.

Remember, perceptions act as filters or funnels. They set the paradigm in which we live, which produces (not creates) what we experience. Because our perceptions only let in what matches what we have agreed—consciously and unconsciously—to be true.

Everything else is blocked from our view. Our senses do not create our perceptions. They report them. And that becomes a self-fulfilling prophecy. We see, smell, taste, and experience something, and then we believe it. That belief produces more of the same.

You can see how easy it is to get stuck in ruts of all kinds. From the foods we eat to the way we earn a living.

Perceptions filter out what they know we don't want or agree with and only reveal to us what we have chosen to be interested in or think we need to know. How do our perceptions know to do that? We told them to.

And please note. Perceptions and beliefs don't know when we are teasing. They don't understand jokes. They don't think things through. They just filter and give us what they think we want.

Perceptions are fantastic servants but terrible masters. We have to learn how to be the masters of our perceptions.

All of this perception filtering and seeing happens at the point of our own consciousness, not outside ourselves, but within ourselves.

And we have to be willing to shift them.

We have all experienced conversations with someone trying to explain something obvious to us but not to them. The problem and solution, once again, lies within perception.

If they are unwilling to shift their perception, nothing will change, no matter how hard we might try to change their minds.

It's easy to see the block and ruts when dealing with someone else. But within ourselves, well, that is another story. Since we can only see what we believe or currently know, we will see nothing other than what we expect to see.

If you were wearing blue lens glasses and I told you the room was green, you would not believe me unless you took off your glasses. So first, I have to convince you to take off those blue glasses.

We have to expect to see something different for things to be different. We have to train ourselves to perceive more. We have to shift. Or pivot.

Since this is a proven fact, it is imperative to learn how perceptions work and what ones we agree to consciously or unconsciously.

Remember this fact: All change begins within and is witnessed without. Thought precedes the outcome.

Our happiness first begins within. And with the decision to be happy. No reason needed.

ONE HUNDRED

— · —

THE TWO MODES OF PERCEPTION

*B*e happy with what you have and are, be generous with both, and you won't have to hunt for happiness. — William E. Gladstone

It makes it easier to understand the concept of perception when we realize that there are two modes of perception; a Point Of View (POV) perception and State of Mind (SOM) perception.

We must fully align both modes of perception with each other to experience the outcome we desire.

Let's use our garden as an analogy. What if we purchased the perfect soil and then poisoned it? The perfect soil is our ideal point of view. The poison is our often unseen and unknown state of mind.

Point of view is simple to understand, and sometimes it is simple to shift. It's like reprogramming a computer. When you know how to do it, it's easy. When you don't, it takes more time.

However, it is the most valuable skill we could learn because what we decide and perceive to be true is what we experience.

If you don't know your point of view perception, look at what you are getting. This is not a guilt thing—it's a mirror thing. Don't judge. Just observe.

Remember, there are hidden points of view, ones we don't know we have until we explore, but before we do that, let's choose a point of view on purpose and work out from there.

In this book, we are choosing to be happy.

Our point of view is that not only is it our right to be happy, but that happiness is innate. Happiness does not need to be created because it always exists. What we are doing is revealing it to ourselves.

So let's reveal this point of view to ourselves: everything we need to be happy and prosperous is present now. This is a beautiful plot of soil—point of view—in which to plant ourselves.

We know that *what we perceive to be reality magnifie*s. A truth that quantum physics, prophets, philosophers, and spiritual teachers have taught throughout the ages.

And that is why I have chosen the point of view that the Master Gardener, whom we'll call Divine Love, *has done the perfect job of providing for everybody and everything in every moment.*

That's our point of view. You don't have to believe it. Just be willing for it to be true.

Now, how about our state of mind?

Suppose I have chosen the point of view that everything I need is present now, but I am not experiencing it? Instead, I feel discouraged, upset, sad, afraid, frustrated, or angry.

These emotions are all a by-product of a state of mind and they produce a poisonous state of mind. It's a vicious cycle or perpetual loop.

No matter what our point of view perception is, it's our state of mind, or emotional perception, that is running the show called our life.

We must get our point of view and state of mind to be in harmony and sync with each other.

Which brings us to the second key to shifting perception.

Become aware.

And within awareness, we learn how to recognize our state of mind and bring it into harmony with our point of view. No poison. Only nutritious supplements.

We'll talk more about ways to shift our state of mind throughout this book.

But one way to shift our state of mind fits perfectly into our garden analogy.

Step into nature. Listen. Feel what is happening. Let nature speak to you and align your state of mind with your point of view.

Remember this: perception either makes us blind or reveals what is present.

The world does not shift. We do. You do. You will choose to be happy, expect to be happy, and bloom within your life. And that shifts the world. It starts within, and is witnessed without.

Observe and witness the outcome of this conscious shift. You can prove the power of perception to yourself, and once you do, life-blooming becomes much simpler.

And that, in turn, my friend, will shift the world that we experience. For me, that's what this is all about. I bloom. You bloom. The world blooms. Joy reigns. It's possible!

ONE HUNDRED ONE

— · —

LET GO

The lust for comfort murders the passions of the soul. — Kahlil Gibran

It was a beautiful fall day, a perfect day to work in the garden. I planned to move two hosta plants growing in an area that received direct afternoon sun and move them to the morning sun area of the garden, their preferred location.

I prepared the new holes for both hostas and then went to dig them up. The first hosta released its roots easily and quickly, and within a few minutes, I had it resting happily in its new home. The second hosta, planted in the same area, would not let go.

I struggled as I tried to dig it out while talking to it, saying, "Please let go. I am moving you to a happier place. You are hurting yourself by holding on. Please, just let go!"

Every minute that went by was harder and harder on both the plant and me until finally, I could pull it free.

Although now planted by the first hosta, I know one of them will have an easier time recovering from the move.

Isn't this how we are sometimes? We won't let go.

We won't let go of how it was, how we think it will be, what we own, or what we want. We hold on with every fiber of our being while the infinite intends to move us lovingly to a "happier place."

Something has to give because that is how we expand and evolve. We can choose to give up how we want it to be, how it should be, how it was, how it could have been, or hold on and make it hard on ourselves.

The sooner we let go, the easier our life is during and after the move.

It reminds me of the phrase, "what gives?" Isn't it interesting that we use this phrase as we greet someone?

But take a moment and think about what we are asking when we say, "What gives?"

It could mean a few things. What are we given, or what are we letting go of, or what is giving way to something else?

As we let go, we get the answer to the question of what gives. We discover that what gives way are limitations. By giving up how we want it to be, we can hear the Infinite say, "I Am what gives."

There have always been times when we have needed to let go and let God, but the past years have forced the issue for many of us.

Now we need to decide if we will hold on to how it was or let go and move into a new awareness. We can throw away what the worldview says our life has to be and enjoy what is being given at this moment to us.

For many of us, when a new direction opens up, instead of letting go, we hold on. It's painful to hold on. As people, places, and things evolve and change in our lives, we must let go.

We can not hold on to our material-based version of love, abundance, supply, and peace because they are not the real thing. They are prepackaged perceptions the worldview wants us to buy with our time, money, and hearts.

They are not what gives. What gives is the pure sense of happiness that is not derived from anything but from Itself. It gives completely, fully, and practically at all times.

As we let go, we discover that letting go is not painful but is full of adventure and joy and security found nowhere else.

ONE HUNDRED TWO

— • —

GIFT YOUR FUTURE SELF

For one human being to love another: that is perhaps the most difficult of all our tasks, the ultimate, the last test and proof, the work for which all other work is but preparation. — Rainer Maria Rilke

When my children were little and Christmas was coming, it filled me with happiness and joy to prepare for their perfect Christmas morning.

Joy and happiness lay in the preparation and anticipation. Even working additional jobs took on an element of excitement because I was preparing a gift for their future self.

We can all remember when we found joy in preparing for our, and others, future selves.

However, we live in a world of right now—a world where we expect immediate entertainment. Where we are so overwhelmed with current tasks, we don't have the mental or physical space to enjoy preparing for anyone's future self, let alone our own.

But, I propose that preparing gifts for our, and others, future self is where happiness lies.

We can prove it to ourselves with a few elementary steps.

At night, as I "close shop" in my business and our home, I walk around the house and put things away that we used during the day. I am doing it for my future self.

When I get up in the morning, everything is clean and fresh and waiting for me to start the day. If I am the first up, I press the coffee maker button for my husband's future self when he gets up.

These are small happiness moments, but happiness lives in small happiness moments.

All tasks that we do are really for our future self and the future self of those that we love. But we forget that and instead think of these tasks as chores or problems.

If we turn our attention to each task as a gift to the future, they are no longer just a thing that needs to be done; they become a happiness producer.

There is a caveat here.

Sometimes we do things for a future self without caring about our present self.

When we overwork, do wrong things to get more money or power, don't take time for thinking, or enjoying the present, we are not producing happiness for ourselves now or for the future.

We may sometimes forget this, but we know in our hearts that it is true.

It's the small things that spring from love that mean the most. I think some of the best presents I ever gave my kids were handmade coupons. They were for their favorite dessert, a health day off from school, or a private lunch or movie date with me.

Every day brings many ways to gift our future selves. Would your future self like it if it was healthy and strong? If it had a cared-for place to live within?

These are things our current self needs to take care of now.

When we don't care, when apathy takes over, when it seems as if we have no power to change the future, that's when we most need to rebel.

We need to rebel against apathy and lack of interest. We need to rebel against the resistance to doing what will gift our future selves.

Right now, what can you do for your future self?

It doesn't have to be far in the future. It could be an hour from now. Start there. Keep going. Then choose another simple project.

Move a piece of paper to where it belongs. Prepare some food for later. Plan a trip to a garden. Plant something and watch it grow. Clean the closet one section at a time.

It's the little things that make up the future. And it's those little things that make us happy now.

We find current happiness when we view our day as future-self projects.

It's a win, win, win, and win situation. Choose your own personal happiness project. Your future self is already smiling in anticipation.

ONE HUNDRED THREE

— • —

THE GOOD THAT WE NEED

*I*n the small matters trust the mind, in the large ones the heart. —
Sigmund Freud

When I first heard it, I had no idea what it was. I thought someone
was tapping at my door, but there was no one there when I looked.

I followed the sound and discovered a beautiful bluebird tapping
on the glass door leading to my office. Thinking it was a
one-of-a-kind event, I shooed it away. However, he came back
tapping at the windows in the living room, flying from one to
another.

I closed the curtains. I spoke to him at the windows and tried to
shew him away. Not because I didn't enjoy seeing him, but I thought
he must have better things to do.

My friend the bluebird circled the house all that summer, tapping
gently at the windows and hopping up from the deck to tap at the
office door.

Of course, I heard all that tapping as a message because haven't
we all behaved this way? Tapping, tapping, and tapping to get
something we want?

Yes, our tapping looks different than a beak at the window. Our
tapping takes many forms. Nevertheless, it is always that insistence

that we know what is good for us, and if we try hard enough, we just might get it.

Then we wonder why we don't.

Perhaps the door or window doesn't open because what we want is not in the house. Maybe Divine Love keeps us safe by not opening that way.

As the bluebird made his rounds that summer, I asked myself, what is he reminding me to do, to think, to be aware of, to accept into my house, my consciousness?

It was pretty obvious. After all, he is the bluebird of happiness, the symbol of contentment and renewal.

Remember that wonderful song written in 1945 called *Zip-A-Dee-Doo-Dah*? It joyously declares the present good and the good that is coming.

This is what we can let into our house. This is what we can declare: "It's the truth, it's actual, everything is satisfactual."

That summer, as the bluebird tapped at my window, I kept him safe by not opening the window or door.

In the same way, Love keeps you and me safe from what we think we want and leads us instead to what we need to bloom as ourselves.

One Hundred Four

— • —

Practical Blooming: Step One

Prepare To Grow

Spend time with these questions. Let yourself background the answers. This book isn't meant to be a one and done event. It's an ongoing exploration, a constant tending of the garden of your life.

It is meant to spark questions and impel conscious action.

Take the time to listen for answers so that you can choose what perceptions you want to keep and which ones you want to shift.

It's not the end result we are after, it's a quality of life.

1. Is it my intent to have my life bloom? Yes — Not Sure — No
2. The two modes of perception are:
3. Using my life as a mirror, I see that I have these perceptions.
4. When do I find myself in a frozen focus?
5. These are the times when my state of mind does not match my point of view.
6. What gifts can you give to your future self?

(Don't forget, if you want a workbook, you can find the link for it in the Resources channel. Otherwise, be sure to write them down somewhere.)

ONE HUNDRED FIVE

— · —

RENEE: STEP ONE

R *eality is that which, when you stop believing in it, doesn't go away.* — Philip K. Dick

Renee was not particularly happy about the questions posed in this first step.

If she answered them, it would mean that she would have to think about things she had decided not to think about anymore. She wanted to believe that it wasn't affecting her if she didn't notice what was happening. Of course, she knew she had been fooling herself, but it had been so much easier that way. Or so she had told herself.

However, when Renee started this book, she agreed to be happier, which meant she had to stop hiding from herself and do the work. Renee knew that not keeping agreements she had made to herself was a dangerous thing to do.

If she couldn't trust herself, could she trust anyone? And she knew trust is an essential part of allowing herself to be happy.

Reading about how perception works, Renee could see how perception was the cause, although not the creator, of what she experienced. So if she was serious about making changes, she had first to find out what she believed to be true.

After that, she could shift her POV perception to one that made her life easier and happier and would affect all the people she cared about.

However, using her mirror as her life made her nervous. She didn't like what she saw in it. She didn't like what she saw in the actual mirror, either. Renee supposed they were the same. It was hard to remember that the mirror didn't reflect what was real. It only told her what she believed.

Although many things weren't working well in her life, she had a mostly good life. But this book asked if she was thriving. And if she was going to be truthful, she knew she wasn't.

It was time to care for her future self. And Renee realized that her future self was not just a few years into the future but an hour from now or the next day. It was simple things. If she didn't get enough sleep, her tomorrow self wouldn't function well. Or if she overate or drank what wasn't good for her, her tomorrow self would pay for it.

Renee decided if she thought of her future self as her child, she would take better care of it. Instead of her future self paying for her actions today, it would be grateful for the gifts that she was giving it.

Thinking of it that way made Renee happy. Perhaps all of her wasn't thriving today, but she could take action towards ensuring that her future self would. It occurred to her that it meant more significant issues than taking care of herself. It would also mean taking better care of the world she lived in.

But for now, she'd start small. She would pay attention to what her life was telling her and then adjust her POV and SOM to reveal an improved outcome.

Renee decided not to focus on what wasn't working but on what was. It didn't mean she hid from what the mirror of her life told her. It meant she noticed it and then did something about it.

ONE HUNDRED SIX

STEP TWO: PUT YOURSELF WHERE YOU GROW BEST

·♥·♥·♥·♥·♥·

One Hundred Seven

— • —

Designing Your Excellent Life

B *eware the stories you read or tell; subtly, at night, beneath the waters of consciousness, they are altering your world.* — Ben Okri

Obviously, to put ourselves where we grow best, we need to know who we are. Not who we have been acting like or trying to be, but the individual, unchanged, can't duplicate, wonderful essence of us that is our true spiritual nature.

Dolly Parton, that delightfully unique individual who obviously lives with an intent to bloom, says it clearly. *Find out who you are and be that on purpose.*

Or, as a food network star said, *Be yourself; control the opposite of who you are.*

Or, as Oscar Wilde said, *Be yourself, everyone else is already taken.*

To do this, we need to put ourselves where we grow best. It sounds simple, doesn't it? But we rarely do it.

It is not what we have been taught. We don't believe that it is our right to choose. Instead, we often act like lemmings following the worldview belief system that we can, and must, all live as if we were all the same plant.

Whether or not you are a gardener, you understand that all plants don't bloom well in the same conditions. We know that a violet likes shade, and a rose loves the sun. If we made the mistake of reversing these two plants, thinking the rose liked the shade and the violet loves the sun, then we would have killed the plant or severely limited their ability to grow, let alone bloom.

Most of us are not completely conscious about what kind of plant we are, let alone where we best bloom. Even those of us who are highly successful are often doing it through human willpower. And despite our training that human willpower is a good quality, it's not. It is not the way to thrive. Sooner or later, it will fail. It's human, after all.

If you have reached a point in your life where nothing seems to work, and all that human effort and willpower is fading or entirely gone, it's a time to rejoice, not despair.

Now, instead of working hard to make things work, you can let your life bloom by shifting to a point of view and state of mind that grows your happiness in a sustaining and supportive way. Not just for yourself, but for the world.

Is it possible to be successful and happy by planting yourself in the perfect garden, life, and conditions? Absolutely. We can all experience a life with less stress, sadness, lack, frustration, or anger. Imagine that!

But first, you need to discover what type of plant you are in order to create the right environment. One place to start is with your USB. Not the marketing USB which is the Unique Selling Benefit. I mean your Unique Spiritual Blessing.

And what is your USB? It's who you are with no work on your part. It's the gift of you. It's what you can't stop being any more than a rose or a violet can stop being a rose or a violet.

Perhaps roses and violets could put on costumes or masks if they were as "capable" as we are, but they would still be what they are underneath that mask. And all that effort to hold on to the costume or mask would slowly but surely tire them into death or, at best, stagnation.

Let's uncover who you are and what you have always done that is easy for you. This means, being human, you have probably not placed much value on it or nurtured it as well as you could.

One way to discover your USB is to notice the effect you have on others. Because we are not used to valuing the essence of what we are, in the beginning, we may find it easier to notice what we consider its "negative effect."

Perhaps it often drove people around you crazy and probably still does if you haven't learned how to be it with an artist's grace.

I have always shifted perceptions, but I didn't know there was an art to it. So even as a very young child, I would attempt to shift people's (adults too) perceptions to something better than what I thought they were experiencing. I didn't do it well. I was pushy about it, and it made people upset with me.

I am learning to be better at expressing this gift. Since I started officially teaching *The Shift System*, I have found it fulfills my need to shift perceptions, and now I try to limit my advice to those who want to shift. And I leave everyone else alone—most of the time.

The idea of knowing what you do without effort is one element of planting yourself where you grow best. But there are more things to consider.

For example, do you need people around you to thrive? Or do you need lots of private time? Or do you promote change or manage change? Or do you like to do things step by step, or do you like to fly to the conclusion?

These and many more questions need to be answered and as you answer them, move your life to match the answers. It's Designing Your Excellent Life—on purpose, as Dolly Parton said.

As you bloom as yourself, you will find that you have no need or use for willpower, ego, or false personality because you know yourself as beautiful and valuable. There will be no need to put on airs, hide, or manipulate because you know who you are.

You won't need to fight every day for a sense of worth because just being who you are will feel deeply fulfilling, secure, and safe. You will feel relaxed and inspired because you have chosen to plant yourself where you grow best.

When someone says, "just who do you think you are," you will no longer answer, "not much, or I don't know." Instead, you will know the answer and be proud of it.

One very exciting side effect is that when we live as our Unique Spiritual Blessing, what we have to offer and share is noticed and desired. As Coco Chanel said, *In order to be irreplaceable one must always be different.*

The good news is that we are already different and irreplaceable. All we have to do is drop the part that is not us and let ourselves grow as our true self.

The question we are asking today is, *where is that for me?*

One Hundred Eight

— • —

Create Your Habitat To Thrive

*Y*ou cannot begin to preserve any species of animal unless you preserve the habitat in which it dwells. Disturb or destroy that habitat and you will exterminate the species as surely as if you had shot it. So conservation means that you have to preserve forest and grassland, river and lake, even the sea itself. This is not only vital for the preservation of animal life generally, but for the future existence of man himself -- a point that seems to escape many people. — Gerald Durrell

Not everyone thinks about creating habitats. My husband has been managing woods for most of his life and, in recent years, has increased his study of how all of nature works in harmony and cooperation.

The problem is, humans destroy nature more than support it. By creating safe habitats, we become part of the solution. We are in the process of turning our yard into diverse habitats that provide support and protection. We leave snags, create wood piles for creatures, and provide bird homes and food, slowly getting rid of our lawn in favor of native bushes and trees.

This idea of habitats for others fits perfectly into the concept of blooming our lives because we want to create habits and habitats where we will thrive.

In order to thrive, different creatures need different habitats. Some need more trees, some more bushes, flowers, and water. We are the same. To thrive, we need to create habitats and habits that match our needs.

However, our perceptions—which produce our habitats—look like green lawns for most of us. Maybe lovely green ones. Pretty to look at, but not very useful for the insects, birds, and animal kingdoms. They don't thrive there, and neither do we.

As we shift our perception, we will begin to see what habitat best supports our individual nature. Some perceptions that we have ignored or been upset with because they didn't fit into our manicured life might be the perfect thing to grow.

However, most of us have to plant more ideas. Get more water. Feed ourselves better. Open more space. Add ideas that we have never thought about or decided we didn't like without giving them a chance to work for us.

Every time we are willing to shift our perception to a broader perspective, we create a better habitat for ourselves.

However, when we decide to accept that we are too old to learn something, don't have time, or worry about what people will say, we create a sterile, flat habitat where ideas can't thrive, and solutions are hard to find.

Diversity is the key—both within our perceptions and nature.

We can expand our perception and create a better habitat for ourselves by learning something outside of our current interests. By listening to opposing ideas. By asking ourselves if thoughts are invasive, and if so, are they harmful?

This is conscious choosing. This is facing and replacing. This is shifting perceptions.

Creating the habitat that you thrive within makes it easier to have a point of view that harmonizes with your state of mind.

Remember, this is all about putting yourself where you can thrive. What habitat suits you best?

Have you ever read a seed packet? It tells you how deep to plant, full or partial sun, etc.

In my classes, I use several profile systems for the same reason. I don't use them to put people into boxes, but to help them learn what conditions best suit them in order to thrive.

Yes, we are much more than a plant. We are actually Infinite Beings. But in this Earth POV perception, we each have a preferred blooming environment, and not only are we allowed to choose that preferred environment, but for the world to thrive, we must.

I have listed the profiles I often use at the end of the book in the Resource channel. Just remember. They are not predictors or limiters. They are servants, not masters.

Note: If you want to do more with habits, *The Four Essential Questions* book might be helpful because it focuses on Choosing Spiritually Healthy Habits.

ONE HUNDRED NINE

— • —

JOY IS WAITING FOR YOU

If you begin to live life looking for the God that is all around you, every moment becomes a prayer. — Frank Bianco

One day in early May, after being away from home for a few days, I took a walk and discovered that spring in my yard and the neighborhood had exploded while I was gone.

There was a riot of color. Flowers, trees, and bushes were blooming in every hue and color possible. Even the lawns were sporting color, with dandelions and spring beauties.

A few days before, I found a note that I had carried around for years but had not seen for a long time.

It was the lyrics to a Lou Christie song given to us by two friends when Del and I traveled the country. It became our theme song.

Lou Christie sings, *Good-bye to things that bore me, Joy is waiting for me.*

Finding the note was an example of the synchronicity of the universe because we had just returned from visiting those friends.

In 2000, my husband Del and I traveled around the United States. Both of us were leaving one life and starting a new one together. As we traveled, we played that song. We were saying goodbye to what we didn't want. We expected that joy was waiting for us.

We explored the country while exploring what we wanted and what was no longer relevant in our lives.

When we returned home from our quick trip to visit our friends in the Berkshires seventeen years later, joy was still waiting for us. Spring had arrived.

However, joy was also waiting for us on the train we took to get there.

It was waiting for us at our friend's home. It was waiting for us at the coffeehouses, restaurants, and baby animal farm that we visited together.

Joy always waits for us. It waits for us as we sleep, work, clean the house, or run errands.

The problem is never that joy is not waiting. The problem is we forget to notice it, celebrate it, and roll around in the pleasure and the feeling of it.

Often it is because we are clinging to what we don't want, don't need, have outgrown, or was never ours.

Things that "bore" us.

Sometimes it's not what is going on in our individual lives that keeps us from noticing the joy that is waiting for us. It's outside events.

People doing mean and unkind and dangerous things to each other can crowd out joy. Illness, whether as poverty or health issues, can cause us to forget joy.

It is even more critical to claim joy as ours in these times. To see it, express it, and share it.

It is an outward sign of our faith that good is the power that can overcome any adversity. It demonstrates that no one has control over how we react or think. When we choose joy, we overcome, we win.

Joy is impartial. It exists. It waits for us to find it.

During those glorious spring days, I exchanged greetings with neighbors as I walked. "What a beautiful day!"

We exchanged joy. It did not embarrass us. We didn't hide our smiles, our light steps, our happiness.

In all things, events, and places, let's find the joy that waits for us and share it. It heals hearts and minds and wins over anything that tries to steal our happiness.

Imagine a world where we sorted our life by how delighted we are and how much joy we can feel at any given moment.

Play the song! Once those lyrics get into your head, they are stuck there. And that is a splendid thing!

The universe laughed at me as I wrote this. I stopped writing this book to jot down something I needed to buy at the store on the shopping pad that I always use.

What I never noticed before was that there was a word at the top of the pad.

Guess what it said. The word was *Joy*.

Yes, joy was waiting for me all along, as it is for you.

All we have to do is notice it and accept its presence. It's not selfish or sinful to feel and be joy. It's precisely the opposite.

Joy is impartial. It exists. It waits for us to find it. It's the pot of gold at the end of the rainbow. Not illusive. Ever-present. Ours to feel and share.

We all grow best in joy!

ONE HUNDRED TEN

— · —

PERCEPTION RULES

We are what we pretend to be, so we must be careful about what we pretend to be. — Kurt Vonnegut, *Mother Night*

Since perception is the reason and foundation of what we experience, let's go through some very simple examples of how perception works before we move on.

Remember—there are two modes: Point of View (POV) and State of Mind (SOM). Let's start with point of view.

Have you ever wanted a new car and had a specific brand in mind? Then, wherever you went, you saw that car? Do you think they made more cars like that and then set them out there for you to see?

No, you can easily see that once your POV perception shifted and expanded to allow that information into your awareness, you noticed what was already present.

Remember, perception is a filter, not a creator.

What about SOM? How does it work?

Let's stick with the car theme. Have you ever tried to find your car keys when you were in a rush? You know you put them right on the counter, but they aren't there, and you get more and more panicked and upset as you can't find them. Later, when you have calmed down, you find them exactly where you left them, right there on the counter.

You were blind to their presence in that rushed and worried state of mind. This is called Perception Blindness.

Now, in the middle of that rush and worry if you would say to yourself and completely embrace the point of view that nothing is ever lost because what we are today calling the Master Gardener, which fills all space, cannot lose anything—and relax into that awareness, that state of mind—and listen to the voice within that guides, at that moment the key's presence may become crystal clear.

I could tell you countless stories of doing just that and then, without conscious thought, walking straight to the item I thought I had lost. Once, after missing my keys for days and searching the entire house, I stopped looking for my keys. Instead, I sat still, letting in the idea of the omnipresence of Infinite Intelligence. I paused, observed, and listened.

Within minutes, I walked to our front porch and, without thinking about it, stuck my hand down into the watering pot I kept there. It did not surprise me to find my keys inside where my youngest daughter, who was two at the time, had put them.

Here's an example of a POV perception and a SOM perception not matching, and one I know all of us experience at least once in a while.

Let's say that our point of view we have chosen is that we have all that we need at every moment. Ah, sounds good. Then we sit down to pay bills. Even before we begin, our state of mind perception often shifts. And if we perceive ourselves to be in a lean time, then as we pay our bills, our state of mind may go from mild discomfort to deep fear.

Once again, remember, perception is a filter, not a creator. No matter what your point of view or state of mind is, it does not create or change anything within the big R Reality of the Master Gardener.

This is a relief because that means the only "job" we have is to shift our perception.

Which brings me to the idea of frozen focus.

Since *what we perceive to be reality magnifies* if we freeze our focus on what is not working, what do we get? More of what is not working.

Don't choose a perception that is frozen on the tiny pinpoint of what is not working. Instead, expand your perception into an awareness of the allness of the Infinite, where everything is already perfect.

When I first wrote the Blooming Your Life course, I was alternating between hours working at my desk to hours working in our yard. It was very early spring, and there was much to be done to prepare the plants for blooming. I had to rake up the leaves I had piled on for winter protection and pick up lots of limbs of trees that had fallen during the winter.

Uncovering hidden perceptions is much the same. We design our lives through conscious and unconscious points of view and states of mind. Uncovering them and keeping only those we wish to experience is part of preparing to grow.

So now we are standing on common ground. The soil is ready for us! We understand perception a bit more, and we have chosen our intent—to grow and bloom profusely.

We are prepared to grow!

ONE HUNDRED ELEVEN

— • —

PRACTICAL BLOOMING: STEP TWO

T$he greatest happiness of life is the conviction that we are loved—loved for ourselves, or rather, loved in spite of ourselves.*
— Victor Hugo

Learning to love ourselves is the focus of these questions. Let it be true that the unique spiritual blessing that you are is a wonderful thing. It's what you are here to do. We need you to do it. Bloom as yourself! It's the place where you grow best!

Remember, these questions are not one and done. Blooming as your USB is a life's work. But like every well-tended garden, it gets more beautiful every year.

1. What is it I can't stop myself from doing?
2. What did I do when I was young that I loved to do?
3. What is it I do that is easy for me?
4. What is my effect on other people?
5. Reviewing my life, I see this was the common element in everything that I did.
6. This is my Unique Spiritual Blessing
7. What is my frozen focus?
8. Is this frozen focus true?
Yes — Not Sure — No

ONE HUNDRED TWELVE

RENEE: STEP TWO

Today I decided to forgive you. Not because you apologized or because you acknowledged the pain that you caused me, but because my soul desires peace. — Najua Zebain

Renee didn't like the question, "What can't you stop yourself from doing?" Renee figured whatever it was, it was probably something she shouldn't be doing. She already felt guilty most of the time. She wanted no more of that.

Besides feeling guilty, Renee also felt as if she was always mad at herself for what she couldn't stop doing. She couldn't stop herself from overeating, sleeping too much, and watching too much TV.

So after reading the question, Renee spent a few days berating herself for her inability to stop herself from doing what she didn't want to do in the first place.

On the third day of looking at the questions, it occurred to Renee that perhaps she was approaching the question from the wrong perception. She believed she enjoyed eating, sleeping, and watching TV too much because it gave her pleasure.

But then, maybe, in the long run, these overindulgences didn't give her pleasure, didn't bring her joy. They only made her mad at herself.

And that realization made Renee look at the question again. *That can't be what the question means,* Renee thought.

So Renee reworded the question for herself. She asked herself what she couldn't stop herself from doing that always made her happy, even if she didn't think it was valuable or others didn't like that she did it.

The first thing she thought of was how much pleasure she got from making things better. Which often drove other people crazy. But she had to admit that she loved doing it and often did it despite what other people felt about it.

Perhaps I only need to learn to do it more gracefully and always make sure that I am not interfering with other people's lives, Renee thought.

Once Renee answered truthfully that she would love it, she knew she was on the right track.

After that, she started paying more attention to what she always enjoyed doing. Sometimes it was simple things like doodling (*don't doodle on your tests,* Renee heard a teacher from long ago say), and she smiled. Yes, she loved doodling.

Renee had a long list of things she loved doing by the end of the week. Things she had told herself to stop doing because either other people didn't like them, or she thought that because they were so easy for her to do, they weren't important.

The idea that she might have gotten it backward, that Life gave her those gifts and wanted her to do them, brought her joy. She decided to look at how to do more of the joyful things, which gave her a lot less time to do the things that brought her temporary relief from what she was realizing had been a boring life.

It was a life she had accepted as her own. But not anymore. She would start growing where she grew best, doing what she loved to do. And she couldn't wait to find out what that would be.

ONE HUNDRED THIRTEEN

STEP THREE: MOVE YOURSELF IF NECESSARY

ONE HUNDRED FOURTEEN

MOVING TO THRIVE

If seeds in the black earth can turn into such beautiful flowers, what might not the heart of man become in its long journey toward the stars? — C. K. Chesterton

Have you ever said to someone, "Why do you stay in that job, relationship, or situation? Why don't you leave?"

Perhaps someone has said it to you. The answer is always the same, no matter what words they use. "I would if I could, but I can't."

Here's the problem. Usually, "bad" or abusive situations are not evident at first. Or we didn't know ourselves well when we first chose the location. So we settle in, put down some roots, and then discover we have been planted where we will not thrive.

Bad situations are always abusive. Abusive situations sap our life and desires from us. They change our point of view and, of course, our state of mind.

Actually, that is the intention of an abusive situation. If we have no life or hope left, we will stay to get more abuse.

Abuse takes many forms.

It is not only physical abuse, but also verbal abuse, yelling, demanding, and degradation.

This abuse is not always from the outside in. It is often from the inside out.

We are all abusive to ourselves in the name of trying to "be good." It is impossible to be as good as the abusive voice in our head—which is not us—claims we must be.

To escape from this situation and find freedom, we must return to the perception we began this garden walk with—because we all know now that *what we perceive to be reality magnifies.* Perception has a guarantee of delivery. It will work in our favor rather than against us when we choose and act from the Reality we wish to experience.

Here's our point of view:

There is only omnipresent Good. Therefore, we are good now and experiencing good now. What appears as not good is the illusion that good is not present.

We have never left omnipresent Good. We have never been less than perfect. We have never been stupid, evil, or bad.

In what we call the big R Reality—which is the Truth of our being—the "bad" story we have been telling ourselves has never been told.

Beginning with this point of view and bringing our state of mind into harmony with it, we can move ourselves if necessary.

When someone else cannot move themselves because they are lost in the worldview's illusion of not enough, or drowning in sorrow, we can rent the van, drive the car, pack the boxes, hold their hand, and stand by them until they regain the sense of themselves.

However, if we force them to move, we are the abuser. See the difference?

Begin with what is True. That will always adjust the situation, and solutions will become obvious.

We can never discover what is good by studying bad and remaining in it. When we begin with good, we can easily see what is wrong. Then we can correct it because by standing with good and in good, we have the strength to move away from what is not good for us. In good, we find the courage to ask for help when we need it.

Once we put down roots into where we do not bloom well, it may feel hard to dig ourselves up and move. Yes, it may—no, it will—be disruptive. Digging out and moving a plant requires some effort. Dirt flies all over the place. Some roots may get left behind. New holes must be dug and old ones filled.

Trust the process of the perception of all good. The disruption will pass, and the sooner we let go and stop holding on to what was and never will be, the easier the re-potting and planting will become.

All newly planted plants must be well watered and well taken care of. When you move yourself, be kind to yourself. Make sure that the basics of your care are handled. There is no need to worry about immediately producing huge blooms. They will come.

While working in the garden one spring, I noticed a plant we had planted in the fall looking very bedraggled. I asked the plant if it would prefer to move to a different place in the yard.

I am constantly moving plants. They need me to do it for them. But you don't.

You can choose to learn more about yourself and your preferences. You can recognize your own seasons of life and move yourself. Of course, this doesn't necessarily—or often—mean moving physically, but move what you do and how you do it.

If what you learn about yourself doesn't feel right, look again. Turn from what others expect of you, what life has required of you, and listen within to yourself and your true feelings and desires.

Once you have found a more comfortable environment, thriving becomes easier.

This step asks us to do something that we often resist doing, even if we know we need to do it order to thrive. But as you make that choice for yourself, it makes it easier for others to do the same. Move yourself if necessary. In the end, you will be glad you did.

Some plants bloom immediately. Others take time. Trust the process. But move yourself if necessary. And sometimes we don't have to move at all, the situation can change, and we are no longer in the wrong place.

One Hundred Fifteen

— • —

Recognizing Abuse

I<i>t is no exaggeration to say that every human being is hypnotized to some extent, either by ideas he has uncritically accepted from others, or by ideas he has repeated to himself or convinced himself are true.</i> —Maxwell Maltz

Because it is sometimes hard to recognize abuse, and it is so imperative to do so, I am including this chapter from *Living In Grace: Chapter 10: Obsessive Vigilance* in this book.

Recognizing abuse in all its forms, even before it becomes abusive, is something we all need to become masters of. And abuse always involves a form of hypnotism. So knowing how that works can stop it before it starts.

When I was in my first year of college, my philosophy teacher gave us the Four Steps of Hypnotism. If we analyze these, we can see how we have agreed to participate in our own hypnotism, or how we succumb to the master hypnotists, our culture, and the worldview.

1. Agree to play by their rules.

This first step is so important. We agree to take part in someone else's stated rules. This is consent. Consent in any culture constitutes contagion. We know it as the power of suggestion.

In October 1998, Oprah staged a demonstration on her show. She told her audience as they were waiting for the show to begin that they were going to release a strong odor. They were told this repeatedly. Although they never released an odor, some of the audience members gave detailed descriptions of what it smelled like.

We agree constantly to the rules that our families, friends, and the world have made. What makes them true? Nothing at all, except our agreement. We have agreed to play by "their" rules in order to fit in and survive.

2. Agree to something that you know is not true.

The stereotypical hypnotist tells patients they are sleepy. They agree even if it is not true. How many times daily do we agree to something we know is not true? For example, an overwhelming number of us have agreed that there is not enough—of anything. We believe and accept the worldview of lack. We don't have enough time, money, love, patience, joy, peace, food, pleasure, understanding...Yes? And yet, in the core of our being, we know this is not true.

Even if we have had only the briefest glimpse of God's State of Grace, we know that there is an infinite amount of everything. In every glimpse of God, we gain a deeper conviction that the Infinite Loving One is All, and as Its reflection, we have all that It is.

3. Turn your thought inward.

This is a surprising part of hypnotism, but on closer analysis, the truth of it appears. What the hypnotist is asking us to do is close our eyes and become alone. When we pull back and turn inward to where we no longer feel the connection to others, we have separated ourselves from Divine Love. In this state of mind, we isolate ourselves, thinking no one would understand.

We hide in our homes and our bodies so that we will not have to participate or come out and play. When things get worse, instead of seeking help outside ourselves, we retreat, hoping no one will notice. Actually, we believe that no one is noticing, and that's why we retreat. Like babies who think they are hidden when they cover their eyes, we think that when we can't see out, no one can see in.

This state of mind keeps us from seeking both physical and spiritual assistance. Hypnotic suggestion gains power when we are isolated.

4. Agree not to do something that you know you can do.

Finally, our hypnotist says something like, "You can't raise your arm." We agree even though we know we can raise it. Think back. What did you love to do as a child that you thought you were pretty good at? Did anyone ever tell you either that you couldn't do it or that it just wasn't done the way you wanted to do it, and you agreed?

When I started college, I thought about being an architect. A counselor actually took me around the college and showed me the rooms where the architects were studying, so that I could see that they were all men. He also reminded me that my weakness was math, and of course, I would need a lot of that. Without a fight, I backed off and switched to interior design. This turned out not to be what I wanted, and I continued to switch majors for a while, looking for what felt right. It might have been architecture if someone had encouraged me, or if I had not already agreed that I could not do it.

Let's wake up to Truth. To correct a habit or move into Truth does not involve more hypnotism. Using hypnotism to cure something is like altering a shadow. It is trying to solve what appears as a physical problem with another, even deeper physical problem. Let's add more light to whatever appears as a problem. We are waking out of our darkness and moving into light, not fixing a symptom.

Break the spell.

To break a spell, whether cast intentionally or unintentionally, we must first recognize that it is not a spell at all. It is only a suggestion, an illusion. It has no power but the power we give it by believing in its reality. Remember, since there is only One power—God—then there is no reason to fear another power that actually does not exist.

If someone says we can't do something, we don't have to agree. We start first with who we truly are—each of us is the expression of Divine Mind. We listen to the Angel Ideas' guidance as to our motivation. We declare what we know to be True, and the spell is broken.

Sometimes the hardest thing to do is to continue stating and believing that we do know even when it feels like we don't. Repeating to ourselves "I don't know" puts us into the hypnotic mental state of not knowing.

Wake up. State that you do know. Don't continue to fall into the loop of untrue suggestions. In the core of yourself, you know. There is no other Truth.

Since we are the Am in I Am, we do know. When the spell is broken, we will remember.

Do not believe what your teacher tells you merely out of respect for the teacher.—Buddha

445

ONE HUNDRED SIXTEEN

— • —

YOU CAN REWRITE THE PAST

The universe is made of stories, not of atoms. — Muriel Rukeyser

When I was a teenager, I alternated between happiness and depression. When I was depressed, I wrote poems about depression and left them around where I was sure my mom would see them since I believed that much of my unhappiness was my parents' fault.

Perhaps all teenagers think it's their parents' fault that they are unhappy. But we are adults now and able to take full responsibility for our own happiness.

To shift our past perceptions affecting our current happiness, we can "revisit" scenes from the past and see them through fresh eyes.

Instead of the person we were then, we can be the wiser awareness that we are now.

Don't worry about which scene from the past is the most important; just take the one that occurs to you now and re-see it. Rewrite it.

Visit it now as an aware adult who understands that Divine Love has always been present.

See it with the Truth that you have never been abandoned, betrayed, or damaged.

Yes, I know that because our human nature is often fixated on the negative, we may want to remember what wasn't good. However, if we want to be happy, we need to rewrite the script.

It is not changing Truth. It is re-seeing what happened as a lie about the Truth.

You'll get better at this as you let go of the idea that what happened was real and must be suffered for or paid for. It's not, and it doesn't.

What can you lose? Try out a scene and see what happens.

Move on to the next one. Would you rather be right about the past or happy in the present? You choose.

ONE HUNDRED SEVENTEEN

— • —

HABITS AND HAPPINESS

Facts do not cease to exist because they are ignored. — Aldous Huxley

Every week for over six years, I made up a big pot of mixed spices, nuts, fruit, and grains that Del and I enjoy eating. I used a Teflon-coated pot and a spoon that wouldn't scratch the Teflon coating for the first four years. The spoon was the perfect height for the pot.

Then Del bought me a new pot. It wasn't Teflon, and it was six inches taller than the first one. However, I continued to use the same spoon, even though it meant I had to reach down into the pot to get the spoon to work.

Then one day, that spoon was dirty, so I picked up a long metal spoon, stuck it in the pot, and started stirring. It was the perfect spoon, the perfect height, for that new pot.

It took me two years to stop using something that no longer worked for the situation and switch to something that did. I was stuck in an unthinking habit.

On a visit to my mom, we decided to watch a football game together. It meant that we couldn't go to a movie that she wanted to see because she would miss the beginning of the game.

No amount of persuasion would get her to agree to let us record the game so that we could do both. Why? Because in her world, we should only watch football live—commercials and all.

I wanted to change her mind, but she was happy with her habit. I had to choose to change my idea about what I wanted her to want, which, in truth, I resisted mightily, so I wasn't happy. I forgot to choose happy.

One year, I had to make an alternative choice about what I wanted to do each morning. I have always told myself that because mornings are my favorite time, that is the only time of the day I can write.

However, I found a Pilates class I wanted to take three mornings a week, and Del needed me to help him with his Taiji class that he taught two mornings a week. And since one morning was a morning we coached, that left only one morning a week to write—if I could only write in the morning.

I had to make a choice. I could choose not to do the classes. That choice didn't make me happy. I could choose not to write, except one morning a week. That choice didn't make me happy.

I could choose to change my mind about when I can write. That choice made me happy. It also proved to be much easier than I thought. So during that time of other morning obligations, I wrote at all times, fitting it between everything else I was doing.

When Del taught that early morning Taiji class, people would tell us they couldn't come to the class because it was too early in the morning. They were in the habit of getting up later.

Because it is so much easier to see the obvious set of choices for other people than the ones we make for ourselves, I kept wanting to convince them that, of course, they could change that habit.

This is where my habit was getting in the way. My habit of thinking that what makes me happy would make others happy.

We all get to choose what we want to do that makes us happy.

However, here's the deal with the spoon and the pot and the change of time about writing—too often, we don't notice what is working and what is not working.

This is where pausing and examining if what we did before is what works for us now is valuable. This way, we can consciously choose the activity and resources that mean the most to us and not default to an old habit that no longer serves us.

Choices and habits. Let's be clear about the ones we are making. Choose the ones that make us happy and let others make the choices that make them happy.

Simple, right?

One Hundred Eighteen

Think Like A Sunflower

*D*on't be seduced into thinking that that which does not make a profit is without value. — Arthur Miller

When their season was over, I pulled out the peas I had diligently planted and tended and discovered a sunflower.

I smiled at it, wondering how it got there. Perhaps a bird or a squirrel or even the wind left a single seed to grow sheltered and nourished by the peas.

It smiled back at me, its bright yellow face bobbing in the wind, and said, "It's so easy to be me."

"Well, of course, it is," I said—out loud because no one was around to hear me talking to a sunflower.

"You know what you are from the beginning. Everything you are is contained in your seed, which is amazing if you think about it. All a plant needs are the right conditions to grow. That's its impulse. To grow and thrive."

"What makes you so different?" The sunflower asked, and then left me to think my thoughts as she raised her face to the sun and danced in the wind. She was done talking.

It's a great question.

What makes us different from the rest of nature that becomes what it is with ease? A duck doesn't try to be a fox. A rose doesn't want to be an oak tree.

Perhaps it's our freedom to choose.

And within the freedom of choice, we make life hard. We accept that life is about getting things, becoming somebody, earning a living, and proving our worth.

We try to be something other than what we are. We conclude that things that are easy for us to do can't be worth much.

It's a strange worldview we have agreed to accept. If it's not hard to do, it's not worth it. If we aren't suffering, we don't deserve it.

These beliefs cause immense pain and stress because we believe doing what is easy for us to be and do doesn't count. Instead, it has become easy not to do what is easy for us to do. It has become easy to forget who we are and what we express in the world is contained in our "seed," just as it is within the sunflower.

As a child, I knew myself as a writer. Yet, as an adult, I ran away from it for years because people told me I could never make money as a writer. As if that was the reason to write in the first place. Or if nobody reads what I write, it doesn't have any value.

I also knew myself as a dancer. I would dance at night in my room after everyone went to bed, singing little songs to myself. But that didn't mean I didn't have to work at becoming a decent dancer. Years of daily classes. Years of practice to learn how to express well what was easy for me to be. But I loved it because it was who I was.

The same goes for writing. Although I knew myself as a writer, it doesn't mean I was born good at it. Every day I work at becoming a better one. I take classes, go to conferences, study programs, and listen to podcasts. And I read a lot of books. (Seriously, reading is a must for a writer and has to be the one thing that makes me say at least once a week, "I have to read," and laugh because it is one of my favorite things to do.)

Just as the sunflower needed all the right conditions to grow and thrive, our "working at" whatever is easy for us to be provides us with all the right conditions. We have the same impulse as all of life—to grow and thrive.

What is easy for you to be? What has always been easy for you? That's the valuable gift to the world that you offer. Choose that and then do the work to be good at it, for the joy and freedom of being yourself.

One more thing. Why not look at everything you do and ask yourself, "How can I make this easier?"

This question alone, asked a few times a day, opens up imagination and curiosity, and breaks the habit of accepting the false worldview that life is hard or not worth it.

Make the sunflower's words your words. Say, "It's so easy to be me."

And then perhaps lift your face to the sun, sway with the wind, and smile. It's easy to do. And that's how it's supposed to be.

ONE HUNDRED NINETEEN

— · —

PRACTICAL BLOOMING: STEP THREE

After you answer these questions, why not spend a little time, and rewrite a story that you have believed to be true. We know that memory is fluid. Nothing is as we remembered. So why not re-remember something, and write a new story for it? Make it a good one.

Note: This is not a writing assignment. Grammar, punctuation, and full sentences are unnecessary. This story is only for you. Don't let the editor-mind take over and try to write the story. Use your imagination.

1. Whose fault is it that I am unhappy?
2. Why?
3. Is that true?
4. What situation would I like to leave or change?
5. Why?
6. What are the reasons I can't leave or change it?
7. What does the voice in my head say about me?
8. This is how I would describe my perfect blooming life.

(Don't forget, if you want a workbook, you can find it in the resource chapter. Otherwise, be sure to comment on your answers in a journal of some kind.)

One Hundred Twenty

Renee: Step Three

A single act of kindness throws out roots in all directions, and the roots spring up and make new trees. — Amelia Earhart

Renee wanted to answer that it was everyone else's fault that she was unhappy. She could prove it, too. The daily news was terrible. The work that she was doing was not satisfying.

She didn't feel appreciated by anyone, and more than one person she worked with picked on her. Plus, she was sure that people laughed at her behind her back because she didn't always understand what they wanted from her.

She didn't like her neighbors either. She thought they were all judging her.

All of it made her think she should move. She could get a new job and find another, more welcoming, place to live. After all, this happiness step was to move yourself if necessary.

Which meant she had to ask herself if it was necessary. What if she was the cause of it all? What if everything she thought was wrong started with her perception of the people, places, and things around her?

Was it their fault she was unhappy? Could she choose to be happy now? Would it make a difference?

Renee took out the list she had started about what made her happy. It wasn't very long. How could so few things make her happy?

Perhaps much of her unhappiness stemmed from not knowing who she was or what she wanted to do with her life. And as hard as she thought about it now, there was nothing in her head about what that could be.

So even if it would be a good idea to move herself, where would she go? If she didn't know what made her happy, how could she make the right choice?

Yes, she told herself. *I am in an abusive situation. But it's not someone else that's doing it. It's me that's doing it to myself.*

Taking out her workbook, Renee started answering all the questions. At first, she judged her answers and got stuck.

Then she decided to set aside the judgment and just write what came to mind. Perhaps something in that stream of consciousness would lead her to what her perfectly blooming life would look and feel like.

In the meantime, she would think like the sunflower. Yes, she was buried behind other plants and sitting in a pile of weeds, but she could still enjoy being herself.

Renee started laughing at that idea. Enjoy being herself? That was a novel idea. It would be interesting to observe, not judge, what grew out of that point of view.

If, after getting to know herself, and observing her interactions with people, showed her it was time to move, at least she'd have a better idea about where to go from there.

ONE HUNDRED TWENTY-ONE

STEP FOUR: FEED YOURSELF THE BEST FOOD POSSIBLE

ONE HUNDRED TWENTY-TWO

WE ARE WHAT WE EAT

Every one of us needs to show how much we care for each other and, in the process, care for ourselves. — Princess Diana

We cheat ourselves by cutting corners and choosing quantity instead of quality. We have grown into a "making it easy and having a lot" society. The result is we put minimal effort into the initial stages of projects, which means we must put a massive effort later into fixing it.

Let's go back to gardening. If we put a plant in poor soil because "who has the time to get that right, besides what difference will that make," and then not water it or feed it, can we expect our plants to grow well, if at all?

Yet, that is our habit in today's society.

Yes, I can be literal and say feed yourself with the best food possible, and we may all stop eating so much nutritionally useless food. I didn't say none of it, but for sure, less of it.

But food means more than literal food. What about what we think about, study, read, watch, spend time on, and hang out with. What about that food?

All plants have different kinds of soil in which they grow best. When we fertilize them, we pick the type that matches who they are. The same applies to our food and how we "eat" it. We are each individual, and we know what is best for us within ourselves. We just don't trust ourselves to listen and act on that wise little voice within.

Let's go back to the idea of perception. My "signature" statement is what you have heard throughout this book—*what you perceive to be reality magnifies.*

This is absolutely true. There is no wiggle room. It has a GOD: *Guarantee Of Delivery.*

It makes sense then to make paying attention to our perceptions a priority. What are they? How are they formed?

We formed many of our perceptions unconsciously. We "inherited" them from parents, the environment, school, and things that happen to us. A soup can fell on our heads when we were three, and we hate soup forever after. That perception shuts the door on any other information about soup, cans, doors opening, and things following.

We have to choose to be conscious, become aware, and be willing to shift our unaware, false, and limiting perceptions and let go of anything that isn't fitting into the infinite perception—my choice and hopefully yours—that good is omnipotent and omnipresent.

When we eat junk perception food, digest it, and hang on to it, we are not building that cool, "I can be happy" perception. We are feeding ourselves small r reality junk perceptions, and then, it's true, "we are what we eat."

What we *perceive—eat—to be reality magnifies* and becomes the life we experience.

Feed yourself the best perceptions you can find. Keep upgrading. This kind of food costs nothing except letting go of false ideas about who you are, which is actually a freedom and not a cost.

ONE HUNDRED TWENTY-THREE

— • —

CONSCIOUSLY CHOOSE HAPPINESS

The smallest fact is a window through which the infinite may be seen. — Aldous Huxley

In *step three*, we asked ourselves, "Whose fault is it that I am unhappy? Why? And is that true?"

We often feel as if someone or something else has done something that has caused us to be unhappy.

We can be unhappy because of our jobs, income, parents, spouses, children, living conditions, health issues, too much or too little money, governments, terrorists, mosquitoes, too hot or too cold—okay, you and I know I could go on with this list forever.

Nevertheless, doesn't everyone face most of these issues at one time or another, and yet some people are always happy, anyway?

So if we have to assign fault to anyone, it really must come back to us.

This is actually good news because it makes it easier to be happy since we don't have to fix anyone or anything else.

All we have to do is shift our own perception to an awareness and acceptance of happiness. It sounds easy enough, but we all have experienced times when happiness felt entirely out of our reach. Times when we have felt so unhappy, we couldn't remember what makes us happy.

This is where a happiness list of why and what makes us happy comes in handy.

I made my first list one day when I was sitting in a cafe and realized that I was happy for the first time in weeks.

I grabbed a piece of paper and a pen and started writing what made me happy so that if I forgot, I could get out that list and remember.

There were simple things on that list, starting with sitting in a good cafe by myself, and then I added reading a good book, going to the movies, getting a child to smile at me, etc.

None of what was on that first list and following lists were "profound." They were all simple activities. I kept that list, and every time I felt unhappy, I did something on the list. It always worked.

As I expanded my awareness of the quality of happiness, I rarely needed to look at the list anymore, but it was a great place to start.

Once upon a time, when women were birds,
there was the simple understanding that
to sing at dawn and to sing at dusk
was to heal the world through joy.
The birds still remember
what we have forgotten,
that the world is meant to be
celebrated. — Terry Tempest Williams

One Hundred Twenty-Four

— • —

Happy To Want Less

S implicity of life, even the barest, is not a misery, but the very foundation of refinement. — William Morris

Once upon a time, a coach I was working with told me I could be another Tony Robbins.

I said no. I had no desire to be the person I would have to become to do that.

He didn't understand, and not long after that told me he couldn't work with me anymore. Well, his actual words were he couldn't help me anymore.

I suppose, in his mind, I was beyond help.

But it wasn't that. What he wanted for me, I didn't want for myself. And not for one second have I ever regretted that decision. But what did I want?

Less. And more.

Less need. More grace.

Having worked in the financial industry for years, I knew that all the money in the world, the biggest house, the biggest company, couldn't buy grace. Didn't bring happiness.

We find grace and happiness elsewhere. And once found, wealth doesn't rob us of them; it serves them.

As the world is in reset mode and people decide whether kindness is more important than winning, most of us are also resetting our wants, needs, and priorities.

But, when it is all over, what will we go back to? Do we have to choose overwhelm?

For me, in that moment when I said no, I decided to want less and be happier. But I still constantly re-examine exactly what that means for me.

It doesn't mean I don't plan on doing more. Happiness and expansion are not exclusive. It's how it's done.

Expansion and sharing are the essences of life. From the expansion of the universe to the continual growth of a forest, we understand that to be true. All life expands. But nothing in nature does it by itself. Each element intertwines within the whole.

All our lives are also intertwined. My need can not override yours. My expansion can not destroy yours. And the way we each expand is personal and uniquely individual.

I expand and share as a turtle, and I am happy to be one.

Every day I write a little of the next book. Edit the one I just finished. Record the audio of the book before that. Edit that recording. Learn something new. Spend time on ads and marketing. Coach. Teach classes. Work on websites and merchandise.

And I also work in the garden, walk, do yoga and pilates, make a meal or two, read, watch TV, talk to Del, check in with family.

Step by step, plodding along. Wanting less, being more happy. But still with big dreams about what I want to do in life.

Nelson Mandela said, *It always seems impossible until it's done.*

It's all about intent. The goal and the to-do list follow. They don't drive the action; they are the action.

Did I want to be the next Tony Robbins? No.

But I did, and do, want to shift people's perceptions and lives towards the infinite. That's my intent. That's my mission. That's the dream I follow. How big or small that becomes is not what is essential.

Doing it well is.

We don't have to choose overwhelm. We can walk away from it. We can want less. And still do more—in our own way.

Be the next Tony Robbins, or Oprah, or Steve Jobs, if that is your calling. I'll be rooting for you. But do it your way and don't give up the essence of your life to do it. It won't be worth the price.

And every day, each of us has to ask ourselves the same question. "What is more important in this moment, and will it be kind and helpful to others?"

If we do that, we may find ourselves in that state of mind called heaven on earth. And really, what could be more important than that?

One Hundred Twenty-Five

Choose Consciously

*C*hildren *have never been very good at listening to their elders, but they have never failed to imitate them.* — James Baldwin

Part of choosing consciously is becoming aware of what we have already chosen or accepted as our choice when it really isn't. Either it's come from a worldview, or from a local view, like parents, teachers, friends, and trying to fit it.

Eventually, we need to make our own choices to live as our unique spiritual blessings. Design our own perceptions and choose our own point of view and state of mind.

This is a simple exercise to help you do that. I use I Choose sheets in every class and mention them in almost every book in *The Shift Series*. Why? Because doing them makes an enormous difference. They don't take much work. It is not necessary to study them, keep them around, or worry about them. Just do them. And then let go.

This is what that looks like taken from the book *Perception Mastery*.

I choose, therefore I am. — Amit Goswami

Did you know there's a voice in your head constantly telling you why you can't do something? This voice is called many things: the monkey voice, the ego, the shadow—whatever you call it, it's imperative to know and understand one thing. That voice is not your voice. I know it sounds like you, and it says things you think you might say to yourself, but it's not.

So, why is it there?

That's like asking why do we believe we are human. Who knows? At this point, it's all someone's story. Believe them or not, it changes nothing.

Here's what we do know, and it does change things. The voice in our head runs the paradigm we think we must live within, and unless we know what it is saying to us, we are stuck in its prison. It drives the car we call our life. It has us choosing things we may or may not want anymore, or perhaps never wanted.

However, we have free will, so let's put that freedom to work.

Let's find out what that voice is saying and then replace it with what we consciously choose. Being willing, becoming aware, and consciously choosing breaks open our current paradigm. It shifts our perception. And as a result, the world we experience shifts to match our new perception.

Remember, perception is reality. *What we perceive to be reality magnifies.*

Therefore, since we can make conscious choices, let's shift our perception to the best version of what I call big R Reality that we can get to right now. Which, for me, and perhaps for you, is a gloriously Loving One Intelligent Reality, because that's the one I want to experience.

Now that we know what we would consciously choose, let's do an I Choose sheet. Doing this is so simple it might seem ineffective. However, I promise you it works if you do it.

Here we go:

Get out a tablet of paper and a pen. Notice I didn't say get your computer. I love writing on my computer. But I Choose sheets work much better when they are handwritten. Besides, when you finish with one, you can burn it. Very satisfying. Or write in a tablet and then clear the page when you are finished.

Begin by stating what you want as a choice.

How do you know what you want? Look back in this book and choose one of the things that makes you happy.

After that, there are just two steps to learn.

- First, pause, and listen for the voice in your head telling you why you can't have it or why it won't work.

I guarantee you that the voice is there. Don't worry. It can't hurt to hear it now. In fact, you want to listen to what it's been telling you all along, and you have been accepting as true.

Once you hear that voice telling you why you can't have what you want, don't write what that voice says. Please don't give it any power by agreeing with it.

- Next, choose and write the opposite of what it's saying. I call this "face and replace."

Face what it says, and replace it with what you consciously choose.

That's it … just keep going until there is nothing left to face and replace. It may take pages and pages. After you are done, there is no need to keep the pages around!

ONE HUNDRED TWENTY-SIX

—·—

PRACTICAL BLOOMING: STEP FOUR

*P**erfection is like chasing the horizon. Keep moving.* — Neil Gaiman

Think of this as a clearing out of your closets and cupboards. Just as you might say, I don't eat this anymore, or I don't wear this anymore. This is an "I don't think or live this anymore" cleaning out.

If you aren't sure you don't want it, go ahead and keep it. But put it aside to be examined later. Don't put the cans of food, the clothes, or old perceptions back in the same place. Store them somewhere you can observe them after some time has passed.

Make your life an endless series of "Spring Cleaning," and let go of what is not working.

Think of it as a gift to yourself, and have fun. Please do your best to enjoy the mess it might make at first, knowing that everything will feel better once it's done.

1. I notice that I have "inherited" these perceptions.
2. Observing my life, I see I have these unconscious perceptions.
3. I realize I am carrying these perceptions from my past.
4. I am willing to choose my own perceptions. Yes - Not Sure - No
5. I am willing to let go of any perception that does not bloom in my life. Yes - Not Sure - No

6. I choose this point of view perception.
7. I choose to remain in this state of mind perception.
8. This is what makes me happy.
9. Do an I Choose sheet on at least one thing that makes you happy.

Things to do as you make your happiness list:

- See yourself as happy.

- What are you doing?

- What are you thinking?

- Take notes, so you remember.

Thank you for taking this time for yourself. This is feeding yourself the kind of food that will radically change your life.

Once you have answered the questions in your workbook, join me in the next step.

I'll be sitting on my bench under the apple tree, listening to the music and rhythms of nature, and waiting to walk the garden with you.

ONE HUNDRED TWENTY-SEVEN

— • —

RENEE: STEP FOUR

A ll God's angels come to us disguised. — James Russell Lowell

As Renee built her list of things that made her happy, she decided to try a little experiment with her neighbors. Instead of trying to ignore them because she knew they didn't like her, she waved and smiled at them. A part of her got a kick out of it, thinking that if they didn't like her, that would make them anxious, wondering what she was up to.

But she recognized that was just another version of her thinking the world was against her and did her best to let that thought go, and instead chose the POV that cooperation and community existed in her world.

What surprised her was that because her neighbor smiled and waved back, it made it onto her happiness list.

That gave her the impetus to choose to see herself as happy and act as if she was, even if she wasn't. She realized that what she told herself or allowed herself to believe that was negative about people, places, and things didn't give her impetus to change. It only increased her feelings of isolation and unhappiness. She decided they were junk food thoughts.

That day she ran across Albert Einstein's quote, *The ideals which have lighted my way, and time after time have given me new courage to face life cheerfully, have been Kindness, Beauty, and Truth*, and realized those were good food thoughts. She could choose them for herself and see what happened.

Renee still wasn't sure if she needed to move, change jobs, or change homes, but she knew she needed to be healthier in her thinking. She wasn't living in a dangerous situation. Her work was okay, so it was safe to take the time to think and eat better first. For that, she was grateful.

That night, she started writing out what she imagined her perfect life would look like and feel like. She had so few ideas she had to use bits from books and movies to make it up. Renee was sure it wasn't what she really wanted, but she had to start somewhere.

Over time, she could rewrite the story as she got to know herself better. And whatever the voice in her head was trying to tell her, she would tell it to shush. She was done thinking it was telling her the truth. Renee decided to trust her still small voice within instead. The one she hadn't been listening to for a long time, but she could start now.

That thought made her happy. She added it to her happiness list.

ONE HUNDRED TWENTY-EIGHT

STEP FIVE: GROW IN YOUR OWN TIMING

ONE HUNDRED TWENTY-NINE

YOUR TIMING IS PERFECT

I am not a complainer. If I was that type of person, I would be cluttering the path that God has laid out for me, and I wouldn't be able to walk it. — Regina King

Sometimes we are happy, but we act unhappy and don't realize it.

I had a vivacious grandmother who was a lover of life. However, she constantly complained under her breath. I am sure she didn't know she was doing it.

I have a clear memory of her looking under the sink, trying to get something out and the running commentary of her complaining while she was doing it. I do that same thing sometimes. When I am observing myself, I am amazed that it is happening.

She was happy. I am happy. However, if you heard that complaining, would you know?

Family habits! We can dissolve them!

When we complain, either consciously or unconsciously, we reinforce the human-computer program that produces what we perceive as our life.

This program doesn't know that we are happy; it doesn't know we don't mean what we are complaining about.

It hears unhappiness and assumes that is what we want more of, and so it shrinks our perception down to what it thinks we believe, actually reducing the possibilities of our lives.

Or, said more simply: *What we perceive to be reality magnifies.*

It's up to us to choose a different reality.

I know you either want to, or already have, chosen the point of view of the big r Reality of Infinite Mind. However, the crucial step is to live in big r Reality by consciously choosing the state of mind that reinforces this point of view.

Consciously choose happiness, consciously stay in the state of mind of happiness, and it will reveal what is already true—that happiness exists because divine Love is.

To help us get to, and stay in, this state of mind, our new habit will be to observe happiness and trust ourselves to see it.

Spend the time to grow a strong root structure.

No matter how quickly or slowly you are doing the work in this book, you may become impatient with the "outside" results.

So let's talk more about being kind to yourself and trusting in your timing.

I thought about these seven simple steps after observing some Narcissus bulbs that I was forcing into bloom so that we could enjoy their beauty along with the snow falling outside.

One year, I put the bulbs in different glass containers on top of rocks, added water, and placed them around our combo kitchen-living room, which is full of light.

Although they all experienced the same conditions, something strange happened.

Within days, one bulb started sending out roots, and the others just sat there. Nothing, nada. I waited for over a week, thinking that they were just different, but still nothing.

Then I started wondering what was different about their living conditions that could cause the delay.

After much pondering, I realized the simple answer was their containers. The bulb that had developed roots was sitting in a fairly shallow container. The others were in a deep one because I thought it would be beautiful to see them grow though the glass.

Do you see what the problem was? It took me a while to figure it out, but then I realized they were getting different amounts of oxygen.

I took all the bulbs out of the deep container and put them all in shallower ones. Within a day, one of them had sent out its roots.

But not all. It took weeks for some of them to grow again after their not-so-perfect first place planting. This goes back to the step - Plant Yourself Where You Grow Best.

Another interesting thing happened. One bulb grew and then bloomed even faster than the first bulb, which had the few weeks' head start.

I love to grow these bulbs in glass containers because it makes it possible to see their beautiful root system. One little root reaches out and touches the water. Discovering support, it is quickly joined by other roots growing so fast you can almost see it happening.

They spread out into the rocks and water to support the growth that is happening above. The leaves and the bloom are the "payoff," but without that root system, they could not grow at all.

Here's what this is all about to me: blooming lives, or not blooming lives.

For each of us to bloom, it is always important to notice where we are planted and decide if we are getting enough "oxygen."

The bulbs needed me to notice their situation and move them. We can not only notice what we need, but move ourselves to a better place to bloom.

We also need deep roots to grow and bloom well and long. Sometimes we question if our lives will ever bloom and forget to notice the beautiful growth of our roots beneath the surface, preparing to support what will become visible.

During a cold snap, the plants that were growing rapidly stopped growing. At least on the surface. They were increasing their root system while they waited for the warm weather to return.

Timing is different for each of us. Some of us are fast growers, but slow bloomers. Others are slow growers, but speedy bloomers.

However, what is true about each of us is that when we give ourselves the support, patience, and substance necessary to bloom, we will bloom—in our own timing.

There is a worldview that if we haven't reached our full potential or bloomed by a certain age, we haven't succeeded. This false perception starts early in life.

We are supposed to talk by a certain age, write by a certain age, speak by a certain age, date, get married by a certain age, have babies, buy a house, and be successful—all by a certain age. The idea of specific blooming periods is all timed out and predetermined by an arbitrary scale, none of which is true or relates to our USB and finding our path.

I always have to stifle a giggle when I hear a teenager or someone in their twenties lamenting that they do not know what they are supposed to be when they grow up.

Be? By that, they mean to be successful at something which we often determine based on the erroneous measurement of money.

What if we measured success by how happy we are? Would there be a time requirement for that? Could money measure it? No!

Although money is a good thing and makes life easier, it is not the source of our happiness.

For most of us, we are too busy doing the outside work of growing branches and leaves that we never take the time to put down deep roots into the soil of our unique self. A self that will absolutely bloom in its proper season if we have given ourselves the time and attention we deserve.

We will also bloom repeatedly. It's not a onetime thing. Each season of life produces unique blooms.

This all goes back to the concept of knowing who you are, valuing it, and following all the steps that we have talked about in this book.

As I write this book, it's spring and I have seeds growing in my kitchen waiting for warmer weather. They are happy sitting on warming pads with a light hanging above them.

My husband and I love stopping by a few times a day to check what has popped out of the ground. And yes, we both talk to them, encouraging them along, telling them how happy we are to see them grow.

Watching the birth of these plants always reminds me that ideas are like that. Some come up right away, bursting out of the ground loudly, others wait and we have to look closely to see that they are there.

Give your ideas water, warmth, light, food... and then... like plants, most of them will grow. You can thin them out later—choosing the ones that will grow best.

Every seed has everything in it that it needs to grow. The same thing is true for each of us.

Be patient, tender, kind, and loving to yourself. Pay attention to what you need, and make sure you provide it. Each step in this process will bring you more ideas and inspiration.

And perhaps, spend a little time thinking about the happiest person you know. Why are they? Perhaps ask them. And if you answer that you are, celebrate that fact. If that's not true yet, keep growing. It will be.

ONE HUNDRED THIRTY

— · —

WHAT THE PAST REVEALS

*H*ofstadter's Law: It always takes longer than you expect, even when you take into account Hofstadter's Law. — Douglas Hofstadter

All winter, the blue storage box sat alone on the garage floor, calling me.

Years before, my husband and I had left it with my daughter for safekeeping on our way to more traveling. When we finished traveling, she returned it, but I didn't open it, knowing it would require something from me I didn't feel ready to do—face all those memories from the past.

Finally, on a beautiful spring day, I opened the blue box. Out came yearbooks, a bunch of videos—destined to be converted to DVDs after tearful watching—my dance thesis, and a gaggle of picture albums.

Underneath all that, I glimpsed the scrapbook that I had once treasured and had thought I had lost. It was a treasure trove of myself from the past. On the first page, I found something I had saved from when I had just graduated from college and, along with my children, was headed off into a new adventure. I was leaving the dance world (mostly) behind and heading into the business world. Scared and excited, but willing.

Also on that first page was a poem by Victor Hugo that I have carried with me for years. And there was a note from my now-grown daughter, written in 5th grade, promising me she would not give me any trouble when she was a teenager. I laughed—happy that she now has her own daughter—and that she had kept her promise the best that any teenager could.

However, the treasure that filled most of the pages were essays from my favorite writers, cut out of magazines and newspapers. They fueled my childhood desire to write and move people the same way those writers moved me.

I read one. It was even better than I remembered. I had to stop looking through the scrapbook for a few days because I was so overwhelmed with the happiness of this discovery.

The scrapbook contains many inspirations that helped me develop my first class on perception, first called *The Power Of Perception* and then *The Shift*, that I began teaching in 1992. Later, I wrote a book based on what I learned teaching that class, and I added those ideas to the scrapbook. I could see little notes to myself telling me on which page of the first draft of the book I had used specific quotes.

The length of time between each of those memories proves to me, once again, that life isn't a disconnected series of events, but it expands as a complete unit, each spiral adding deeper and higher meanings to every event.

It reminds me of our garden. Each year we add more nutrients to the soil, and each year it is a richer environment in which seeds can grow.

Our lives are like that too.

What I was as a child is still here with me now as a grandmother; just more of it, deeper and richer. What I wanted to do, what I believed in then, and wanted to be, is still present, and the scrapbook is my witness.

That book, which first came from the scrapbook, is *Living In Grace: The Shift To Spiritual Perception*. I developed it from a lifetime of observation, listening, and collecting ideas, as contained in that scrapbook, plus much more.

When I finished that book, I thought I had done my job, and that was all the writing I was going to do. Of course, now I know it was only the beginning.

Sometimes it helps to look back and see how the events in our lives unfolded because it helps us remember that we can trust that our lives, properly tended and cared for, unfolds in its own timing bringing even more extraordinary beauty as what we call time moves on.

Be like the bird, who Halting in his flight On limb too slight Feels it give way beneath him, Yet sings Knowing he hath wings. — Victor Hugo

ONE HUNDRED THIRTY-ONE

LIVE YOUR WHY

To laugh often and much; to win the respect of the intelligent people and the affection of children; to earn the appreciation of honest critics and endure the betrayal of false friends; to appreciate beauty; to find the beauty in others; to leave the world a bit better whether by a healthy child, a garden patch, or a redeemed social condition; to know that one life has breathed easier because you lived here. This is to have succeeded. — Ralph Waldo Emerson

The end of this quote has always struck me as the perfect why of being alive. To know even one life has breathed easier because you have lived. This is to have succeeded.

How simple this would make all our decisions if we followed this idea. And although each of us achieves this in our unique way, it can be the perfect "why" for each of us.

However, "the what-or the what's in it for me point of view," is celebrated instead. Get rich, get famous, get, and more get. This is the false manhood come into power, unchecked by true womanhood. It's going after that "what" and not following the "why."

The why, asks us to consider the underlying reason for our sharing our days with each other. What do we most bring into life that means something? What differences do we, and can we, make?

In 1964, Bob Dylan wrote, "The times they are a changing."

As we change, let's make sure that we move away from a false sense of male as conqueror and controller, and into both the true sense of manhood as protector, and action taker, and true womanhood as the guide to wise action.

Let's move into choosing the why as the motivator, not the what.

I am a lover of all design shows. I love watching the design unfold and the contestants find themselves and become more of their unique spiritual blessing. However, sometimes they lose their way. On a fashion design show a few years ago, an additional $10,000 cash prize was announced for the winner of the week's competition.

At which point, one woman in the competition, who previously had done well, stopped being able to create anything. She cried, and worried, and blamed others, and couldn't stop thinking about how much she needed the money.

She had turned into wanting something and completely forgot her why. Her creation, and the process of creating it, was a disaster.

Remembering, and expressing, our why, and not getting caught up in the temptation of the what is a practice. We admire people that don't forget their why. Perhaps we don't always agree, or like what they do, but we admire their clarity and honesty.

The vehicle of expression is not the important part, it's knowing, and expressing, the why that is important.

I watched our family move another member of the family into their new home. I witnessed how each member easily and gracefully worked their why throughout the day, and no one said what's in it for me.

Doors were removed so a refrigerator could come through, plumbing was fixed, new locks were installed, cleaning took place, clothes put away, and beds made so that sleep was possible at the end of the day. Everyone did their part, without division, as one unit working in harmony.

Imagine this happening everywhere, all the time—everyone choosing to make someone else's life easier!

Let's make sure that all our changes are being fully directed by our why, and that why is always based on kindness and respect for all living things. When the why, based on each unique expression of the Divine, is the raison d'être, we all thrive and we all find happiness in the process.

ONE HUNDRED THIRTY-TWO

— · —

PRACTICAL BLOOMING: STEP FIVE

T hank you all for being such faithful tenders of your garden. We are preparing for an abundant harvest, now, and far into the future.

As you answer these questions, think about walking to the open door that has always been there for you. The one that calls to you with love and abundance. Let yourself move to that door. You will know that you are moving towards it by the joy you feel rising in your life.

When you are ready, I will be waiting for you in the garden.

1. What did I learn from my past?
2. How is what I learned nourishing my life now?
3. Where are my current roots?
4. How deep are they?
6. Am I allowing the roots to go deep?
7. Am I rushing the process? Yes - Not Sure - No
9. What ideas am I currently growing?

ONE HUNDRED THIRTY-THREE

— · —

RENEE: STEP FIVE

*H*appiness *is not a matter of intensity, but of balance, order, rhythm, and harmony.*—Thomas Merton

The question, *what did I learn from my past*, threw Renee for a loop. If she really answered what she learned from her past, she could answer that question for days. *Besides,* she asked herself, *what is the past? Does it mean yesterday, or when I was two, or before I was born, or maybe just a minute ago?*

All those things were in the past. *Pick one*, she told herself. *Then go pick another*. So she started with what she had learned a minute ago. That she was very analytical, and that wasn't a bad thing. But it could stop her in her tracks by getting stuck on questions that had either no answer or multiple answers.

Good to know, she said to herself. *Use it correctly, so it serves me. Use that skill when it's helpful and let go of it when it isn't.*

Moving back to something she learned from her mother, she realized she used food as a requirement, comfort, and a reward. With that realization, Renee decided to eat the best food possible when she was hungry and not reward herself with it anymore. Or at least notice when she did.

Observe, don't judge, Renee reminded herself. Otherwise, guilt or shame would make her want to eat more to comfort herself, which would only bring her back full circle.

Each time Renee asked herself what she learned from her past, she realized she had a choice of whether or not to keep that perception. And she could change her mind as she evolved in her understanding of herself and what brought her joy.

Bringing herself to the present, Renee wondered what brought her joy because that was where she wanted to spread her roots. She took out her what-makes-me-happy list to find out.

That's when Renee realized there was something not on the list that always used to make her happy. She loved going to classes and doing things that involved creativity.

Wow, Renee said to herself, *I am happy when I create something. And I like being around other people doing the same thing!*

Does it matter what I create, she asked herself. The answer was she didn't know. But she remembered how much she enjoyed going to art class. She'd start there and see where it took her.

Since she remembered that she learned best in groups, Renee found a local art class and signed up. It was a beginning. She had planted a seed, and she expected it to come up in its own timing and in its own way.

ONE HUNDRED THIRTY-FOUR

STEP SIX: EXPECT TO BLOOM

ONE HUNDRED THIRTY-FIVE

— · —

YES, IT WILL COME UP

The future belongs to those who believe in the beauty of their dreams. —Eleanor Roosevelt

It was spring when I first wrote these seven steps of happiness.

Although I grew up in Pennsylvania, I lived in California as an adult. Every spring, I would say to my family in the east, "Yes, it is spring here too," and they would smile and say, "Hum."

And now that I am back in the east, I know what they meant. The spring in a place where there has been cold and snow for months arrives with more intensity, and the search for spring is a daily activity.

In February, I look for signs of spring, and I find them. The preamble to the season hides within the cold, but it's there.

However, when true spring arrives, it sweeps in like the wind. One day it is dark and dreary, and the next, the trees are wearing gorgeous halos of red and yellow buds.

The daffodils are not visible one day and nodding their golden heads in the breeze the next. You have to carefully observe each day not to miss spring as it bursts forth from winter.

The harbingers and celebrators of spring are the birds. They sing with every fiber of their being, belting out songs with abandon. They glow with happiness.

Yes, this is all about happiness.

Buried beneath what may appear as a winter of unhappiness are the seeds of happiness—just waiting for the warmth of love to burst forth.

I can see each of you on your tree of life, singing of joy with every fiber of your being.

Before the sun comes up, birds begin their dawn chorus. You can start now, too, knowing that nothing can stop the sun, or your happiness—in its multitudes of forms—from rising and being known.

Because it is always within you.

We contain within ourselves, as the bulb and the acorn contain its substance within, all the elements of a beautiful blooming life. Like the bulb and the acorn, we are designed to grow and bloom into our lives as the Unique Spiritual Blessing that we are.

So what stops the process?

Years ago, I heard a fable that has become a favorite of mine because it illustrates so clearly why we often stop expecting to bloom, and in not expecting to, we do not.

At one time, the devil was said to be going out of business. His tools would be for sale to anyone who would pay his price. On the night of the sale, they were all displayed—malice, envy, hatred, jealousy, sensualism, deceit, and all the other implements of evil.

Separate from the rest lay a harmless-looking, wedge-shaped tool. It was much worn and priced higher than any of the others.

When someone asked the devil what it was, he said, "That's discouragement."

"Well, why do you have it priced so high?"

"Because," answered the devil, "it is more useful to me than any of the others because I can pry open and get inside someone's thought with that when I couldn't touch them in any other way. It is so worn because

I use it with nearly everybody, as very few people know that it belongs to me."

"Is there anyone on whom you can't use it?"

The devil hesitated a long time and finally said in a low voice, "I can't use it in a grateful heart."

At the sale, the devil's price for discouragement was so high that it was never sold. The fable concludes, he still owns it, and he is still using it.

When I was a little girl, I had a favorite little book and record that went with it. It was about a boy who had planted some carrot seeds. He waited and waited, but they didn't come up. He expected them to.

However, his brother teased him constantly, saying, "Naw, naw, it won't come up."

How discouraging. This is exactly what the worldview says about living happy lives. "Naw, naw, it won't come up." All the time. It's constant, just like the sibling's constant "Naw, naw, it won't come up."

And since it takes a while for carrot seeds to sprout, it was hard to hold to the fact that they would.

He stared at them every day. Made sure they had the proper soil, light, and water and waited as patiently as he could.

The "Naw, Naw" kept up, and he sometimes rebutted it, sometimes said nothing, but kept on watching for the seeds to sprout.

I have never forgotten that story because of his courage, and vision, and faith. And, of course, those carrots came up. It is within a seed to sprout, and it will when given the right conditions.

There are some other key points here.

The little boy didn't fool around in the soil, checking to see if the seeds had roots. When they began to sprout, he didn't pull them up to see how big the roots were because both actions would have killed this tender sprout.

The same thing is true with ideas. Be careful with whom you share your plans to bloom. Actually, this is one reason we have a thriving a community of like-minded souls shifting from the limited to the unlimited, and is a safe place to share and get help to bloom.

Take care not to worry and fret, which is the same thing as pulling up the roots. Everything that we are talking about, the entire universe of blooming, is happening within.

If fret, worry, doubt, and discouragement are part of your inner world and you haven't yet learned how to shut it down, dissolve it, watch it float by, or at least stop believing it, you will struggle instead of thriving.

It is within you to bloom, given the right conditions. The good news is that these right conditions are all within you now. You have a right to change what everyone else might say are the rules and be happy.

Plants in the wrong situation can't move by themselves.

But we can, and in a very real sense, we must so that others can thrive too.

Without every bulb blooming, the complete picture of the garden is not present. Following this metaphor, each of us blooming is necessary for the garden called God—or Infinite Intelligence, or Divine Order, or Love—to be seen and experienced.

Sometimes, what seems complicated is actually quite simple. These seven steps help us see and live that simplicity.

Can you feel the quality of ease present within the seven steps? Happiness is already present within you. We are shifting our perception to this fact and taking steps to reveal it.

After Will Smith's now-famous misbehavior at the 2022 Oscars, Denzel Washington reminded him that, "At your highest moment, be careful. That's when the devil comes for you."

But that pull to bring us down also happens at our lowest moments.

Being happy for no good reason is a great defense against the "devil."

Choose happiness, my friends. It's an open door to the Divine, the Universe of Infinite Intelligence and Love.

One Hundred Thirty-Six

— • —

Designed To Be Filled

The rain begins with a single drop. — Manal al-Sharif

Have you ever stood in an empty football stadium? The experience of standing in that open space is awe-inspiring. It's a space just waiting to be filled. It's a space that understands its purpose and is perfectly designed to fulfill that purpose.

I had this experience during a high school reunion when we visited the Penn State University football stadium. We took the elevators that are accessed only by a special key to the top level, and stepped out into the empty, light-filled stadium.

Our tour guide shared the history of the stadium's expansion. He took us from its beginning and its move to the present location. Throughout the years, the stadium has expanded in progressive steps, always improving.

It continues its purpose, to provide a space for many people to bring their hopes and dreams, and to make memories. Each step of its expansion has cost time and money, and has involved collaboration between a wide diversity of people and talents.

Instead of closing down and doing less as time moved on, the stadium has expanded and accepted new ideas, providing more space to be filled with the qualities of joy, happiness, expectation, intent, and celebration.

As I stood in that empty stadium and listened to the tour guide, I felt the correlation of the stadium to the way we live our lives. Like the stadium, our lives are also a space designed to be filled. But, unlike the stadium, we are not always clear about our purpose, or willing to fulfill it.

As time moves on, we are often tempted to do less. We stay stuck, or comfortable, in our patterns of beliefs and judgments. But like the stadium, our lives are designed to be filled with ideas, hopes, love, joy, happiness, compassion, intents, caring, gifts, memories, people, and celebration.

Being exclusionary, and shutting down, is counter to our purpose.

Recently, two new digital boards were added to the PSU stadium. This new technology will enable everyone in the stadium to see a clear picture of what is happening on the field. The stadium continues to move with the times, with a cost of time, money, and patience and with a strong willingness to go forward into the future.

Do we do the same? Do we allow our lives to grow and expand so that we can be more of what we have been designed to be? Although our lives are designed to be filled, we are responsible for the expansion that enables that to happen.

As in all things, size doesn't matter. Some people's lives are as full as a stadium; others are smaller and more intimate. But, in all cases, we are the ones who must be willing to expand to allow more ideas and people into our lives. It takes work. Sometimes it takes money. It always takes patience.

However, that has always been our purpose, and in the end, it is what blooms our lives in joy, and where we find fulfillment. Yes, we are designed to be filled with happiness.

ONE HUNDRED THIRTY-SEVEN

LET GO AND RISE

For he shall give his angels charge over thee, to keep thee in all thy ways. — Psalm 91:11

One spring, I hung a suet feeder on a branch of a tree right outside my office. I hung it there because it was visible as I worked at my computer. It was delightful to have the company of birds like woodpeckers, blue jays, nuthatches, titmice, chickadees, and cardinals as they pecked away at the suet.

When I needed to fill the feeder, I would grab a lower branch, pull it toward me and bounce it. That would bring down the branch with the feeder to my level.

As fall approached, I noticed something I had never realized before, but seems perfectly obvious in hindsight. Did you know that as leaves drop off branches, the branches rise? Not just a few inches, they really rise.

One night, as I took the feeder off a branch that had dropped its leaves, it popped back into the air at least five feet. I laughed in delight at my discovery, and in the realization that I would have to find another way to grab the branch!

My imagination took off as I thought of how the tree must feel to be free and clean to begin again, to be able to lift itself up higher into the sunlight. As the trees let go, the display of beautiful color and raining leaves is stunning. It's not a sad time, it is a season of harvest and abundance and rising!

We, on the other hand, tend to hold on to what is over, or is no longer useful. In fact, not only do we hoard, we gather what we don't need, just in case we need it someday.

Imagine trees acting like us, keeping their dead leaves, and then growing new ones, keeping them when they die, growing more, and keeping them, too.

As the cycle continued, instead of rising, the branch would droop lower and lower until eventually the weight of it all would bring it down. Or what if the tree let the leaves go, but then gathered them up, and tried to reattach them to themselves?

The trees, knowing that all that it needs is within and will create anew, releases, and rises, and restores, and glories in its freedom. Each tree has its own timing when and how it lets go, but it always does. As it lets go, it reveals its true structure, its limbs tracing beautiful shapes in the air and sky.

We are afraid that we are not like the tree, with all that we need already contained within our true nature. So we hold on to beliefs, ideas, and decisions that weigh us down, until one day we break under their weight, or simply stop growing exhausted from the effort of holding on.

Every leaf that dropped off the tree branch made a difference in how high the branch would rise. I could see the branch lift a little more each day. Just a light little leaf, one at a time, makes a difference, and once they were all gone, the branch leapt into the air!

Sometimes we may feel discouraged that all we can do is let go of little things, like a small unwelcome belief, a tiny fault forgiven, a false memory dissolved. Perhaps we think that we have to do big things to make a difference. Each leaf says otherwise.

In our fireplace, the logs were carefully placed, but not burning. Deep underneath them, I glimpsed a small red core, so tiny it was hardly visible. As I watched, within minutes, the fire exploded into action; the flames leaping up to the ceiling of the stove.

We might only have a small deep core within that is holding to what is true and beautiful, and perhaps it feels as if we have been doing that forever and yet nothing has happened. The fire says otherwise.

Life is about the little things. Each moment gives us something to affirm as Truth, or to let go of because it's no longer needed or wanted.

All that we see and know gives us a message. Everything that we experience is a symbol, not a thing. Whether it is a person, a spark, or a leaf, it is a symbol of the qualities that make up its true substance.

As we understand this idea, it becomes easier to let go and rise and feel the freedom of knowing that all that we are contains all that we need in every moment. Feeding the fire of this knowledge, the core of our being warms and then leaps into action, and that benefits not only ourselves but also those whose lives we touch.

So go ahead, let go, rise and enjoy the lightness of being, the sunlight of love, and the comforting warmth of the knowledge that you are the idea of Divine Love and therefore always and eternally safe and free.

ONE HUNDRED THIRTY-EIGHT

— • —

THE QUALITIES OF WHAT WE DESIRE

A bird does not sing because it has an answer. It sings because it has a song. — Chinese Proverb

No book in *The Shift Series* would be complete without talking about why and how to use quality words. In this book, our focus is on blooming our lives. To what end, though?

As you take yourself through these seven steps intending to bloom, hopefully there will be things you want to change, places you want to go, and things you desire.

All of which is part of the process of blooming. The problem lies in that although we may believe that we do—we don't really know what we want. We have a picture in our head about it, a story that we have told ourselves. Outside forces, or internal patterns and habits, perceptions, that we accepted as truth, have influenced and driven that picture and story, and although they once were useful, they no longer serve us.

For example: We may decide we want a red car, go out and buy one, but it never satisfies the actual need. If you examine your life and often find a sense of dissatisfaction, one reason may be that you went after the thing, and not the idea. Or qualities.

But what are qualities? They are what makes up a thing, or idea. One way to say it is they are not nouns. They are describers.

Sometimes we make a quality word list on how something would look. Sometimes we make a quality word list on how something would feel if we were doing it, or had it. But we use describers not nouns.

Remember, we talked about POV and SOM perceptions? Making a feeling quality word list brings our state of mind into harmony with our point of view.

Using the car example. Let's say we realize we need a better way to get ourselves from here to there. Instead of saying we want a red car, we say something like this: "I desire transportation."

This statement is shorthand for all that lies behind it. But you, as the writer, would have all the feelings and needs internally, so it's just a holding place and symbol of all that you mean by it.

Now. Instead of stating a noun, describe first how you would feel if you had the perfect transportation for yourself.

Maybe your list would include safe, secure, easy, clean, comfortable, and quick. Notice that these are simple descriptors and not nouns.

What may happen after making this list is you realize this is not a car. It's a bike, a bus, a train, walking, or riding with a friend.

But, let's assume you decide it is a car. Perhaps then you could make a list of what it would look like. No nouns, though. However, when I make a list like this for a car, it's usually very short. The last list went something like this: not red, white or black. Heated seats. Rated high in safety. Good mileage. Room to carry things.

But first, it had to satisfy how I would feel: safe, secure, comfortable. Notice safe was on my list twice. So when I researched my car, I checked how high its safety rating was first, and everything else fell into place.

If you are not in the habit of doing quality word lists before you get or do anything major (or even small things) I hope you will take up the practice. Life will become much more satisfying and you will find that doing all seven steps of Blooming Your Life much easier.

ONE HUNDRED THIRTY-NINE

—•—

QUALITY WORD DETAILS

*H*appiness is when what you think, what you say, and what you do are in harmony. — Mahatma Gandhi

Going back to the car example, here's an excerpt from the book From *Living In Grace* that explains more about how to do and use Quality word lists.

You will notice that you need someone else to help you put the Quality word lists in order. And they **do** need to be put into order. Otherwise, they are in the order of how your intellectual mind thinks they should be and not your heart. And that means you will still end up with something that will not satisfy what you want.

You will find more instructions, including visual instructions, and an ongoing community of people that are always available to order a list in the resource chapter of this book.

Or find a friend and do this together!

From *Living In Grace: The Shift To Spiritual Perception*
  Turning things into thoughts.

Pick anything that you're thinking about, or desiring to see ,and list its qualities. For example, let's say that you were thinking about a car. You want the idea or quality of transportation. So how would you like that transportation to look? You might say that its qualities include safety, effortlessness, speed, security, luxury, grace, convenience, and so on.

You have probably phrased this request as something you want or need. However, if you use the words "need" or "want," they imply that you're lacking something. It is a statement of separation. As an expression or reflection of the Infinite One Loving Mind, how could you lack? If you believe you are lacking, you are.

What we perceive to be reality magnifies, so if we perceive lack, we receive lack. An unlimited Reality cannot lack; therefore, neither can you.

You have never been separated from God. In addition, wanting something often involves our ego, or human will asking for it. When we use human will, or ego, we are walking the mental or physical path. We think we are the cause and creator. We believe that if we do enough, know enough, or work hard enough, we can fix the problem. This is not putting God First. It is putting "me first." To avoid this trap of personal ego, which blinds us to the will of God, we ask instead "to see." Since everything has already been created, we are asking ourselves to wake up to what has already been provided.

Steps to making qualities lists.

Remember again, we are not interested in things here. We are interested in knowing God. Since things are in essence composed of qualities, we translate back into qualities the things of which we desire to become conscious.

Step 1: Take a moment and list 8–10 qualities of something you want to experience. Use one word to express each quality. If you are using sentences, you have not come to the heart or essence of it.

Step 2: There are two kinds of qualities lists: You can either list the qualities of the thing itself, or you can list the qualities of how you will feel when you have it.

For example, let's go back to the idea of buying a car. Your quality list for the thing—or car—might contain ideas such as red, fast, inexpensive, safe, etc.

If you choose to do a qualities list of how you will feel when you drive this car, it might read "wealthy, secure, free, joyful, etc."

If you wish, do both lists. Otherwise, do the list that makes the most sense to you. What you choose to see does not matter. It can be as important as having a home or as simple as setting the table for dinner. It is being conscious of the qualities of these "things" that makes a difference.

Now that you have a list, how do you use it?

1. Use the qualities as a filter.

If something appears you think might be what you are looking for and does not have at least the first four qualities—with the first one first, it is not "it." Think of the time you will save if you can eliminate quickly and easily what is not right for you.

For example, if you find that safety is first on your quality list for a means of transportation and the car you are looking at has a very low safety record, don't buy this car no matter how much you love it. If you buy it, you will eventually be unhappy with it, and somehow you will unconsciously figure out how to get rid of it.

2. See the qualities everywhere.

See the qualities in everything, not just in what you're seeking. Notice that they're always with you in many forms. You have always had and always will have each quality on your list if you just look.

A quality does not have to belong to you. It can appear anywhere. All of what you see is already yours because you can see it. The goal is to notice that the quality you're looking for in an object already exists everywhere, and since you can see it—it exists for you—now.

3. Be grateful for each quality as you see it.

Be grateful for these qualities each time you see them, no matter where they occur.

If the person you dislike most has one of these qualities, be grateful that you have seen this quality in your life. Know that if it is "out there" it was first "within here" and therefore always available.

4. Be and live these qualities yourself.

Now that you have begun to live with God First, no longer is having the "thing" you wanted so important. You have discovered that it already exists as God's thoughts—qualities.

As we express gratitude, we are living in Grace. The result? Sometimes we realize we don't actually need the thing we were asking to see, or it turns up in another package, or it appears in a way greater than we could have dreamed.

Whichever way this happens, we have begun with seeking the kingdom of God first. That beginning cannot help but produce in our world whatever we need at the moment, because we began with the correct premise. We become conscious of always having whatever we need. We have never been abandoned, nor could we ever be. Looking for qualities opens your eyes to what has always been and always will be yours.

ONE HUNDRED FORTY

— • —

PRACTICAL BLOOMING: STEP SIX

Thich Nhat Hanh said, *Our notions about happiness entrap us. We forget they are just ideas. Our idea of happiness can prevent us from actually being happy. We fail to see the opportunity for joy that is right in front of us when we are caught in a belief that happiness should take a particular form.*

And he offered this last piece of advice: *Do not lose yourself in the past. Do not lose yourself in the future. Do not get caught in your anger, worries, or fears. Come back to the present moment, and touch life deeply.*

1. What makes me discouraged?
2. Who or what is saying to me, "Naw Naw, it won't come up."
3. What can I let go of now?
4. What space in my life wants to be filled?
5. With what?
6. My heart is grateful for:
7. I am doing a quality word list on this:

PS: Just a reminder that the place to find videos and more instructions on I Choose sheets and Quality Words are in the resource chapter of this book.

ONE HUNDRED FORTY-ONE

— • —

RENEE: STEP SIX

*Y*ou are filtering reality. We need to open up and let go of the filters *that are not serving us, filters of lack and scarcity, filters of not deserving healing, filters of not believing in miracles. These are the kinds of belief filters that we hold on to that prevent better things from happening in our life.* — Anita Moorjani

For a few days, Renee was happier than she had ever been. Then she wasn't. Normally, she would have just ignored her feelings, but this time, she asked herself how she felt and listened to the answer.

She realized she felt depressed and discouraged. But first, she had been angry. Angry that nothing felt fun, that no one understood her, and she seemed to be alone even when she wasn't. When the anger faded, that's when she started feeling depressed and discouraged.

At first, it surprised Renee that she was angry. Perhaps if she had understood why she was angry, she wouldn't have slid into the other two emotions. At least if she was angry, she might do something about it.

But not when she was discouraged. That shut her down. It had never occurred to her that discouragement was the "devil's" tool. It seemed like a natural part of life. But what if it wasn't? For a moment, she got stuck in the question of if there was a devil, what it looked like, but realized that didn't help make her feel any better. In fact, she became more discouraged.

She decided to put those questions aside for when she felt more clear-headed and concentrate instead on getting undiscouraged. Besides, she wasn't sure anyone knew the answer to the question. She had heard once that the devil was only the claim, perception, and belief that God is not omnipotent. Renee thought that if that was true, it was essential to refute it by choosing a point of view that there was only one power, and it was Good.

It couldn't hurt, she told herself. She even remembered she needed to bring her state of mind into harmony with that point of view. To do that, she stood under a tree and felt its goodness and the community of nature that surrounded it.

Next, Renee did an I Choose sheet that said this: I desire to experience the omnipotence of Good.

Wow. That set off a firestorm of reasons that couldn't be true, at least not for her, which was laughable in a way. Did she think she was better than everyone else? That God didn't include her in his plan? As if she was important enough to be left out?

Laughing helped. It took away the power of discouragement, and she quickly came up with ideas to refute its claims. She kept the I Choose sheet running for a few days until the loud voice saying that she couldn't be happy, that she wasn't part of the Infinite Good, went silent—or at least she could barely hear it. Then she tore the sheet into little pieces and threw it away, feeling better than she had for as long as she could remember.

After that, answering the rest of the questions was easier. And Renee was grateful that she was growing and blooming in her own timing. Besides, what was the rush?

Renee chose to do a quality word list on how she would feel if she felt happy. The first word that popped into her head was *peaceful*.

Other quality words came quickly after that, and she realized that sometimes she felt happy and hadn't noticed.

Realizing that she needed to put her quality word list in order and needed help to do it, she thought through all the people she knew who could do that for her. Finally, she settled on someone she knew at work who seemed open to such things.

She took the list of how to order quality words to work the next day and asked. It surprised her how happy the person was to be asked, and after the list was ordered, they spent time talking.

Renee added having a friendly conversation to her what-makes-me-happy list. And then, with an ordered quality word list in hand, she started using it.

To her surprise, the most challenging part of it all was letting go of how she thought things were and becoming open to the possibility that Good was omnipresent and omnipotent.

But it did not discourage her. She would get there because she was in charge of how she looked at things. That she could do.

ONE HUNDRED FORTY-TWO

STEP SEVEN: CELEBRATE THE UNIQUE BLOOM THAT YOU ARE

·♥·♥·♥·♥·♥·

ONE HUNDRED FORTY-THREE

— • —

STOP RESISTING

To believe in God for me is to feel that there is a God, not a dead one, or a stuffed one, but a living one, who with irresistible force urges us toward more loving. — Vincent Van Gogh

Nothing can stop a rose from being a rose, can it? If a rose could see outside itself and could abuse itself as we can, it may wish it was smaller, lived in the shade, and bloomed in the snow.

However, no amount of wishing will make that happen.

Relaxing and releasing into being a rose, it finds its unique spiritual blessing and joyfully allows itself to bloom. There is no work involved but to let go and be what it is, a rose.

Resisting what we are is so much work. Imagine an apple tree trying to be a grapevine or a violet wasting its life trying to be a lilac. No matter how much they try, they can't do it.

They could convince themselves that it was working, but all of us looking at the tree and violet would only see what they were—unless they did an outstanding job of putting up an illusion, so we could only see the lie.

But this is something humans are good at, producing and living within illusions. Plants—not so much.

In the world today, many people find it easier to succumb to the illusion of the worldview of "how things are." But that doesn't mean we have to play that perception game with them.

We have a choice. It is our perception that determines our reality. Not our self-will. Our perception. No matter how hard we try, we cannot change the Truth of omnipresent abundance to lack.

However, we can allow ourselves to be blinded by the propagated perception of lack. Then we struggle to survive and trade in our freedom of choice for the prison of limited perception.

Many will say "naw, naw," it won't come up. But they are wrong. It has, it is, and it will.

Don't listen to those that don't expect to grow. Inspire them instead by not taking part in the worldview game of fear, sorrow, and lack and move yourself out of those poor growing conditions.

You don't need to experience the bad to experience the good. This is another lie designed to keep us in the cycle of good to bad, from bad to good, sorrow to joy, and back to sorrow. That is not what happens in omnipresent Good.

We can learn from what appears as "bad" if it occurs, but there is no need to suffer to grow in wisdom and understanding.

Instead of the false perception of the need to experience bad to experience good, think of it this way.

There is the experience of good snuggling by the fire in the deepest of winter. And there is the experience of good swinging in a hammock under a shady tree in the summer. We don't have to make one wrong to enjoy the other.

Both experiences are qualities of the Infinite to enjoy and celebrate with gratitude, and in this way, we overcome the devil's tool of discouragement.

We absolutely don't need tragedy to experience omnipresent good. That is a perception that does not serve anyone.

Let your life have a bigger purpose than your ego. Find out who you are and be of service with it. Make yourself visible so others can benefit from what you offer. Accept payment and give payment abundantly.

Albert Einstein said, *Only a life lived for others is worth living.*

As you bloom into your life, this becomes self-evident and part of the joy of blooming as your unique spiritual blessing.

When you become aware that the Master Gardener is blooming Itself as you and that you are entirely necessary for the garden of life to be complete, all anxiety and fear will fade.

Shifting happens moment by moment, thought by thought. The results of this shift from a limited perception to an unlimited and omnipresent good perception far outweigh any time and effort we put into this practice.

One Hundred Forty-Four

— ⋅ —

Go For The Goodness

No one is useless in this world who lightens the burden of it for anyone else. — Charles Dickens

My daughter's family had a rescue dog named Eva. She was a kind, gentle, loving, and a very happy dog.

Watching her, one might have thought that Eva had an easy and happy puppy-hood, but that wasn't the case at all. In fact, it was completely the opposite. It was hard, mean, and by all appearances, cold and lonely.

However, instead of dwelling on her past, Eva went for the goodness. As she lived with her new family, she increased her goodness.

I understand that many rescue dogs are like Eva. They go for the goodness with all of their being.

However, we don't appear to be as good as Eva was at going for the goodness. Instead, we allow our past to direct our present, which is then the architect of our future.

Even though we have so many more opportunities and abilities to choose goodness than a dog does, we don't choose it. We dwell in past hurts, both true and perceived.

To add to the pain, we allow blame—not just to others—but also to ourselves, to fester and grow.

Remaining in this victim viewpoint in any degree leaves us in the same situation that we are trying to forget, or from which we wait to be rescued. However, unlike a dog that has to hope and wait for rescue, we can rescue our own lives and stop waiting for someone else to do it.

In fact, we must rescue our own lives, and not wait for another to do so, because no one else can. No one can "fix" us because it is our own hanging onto a past picture of lack of love that must be resolved if we want to be more like Eva—kind, gentle, loving, and happy.

The question is how to do this?

Most of us have a part of our past, whether it was yesterday's past or childhood pasts, which were painful. They weren't fair. They weren't kind, and they were not filled with joy.

How do we leave that memory, how do we forgive the players, how to we choose the now of happiness instead?

Viktor Frankl wrote: *A thought transfixed me: for the first time in my life I saw the truth as it is set into song by so many poets, proclaimed as the final wisdom by so many thinkers. The truth–that love is the ultimate and the highest goal to which man can aspire.*

With the goal of love in mind, how can we not go for the goodness?

As we rise to the awareness of Love's everywhere presence in the turn of a flower petal, the shape of a leaf, the smile of a child, the dew on the grass, the song of a bird, we begin to dissolve the need to hold on to and reciprocate with anger through either passive or aggressive choices.

What use is there in not forgiving? Can we see the stars when the earth is shrouded in fog? Neither can we see goodness within the fog of victim-hood.

We all yearn for world peace. However, how can there be world peace when there is not family peace? How can we wish for love to be known in everyone's heart when we don't know it within ours?

In order to forgive others and ourselves and reach for the awareness of Infinite Love, we have to rescue ourselves from the false claim of victim-hood. We have to aim for a higher love.

The sad story is that most victims become the abusers, sometimes physically, and always emotionally.

Perhaps it doesn't seem as if we are being abusive when we say we have a right to be sad, lonely, and depressed. However, for the people that love us, it is a hard thing to live with.

Sometimes we are abusive by punishing the other person who we feel has abused us, or other people that act like them, or remind us of them.

And, even if none of this is true for you, in victim-hood we are always abusive to ourselves.

We exist to share, live, and love Divine Love. Anything less than that, we are depriving ourselves of the infinite happiness that has been gifted to us as a result of our being.

We can rise higher. We can rise above the claims that exist within the worldview picture, and lift ourselves into the awareness and understanding that divine Love does not know abuse or lack.

Starting with this perfect sense of Love, we can make day-to-day choices that will begin to dissolve the pictures of abuse in all its forms, past, present, and future.

Let's all make Eva's choice and go for the goodness.

Let's all choose to make a higher love the architect of our future and rewrite the past, letting the hurt and anger dissolve into nothingness.

ONE HUNDRED FORTY-FIVE

— • —

BE UNREASONABLY HAPPY

*W*hen a flower doesn't bloom you fix the environment in which it grows, not the flower.*—Alexander den Heijer

We began walking this garden path understanding that we have a right to be happy, and a dawning awareness that we might have unconsciously chosen not to be.

We followed up with tools that help us recognize and let go of any conscious or unconscious ideas that keep us from living within and as happiness.

There is no reason to stop at a "sort of" happy place.

As we understand the true nature of Love as the only presence, the only activity, the only cause, and creator, then the mist of false perceptions of what claims to be situations and circumstances that produce unhappiness will dissolve.

This allows us to see happiness as a fundamental element and quality of life.

With this understanding of happiness, we eliminated all the reasons for unhappiness in one fell swoop, because they all begin and end from the false premise of duality and separation.

Now that you have prepared the soil, found the perfect place to bloom, watered and fed yourself with what suited you, and relaxed into your personal timing and growth, don't let those old beliefs and perceptions back in.

Be careful about what you choose to perceive.

Don't buy all that stuff and nonsense that claims that suffering is necessary and that we must be unhappy to be good or even to experience happiness. Realize that happiness is a quality of the Divine, as is Harmony. And Love.

When we experience less than happiness, it's not because it doesn't still exist. It's because we have misplaced our awareness of big R Reality. There is nothing to create. Nothing to get back to. Only the letting go of cherished, unconsciously or consciously, stubborn beliefs that hide happiness.

Happiness is experienced in a multitude of ways—an infinite variety of colors. But always we can choose it because in choosing it, we are stepping into the river of God's Joy.

If you were happy, how would you feel? Notice that those qualities are qualities of God. Which means we can't lose them. They are infinitely omnipresent.

Check your garden often for the weeds of discouragement and discontent to make sure unhappiness has not slipped back in without your noticing.

Daily, give yourself full permission to be utterly and unreasonably happy.

Pull out your list of what makes you happy once in a while and do something on it. Sing with the birds at least once a season, and experience what they know.

Continue with this happiness shift so that when you ask, "Who is the happiest person I know?" you will answer without hesitation, "It is me!"

And because you are the happiest person you know, it will be easy to include everyone into your circle of joy so everyone can answer the question the same way. "It's me." And that will be true.

Celebrate happiness every day and watch what happens.

In the spring, the plant called Spring Beauties pops up everywhere. It spreads like crazy. Most of the year, unless you know what to look for, you won't see it. But April and May in the east, you'll say, "What's that," and point to the lawn, and there they will be—spreading tremendous joy at the coming of spring. Tiny flowers with a big message.

Yes, you all are spring beauties: multiple colors and shapes, but all with a big message. Happiness is available to everyone at all times and does not need fanfare or admiration to be present.

You all are gifts of joy to the world. Go ahead, be happy about that!

You have prepared your garden for your future self. Now your "job" is to watch, water, weed, and enjoy the fruits of what you have done.

And as you know, there is always more growth, more perception shifting, and more to enjoy. That's the good news. We are not striving for completion. We are blooming into each day, being unreasonably happy.

ONE HUNDRED FORTY-SIX

— · —

PRACTICAL BLOOMING: STEP SEVEN

*I*n order to be irreplaceable one must always be different. — Coco Chanel

Remember, find out who you are and be of service with it. Make yourself visible so others can benefit from what you offer. Remember accept payment and give payment abundantly.

Answer these questions:

1. What do I have to share?
2. Am I willing to be visible as the unique spiritual blessing that I am. Yes - Not Sure - No
3. Am I willing to appreciate good by staying in good. Yes - Not Sure - No
4. I am willing to shift to fully blooming as myself.

>>Continue doing I Choose sheets.

>>Remember to use your Quality Word lists.

>>>>Go back through the *Blooming Your Life* book and do it again! Life is a progression, not a stop sign. Gardens evolve and become more and more beautiful. This will happen to your life too as you continue to practice shifting your perceptions.

ONE HUNDRED FORTY-SEVEN

— • —

GO FORTH AND BLOOM

*T*here *is no duty we so much underrate as the duty of being happy. By being happy we sow anonymous benefits upon the world.* — Robert Louis Stevenson

Prepare yourself, you have blooming to do!

When you become aware that the Master Gardener is blooming Itself as you, and that you are entirely necessary for the garden of life to be complete, then anxiety and fear will fade.

Shifting happens moment by moment, thought by thought, and the results of this shift from a limited perception to an unlimited and omnipresent good perception far outweigh any time and effort you put into this practice.

Remember, we talked about two of the seven steps to shift lives: Be Willing and Become Aware.

If you would like all seven steps and learn more about them, they are in the book

And now we are ready to see in one place all the *Seven Simple Steps For Experiencing Consistent Happiness* or *How To Thrive In Your Life By Knowing Who You Are And Living It On Purpose*:

1. Prepare to grow.

2. Put yourself where you grow best.

3. Move yourself if necessary.

4. Feed yourself with the best "food" available.

5. Grow in your own timing.

6. Expect to bloom.

7. Celebrate the unique bloom that you are.

I hope you will go back and read this book over and over again. Keep reviewing the steps, because each time you do, you are approaching it from a new normal.

And before we step out into the world blooming as our unique spiritual blessing, let's see how Renee is doing.

One Hundred Forty-Eight

Renee: Step Seven

I think I could turn and live with animals, they are so placid and self-contain'd, / I stand and look at them long and long. / They do not sweat and whine about their condition, / They do not lie awake in the dark and weep for their sins, / They do not make me sick discussing their duty to God, / Not one is dissatisfied, not one is demented with the mania of owning things, / Not one kneels to another, nor to his kind that lived thousands of years ago, / Not one is respectable or unhappy over the whole earth. — Walt Whitman

Renee finished reading this book and doing the worksheets and felt a surge of hope and joy. Now she knew she was in control of how she saw things. She was not at the mercy of other people's points of view.

She understood that when people said cruel and unkind things to each other, they had not chosen to understand the omnipotence of Good and the joy that flowed from that. And although she could feel sorry for them and perhaps in some way be helpful, she was not responsible for their point of view and behavior.

She was responsible for her own. And if she continued to choose a point of view and state of mind that brought joy and contentment to her, it would spread out like a stone thrown into a pond.

Renee understood that living in guilt and shame did not heal anybody or anything. But choosing to be happy did.

Yes, I am willing to be happy, Renee said to herself. I choose a perception of omnipresent Good. And when something doesn't appear to be good, I can do something about it.

Renee took herself through the seven steps each day.

She was prepared to grow. She would put herself where she grew best in every moment. She'd move herself when necessary. Sometimes that was as simple as stepping away from someone being angry and abusive. Other times, she would have to move away from it.

She would feed herself the food of goodness and kindness, and with the abundance that brought her, she'd share it with others. Sometimes that was only a smile, other times a listening ear, and sometimes it meant physically helping.

Each day, Renee reminded herself that she, like all the other blooms in the world, grows in her own timing. And like a beautiful garden, there was always something and someone to celebrate and admire as they expressed their unique spiritual blessing.

Today I expect to bloom with more happiness and then share it, was Renee's favorite thing to say to herself.

And each night, before falling asleep, she would thank you for the day and the gifts she had been given. She could already feel the effects of doing that. It seemed her gifts were growing, or at least she was experiencing them more often.

Yes, there were days when things didn't go well. Renee still wasn't sure about her job or where she lived, but Renee trusted that she would know what to do and do it when the time was right.

Along the way, she met a few new friends who wanted to walk the garden path with her. Together, they started through the book again and often discussed their progress.

What Renee appreciated the most was the proof she felt every day that she could choose how she perceived the world. She was experiencing the world differently, and that was a beautiful thing.

Author Note

This book was a long time in the making. In my life, I have gone through these seven steps repeatedly, each time making my life garden just a little more beautiful.

It was spring as I finished writing this book, so it was perfect timing. I could see how true it is that growth is the propulsion of the universe. And it also reminded me that gardens are never done. They require attention. And that's not a bad thing.

What I love most, though, is that gardeners are about community and sharing, and since we are all gardeners of our own lives, I love that we can share our growth steps together.

The business garden that I am growing is an evergreen garden online where anyone can take my courses at anytime. Plus a community circle where gardeners of perception can meet and get help and support from like-minded souls.

Like all gardens, it's a work in progress and will require attention. But this book reminded me what our life is about. Growing. Blooming. And sharing joy and happiness.

I thank you for walking this garden path with me, and I look forward to seeing you back here again. I will be watching for you. — Beca

PS: If you, like me, love quotes and would like a list of all the quotes in this book—I have you covered. You can find where to download the list in the resource chapter of this book.

RESOURCES

M ore Help To Shift

- *Perception Shifting Courses*, the *Perception Circle*—where you will find someone to help you with your Quality Word lists—and videos on how to do many of the things we discussed in the book can be found at <u>PerceptionU.com</u>

- You can download the workbook for this book for free here: <u>perceptionu.com/the-library/workbooks/</u>

- The list of quotes from this book is here: <u>becalewis.com/books/shift-series/blooming-your-life/</u>or in the workbook section at <u>PerceptionU.com</u>

- All my books are at <u>BecaLewis.com</u>

Books About Nature

- Mary Reynolds: *The Garden Awakening: Designs to Nurture Our Land and Ourselves and Reclaiming the Wild Soul: How Earth's Landscapes Restore Us to Wholeness*

- Michal Polin: *The Botany of Desire: A Plant's-Eye View of the World*

- Robin Wall Kimmerer: *Braiding Sweetgrass: Indigenous Wisdom, Scientific Knowledge and the Teachings of Plants*

- Suzanne Simard: *Finding the Mother Tree: Discovering the Wisdom of the Forest*

- Plant Intelligence and the Imaginal Realm: Beyond the Doors of Perception into the Dreaming of Earth

- The Lost Language of Plants: *The Ecological Importance of Plant Medicine to Life on Earth* **Self-Discovery Tools**

These are a few profiles I use in teaching and coaching. You might also find them valuable. Just remember, they are not boxes or excuses. They are not answers. They are mirrors. They are tools to help you thrive in the garden of your life.

- Enneagram: eclecticenergies.com/enneagram/test

Then sign up for this email and get the one that matches your results. See if you agree. If you had two answers, and you are not sure which one is true, get both emails.

- Myers Briggs. Take the test at the back of the book: *Please Understand Me*. There are a few tests online that aren't accurate and are easily manipulated. Besides, the book will help you understand yourself and others. That's always a good thing. I made a copy of this test. If you would like it, just let me know.

- Clifton Strengths:
  gallup.com/cliftonstrengths/en/home.aspx

- Gene Keys: genekeys.com/free-profile/

- Carol Tuttle's Energy Guide:
  my.liveyourtruth.com/freecourse/

- Gretchen Rubin's: Questioner-Rebel-Obliger-Upholder:
  gretchenrubin.com/2014/03/quiz-are-you-an-upholder-a-questioner-a-rebel-or-an-obliger/

ALSO BY BECA

The Ruby Sisters Series: Women's Lit, Friendship
A Last Gift, After All This Time, And Then She Remembered, As
If It Was Real...

Stories From Doveland: Magical Realism, Friendship
Karass, Pragma, Jatismar, Exousia, Stemma, Paragnosis,
In-Between, Missing, Out Of Nowhere

The Return To Erda Series: Fantasy
Shatterskin, Deadsweep, Abbadon, The Experiment

The Chronicles of Thamon: Fantasy
Banished, Betrayed, Discovered, Wren's Story

The Shift Series: Spiritual Self-Help
Living in Grace: The Shift to Spiritual Perception
The Daily Shift: Daily Lessons From Love To Money
The 4 Essential Questions: Choosing Spiritually Healthy Habits
The 28 Day Shift To Wealth: A Daily Prosperity Plan
The Intent Course: Say Yes To What Moves You
Imagination Mastery: A Workbook For Shifting Your Reality
Right Thinking: A Thoughtful System for Healing

531

BECA LEWIS

Perception Mastery: Seven Steps To Lasting Change
Blooming Your Life: How To Experience Consistent Happiness

Perception Parables: Very short stories
Love's Silent Sweet Secret: A Fable About Love
Golden Chains And Silver Cords: A Fable About Letting Go

Advice:
A Woman's ABC's of Life: Lessons in Love, Life, and Career from
Those Who Learned The Hard Way
The Daily Nudge(s): So When Did You First Notice

OTHER PLACES TO FIND BECA

- Facebook: facebook.com/becalewiscreative

- Instagram: instagram.com/becalewis

- Twitter: twitter.com/becalewis

- LinkedIn: linkedin.com/in/becalewis

- Youtube: www.youtube.com/c/becalewis

About Beca

B eca writes books she hopes will change people's perceptions of themselves and the world, and open possibilities to things and ideas that are waiting to be seen and experienced.

At sixteen, Beca founded her own dance studio. Later, she received a Master's Degree in Dance in Choreography from UCLA and founded the Harbinger Dance Theatre, a multimedia dance company, while continuing to run her dance school.

After graduating—to better support her three children—Beca switched to the sales field, where she worked as an employee and independent contractor to many industries, excelling in each while perfecting and teaching her Shift® system, and writing books.

She joined the financial industry in 1983 and became an Associate Vice President of Investments at a major stock brokerage firm, and was a licensed Certified Financial Planner for over twenty years.

This diversity, along with a variety of life challenges, helped fuel the desire to share what she's learned by writing and speaking, hoping it will make a difference in other people's lives.

Beca grew up in State College, PA, with the dream of becoming a dancer and then a writer. She carried that dream forward as she fulfilled a childhood wish by moving to Southern California in 1968. Beca told her family she would never move back to the cold.

After living there for thirty-one years, she met her husband Delbert Lee Piper, Sr., at a retreat in Virginia, and everything changed. They decided to find a place they could call their own, which sent them off traveling around the United States. They lived and worked in a few different places before returning to live in the cold once again near Del's family in a small town in Northeast Ohio, not too far from State College.

When not working and teaching together, they love to visit and play with their combined family of eight children and five grandchildren, read, study, do yoga or taiji, feed birds, and work in their garden.

www.ingramcontent.com/pod-product-compliance
Lightning Source LLC
Chambersburg PA
CBHW060848120626
46553CB00001B/11